Roman Zykov

ROMAN'S
DATA
SCIENCE

HOW TO MONETIZE YOUR DATA

SCIENCE

Academus Publishing
2021

Roman Zykov

ROMAN'S
DATA
**HOW TO
MONETIZE
YOUR DATA**
SCIENCE

**#NOCODE
#NOMATH**

Academus Publishing, Inc.
1999 S, Bascom Avenue, Suite 700 Campbell CA 95008
Website: www.academuspublishing.com
E-mail: info@academuspub.com

ISBN 10: 1 4946 0026 9
ISBN 13: 978 1 4946 0026 6
DOI 10.31519/0026-6

Cover design & illustrations: Vladimir Vishvanuk
Russian editor: Ekaterina Zykova
Translation to English: Alexander Alexandrov
English editor: Philip Taylor
Layout: Elena Voloshina

Roman Zykov

Roman's Data Science
How to monetize your data

An introduction to the field of data analysis written in jargon-free language that is not bogged down by programming code and mathematical formulas. It covers the most essential topics in the fields of data science, machine learning and business intelligence that you are likely to come across on a regular basis.

The main goal is to help readers get the most out of their data, make business decisions and create information products – all without paying over the odds.

In a career spanning over 20 years, the author has worked as a junior data analyst, headed up the analytics division of an $10-billion company and co-founded a recommendation systems startup. The text was edited by a professional journalist. It contains QR codes and links with links you can follow if you want a deeper understanding of the topics covered.

CONTENTS

ABOUT THE AUTHOR

Roman Zykov was born in 1981. After completing his undergraduate studies in 2004, Roman went on to earn a master's in Applied Physics and Mathematics at the Moscow Institute of Physics and Technology (MIPT).

Roman started his career in data science in 2002 as a technical consultant at StatSoft Russia – the Russian office of the U.S. developer of the STATISTICA statistical data analysis software. In 2004, he was hired as head of the analytical department of the Ozon.ru online store, where he created analytical systems from scratch, including web analytics, database analytics and management reporting, while also contributing to the recommendation system.

In 2009, he advised on a number of projects for Fast Lane Ventures investment fund and the gaming industry.

In 2010, Roman was hired to lead to analytics department of the online retailer Wikimart.ru.

In late 2012, he co-founded RetailRocket.ru, a marketing platform for online stores. The company is currently the undisputed market leader in Russia and successfully operates in Chile, the Netherlands, Spain and several other countries.

Roman ran the blog Analytics in Practice on the now defunct KPIs.ru from 2007 where he evangelized data analysis as it applies to business problems in ecommerce. He has spoken at numerous industry conferences, including the Russian Internet Forum, iMetrics and Gec 2014 (with Arkady Volozh of Yandex), as well as at business conferences in Dublin and London, the U.S. Embassy (American Center in Moscow), and

Sberbank University. He has also published in PwC Technology Forecast, ToWave, *Vedomosti* and *Sekret firmy.*

In 2016, Roman gave a mini lecture on hypothesis testing at MIT in Boston.

In 2020, he was nominated for a CDO Award.

ACKNOWLEDGEMENTS

This book is dedicated to my wife Katya and my children Adella and Albert. Katya was the one who gave me the determination to write the book, and she was heavily involved in the editing – for which I am eternally grateful.

I would also like to thank my parents, who raised me during an exceedingly difficult period in our country's history. Special thanks go to my dad, Vladimir, who instilled in me a love of physics.

Thank you to all those I have met on my long journey into data analytics: Ilya Polezhaev, Pavel Bolshakov and Vladimir Borovikov at StatSoft for the guidance you gave a young man just starting out his career; former Ozon. ru CEO Bernard Lukey and my Ozon.ru colleagues Alexander Perchikov, Alexander Alekhin and Valery Dyachenko for co-writing the recommendation system with me; Marina Turkina and Irina Kotkina – working with you was sheer joy; the founders of Wikimart.ru Kamil Kurmakayev and Maxim Faldin – our meetings in California were a great inspiration for me; Alexander Anikin – you were cool back then, but now you're a stud; and the founders of Ostrovok.ru, Kirill Makharinsky and Serge Faguet, not to mention Evgeny Kuryshev, Roman Bogatov and Felix Shpilman – I had a blast working with you and learning about software development.

I would also like to thank my co-founders at Retail Rocket, Nikolay Khlebinsky and Andrey Chizh. And a special thanks to Impulse VC venture fund (Kirill Belov, Grigory Firsov and Evgeny Poshibalov) for believing in us. To all my coworkers at Retail Rocket, especially my boys Alexander Anokhin and Artem Noskov – you guys are the best!

I am grateful to my therapist Elena Klyuster, with whom I have been working for several years now, for helping me discover my boundaries and true desires. I would also like to thank my swimming coach Andrey Guz for imparting an analytical approach to training in me. Turns out that it works for amateurs just as well as it does for professionals.

I would also like to express my gratitude to all my virtual reviewers, especially Artem Astvatsaturov, Alexander Dmitriev, Arkady Itenberg, Alexei Pisartsov and Roman Nester for their input on the chapter on ethics.

Thank you to everyone who had a hand in the publication of this book, especially Alexey Kuzmenko, who helped me find a publisher in no time by sidestepping all the bureaucratic nonsense.

INTRODUCTION

Give me a place to stand, and I will move the earth.

Archimedes

Give me data, and I will change your whole life.

Data Scientist Archimedes

Data is everywhere – from Tinder algorithms that match you with supposedly (but not really) random people, to information wars waged by politicians. It is of no surprise to anyone these days that every single thing we do is closely monitored, including your internet search history and whatever you might be up to offline too. Something catch your eye when you were passing that sports store? Just wait for the ads to start appearing on you social network pages. Tell a friend at work what your cat's been up to and suddenly there's dry kibble and cat litter all over your feed.

This is where the more impressionable of us might become more than just a little paranoid. But it's not the data that's to blame. It's all about whose hands it falls into. There are many myths when it comes to data analysis, and "data scientist" is one of the "sexiest" and most promising professions of the future. My aim with this book is to debunk these myths and tell things how they really are. And I hope that you, the reader, will find yourself on the "light side" of the Force alongside me.

I graduated from the Moscow Institute of Physics and Technology in the early noughties before going on to head up the analytical department of the online store Ozon.ru, where I created analytical systems from scratch. I have provided consulting services to investment funds and retail and game industry giants. Eight years ago, I co-founded Retail-Rocket.ru, a marketing platform for online stores. During that time, we have become the undisputed market leader in Russia and have expanded our operations to Chile, the Netherlands, Spain and Germany. In 2016, I gave a guest lecture on hypothesis testing at MIT in Boston, and in 2020, I was nominated for the CDO Award.

They say it takes 10,000 hours of practice to become a master in one's field. I've been doing data analysis since 2002, when it wasn't such a hot and talked-about profession. Have I clocked in those all-important 10,000 hours? Well, let's do the maths: 10,000 hours / 4 hours a day / 200 days a year = 12.5 years. Looks like I've actually posted one and a half times this figure! I hope this is enough to have produced a book that the reader will find useful.

This book is about how to turn data into products and solutions. It is not based on academic knowledge, but on my personal experience of data analysis over the past 20 years or so. There is no shortage of courses on data science and machine learning these days, but, as a rule, they are highly specialized. This book is different in that it does not bog the reader down with unnecessary details. Rather, it provides a big picture perspective, offering insight into:

- data-driven decision making
- how systems should work
- how to test your service
- how to combine everything into a single whole in order to create a "conveyor belt" for your data output.

PREFACE TO THE ENGLISH EDITION

This book first hit the shelves in Russia on April 26, 2021 and was the culmination of more than a year of hard work. The initial run was sold out in just three weeks, becoming a bestseller! This inspired me to have the book translated into English and publish it on Amazon.com.

I would like to think that my experience in data analysis will be of interest to readers outside of Russia. To help you understand this book better, I will describe here some of the Russian companies that I refer to in the text. These are Ozon.ru, Wikimart.ru and RetailRocket.ru.

Ozon.ru is one of the first e-commerce companies in Russia, sometimes referred to as the "Amazon of Russia." The company was established in 1998, and by 2019 it was among the top three online retailers in the country. In 2020, *Forbes* ranked Ozon the third most valuable Russian internet company.

Wikimart.ru is an online B2C marketplace that enables Russian retailers to sell a wide range of products, from electronics to apparel. The company closed in 2016.

Retailrocket.ru offers online shopping recommendation services based on user behaviour. I founded the company in 2012 alongside two of my partners. The company has proved to be extremely successful, with offices in Russia, Western Europe and South American providing services for over 1000 clients. I left Retailrocket.ru in 2021.

The book was translated into English by RPK Group (https://rpk.group). RPK's translators, Philip Taylor and Alexander Alexandrov, helped me get my messages across and make the book read as an authentic English text.

WHO IS THIS BOOK FOR?

This book is dedicated to thinking readers who want to try their hand at data analysis and develop data-driven services.

If you are an investor, this book will help you to better understand the potential and infrastructure of the startup team asking you for your investment.

If you are itching to get your startup off the ground, this book will help you find the right partners and hire the right team from the outset.

If you are starting your career, this book will broaden your horizons and help you start applying approaches that you may not have considered.

HOW TO READ THIS BOOK

The beauty of this book is that it does not need to be read in order. The following is a short description of each chapter:

Chapter 1. How We Make Decisions describes the general principles of decision-making and how data affects decisions.

Chapter 2. Let's Do Some Data Analysis introduces general concepts: What artifacts do we deal with when analysing data? In this chapter, I also start to raise some organization issues relating to data analysis.

Chapter 3. Building Analytics from Scratch describes the process of building analytics, from the first tasks to the choice of technology and hiring personnel.

Chapter 4. How about Some Analytical Tasks? This chapter is all about tasks. What is a good analytical task? And how can we test it? The technical attributes of such tasks are datasets, descriptive statistics, graphs, pair analysis and technical debt.

Chapter 5. Data covers everything you ever wanted to know about data – volume, access, quality and formats.

Chapter 6. Data Warehouses explains why we need data warehouses and what kind of data warehouses exist. The chapter also touches upon the popular Big Data systems Hadoop and Spark.

Chapter 7. Data Analysis Tools describes the most popular analytical methods, from Excel spreadsheets to cloud systems.

Chapter 8. Machine Learning Algorithms provides a basic introduction to machine learning.

Chapter 9. The Practice of Machine Learning shares life hacks on how to study machine learning and how to work with it for it to be useful.

Chapter 10. Implementing ML in Real Life: Hypotheses and Experiments describes three types of statistical analysis of experiments

(Fisher statistics, Bayesian statistics and bootstrapping) and the use of A/B tests in practice.

Chapter 11. Data Ethics. I could not ignore this topic. Our field is becoming increasingly regulated by the states. Here we will discuss the reasons why.

Chapter 12. Challenges and Startups describes the main tasks that I faced in my time in ecommerce, as well as my experience as a co-founder of Retail Rocket.

Chapter 13. Building a Career is aimed more at beginners – how to look for a job, develop as an analyst and when to move on to something new.

Chapter 1

HOW WE MAKE DECISIONS

"The first principle is that you must not fool yourself – and you are the easiest person to fool. So you have to be very careful about that. After you've not fooled yourself, it's easy not to fool other scientists. You just have to be honest in a conventional way after that [...]

"I have just one wish for you – the good luck to be somewhere where you are free to maintain the kind of integrity I have described, and where you do not feel forced by a need to maintain your position in the organization, or financial support, or so on, to lose your integrity. May you have that freedom."

Nobel Prize winner
Richard Feynman,
from his 1974 commencement
address at Caltech

Monetizing data is only possible when we make the right decisions based on that data. That said, it is a bad idea to base your decisions on statistics alone – at the very least, you need to know how to read between the lines and listen to what your gut is telling you. The first chapter of this book is thus given over to a discussion of the principles that I use when making data-driven decisions. These are principles that I have tried and tested over the course of many years and I can assure you that they work.

Decision-making is difficult. So difficult, in fact, that scientists have even come up with a term for it – "decision fatigue" [7]. The stress of making hundreds of choices every day builds up to the point where we are so exhausted by the need to constantly make decisions that we just give

[1]   [7]

up and start choosing at random. There's a reason I quoted the brilliant Nobel Prize winning physicist Richard Feynman at the beginning of this chapter, as his words have a direct bearing both on data analytics and on our lives in general.

How can we make the correct decisions while at the same time remaining true to ourselves?

In his book, *Behave: The Biology of Humans at Our Best and Worst*, neuroscientist and Stanford University professor Robert Sapolsky [1] notes that our actions, and thus our decisions, are influenced by a multitude of factors: the environment in which we grew up, childhood trauma, head injuries, hormones, feelings, emotions, etc. We are constantly influenced by all kinds of processes that we are not even aware of. We are incapable of being objective!

It always seemed obvious to me that that it is far easier for us to be biased and thus cut corners than it is to be objective, because objectivity requires serious effort.

Keep that in mind the next time you give someone a set of figures and ask them to make a decision. As my colleagues have to remind me from time to time, I too am guilty of letting my biases get the better of me when looking at the results of certain A/B tests. This helps me stay grounded, and I inevitably end up agreeing with them, as objectivity is always more important than any *a priori* decisions I may make before we have even conducted an experiment.

In today's world, we are forced to make decisions quickly and with a number of uncertainties. This is not inherently a bad thing. Quantum physics teaches us that we do not know the exact location of an electron, but we do know the probability of finding it. In fact, the entire discipline of quantum physics on based on such probabilities. And it is the exact same thing with decisions – no one knows the truth; we're just trying to guess what is "right" and hope for the best. And that's where data comes in, to increase the likelihood of our making the right decisions.

FOUR HUNDRED RELATIVELY HONEST WAYS

Ostap Bender from Ilf and Petrov's *The Twelve Chairs* knew of 400 relatively honest ways to scam people out of money. A professional analyst knows roughly the same number of ways to manipulate the numbers so that they bring about the desired decision. Unfortunately, this is extremely common in politics: just look at how countries reported on the number of people infected during the COVID-19 pandemic. Mortality rates in Russia were artificially low [6]. It turned out that deaths from underlying conditions were not recorded in the official coronavirus statistics. Meanwhile, in most Western countries, a positive coronavirus test was enough to be included in the total number of infected. If we dig a little deeper, it becomes clear that each country has its own methodology when it comes to recording coronavirus cases and deaths that serve different goals. And there are a number of objective and subjective reasons why the numbers are not clear.

The first reason is objective: there are many asymptomatic carriers of the virus who do not get tested. This is why we need systematic testing for asymptomatic infections, where a random sample from the population of a particular area is taken. Testing would be voluntary, which means that many people would not turn up – some because they are demonstrating symptoms of coronavirus and do not want to self-isolate and thus run the risk of losing two weeks' worth of wages. The resulting sample is thus skewed towards healthy people, giving us a lowball estimate of the actual number of cases.

The second reason is also objective: the lack of funds to carry out mass testing of the population.

[2]   [3]   [6]

The third reason, however, is subjective: the authorities are keen to downplay the actual figures in order to reduce panic among the population and calm the international community. A good analyst understands these nuances and knows how to interpret the data with a critical eye, which in turn allows for more objective conclusions to be drawn.

I encounter this all the time in my work. Nowadays, people live and die by KPIs. Managers obsess over figures, as their bonuses literally depend on them. This is where the temptation to fudge the numbers creeps in. A strong leader will take poor results on the chin and try to take corrective measures. As researchers, data analysts are personally responsible for what happens to their figures.

WHAT WE CAN LEARN FROM AMAZON

I love reading Amazon founder Jeff Bezos' annual letters to his shareholders. He was talking about the importance of the personal recommendations feature back in 1999, for example, something that every single online retailer adopts as standard today. Two of his letters in particular spoke to me, though – the one from 2015 [2] and the one from 2016 [3].

In the 2015 letter, Bezos talks about Amazon being an "Invention Machine." And if anyone knows what he is talking about, it is Jeff Bezos, as it is providence itself that has guided Amazon through the vicissitudes of ecommerce. Amazon has been a trailblazer on the market since its inception, bringing us such innovations as the recommendation system, A/B tests (that's right, Amazon pioneered the practice of testing hypotheses for the web), AWS (Amazon Web Services), robotized warehouse systems, press-to-order Dash buttons on refrigerators, and so much more.

In the same letter, Bezos goes on to talk about how large companies go about making decisions on the creation of new products. The approval process often looks like this: everyone involved (usually heads of departments) gives their opinion on the product. If the overall consensus is positive, then the idea or hypothesis is developed further. Here, Bezos warns that there are two types of decision (Type 1 and Type 2) and they should not go through the same approval process.

Type 1 decisions are irreversible or nearly irreversible. They are like one-way doors, "If you walk through and don't like what you see on the other side, you can't get back to where you were before." Decisions of this kind must be made with great care and deliberation.

Type 2 decisions are changeable and reversible. They are two-way doors. These kinds of decisions, according to Bezos, should be made quickly without subjecting it to excessive bureaucratic hoop-jumping.

In his 2016 letter, Bezos contrasts Day 1 of a company, which is characterized by the vibrant atmosphere of a new company creating new products, with Day 2, which he describes as "stasis" followed by "decline" and, ultimately, "death."

Bezos identifies what he calls the four "essentials" for Day 1 of a company:

- customer obsession
- a sceptical view of proxies
- the eager adoption of external trends, and
- high-velocity decision making.

I would say that the last point is particularly important in the context of this book. Maintaining the vitality of Day 1 calls for high-quality, high-velocity decisions. "But how?" as my six-year-old son often asks in such situations. Well, Bezos has developed some rules:

1. Never use a one-size-fits-all decision-making process (there are, as I mentioned earlier, two types of decision). Don't wait until you have 90% of the information before you make a decision, as 70% is enough. Being wrong is not such a bad thing if you are good at course correcting. On the other hand, being slow to make a decision will often end up costing you big time.

2. Use the phrase "disagree and commit." Greenlight ideas even if you are not convinced that they will work instead of wasting time deliberat-

ing them. This is precisely what happened with an Amazon Studios original series. Bezos thought it would be a risky move, as the idea was not interesting enough and the show itself would be complicated to produce. His team disagreed, so he said "okay, let's give it a go." They didn't have to waste time convincing him to go ahead with the project. And he thought, "this team has already brought home eleven Emmys, six Golden Globes and three Oscars, I'm just glad they let me in the room at all!"

3. Recognize true misalignment issues early and escalate them immediately. Different teams may have different views on how to resolve a given issue. Instead of wasting time in exhausting meetings trying to negotiate, it is better to escalate the matter to the top.

ANALYSIS PARALYSIS

Haste makes waste. The biggest mistakes I have ever made can all be put down to my being in a hurry. For example, 15 years ago, I was hired by Ozon.ru to build up its analytics division. Part of my job was to compile a huge weekly data sheet on the company's activities, without actually being able to verify the information on a regular basis. Pressure from above, together with the time constraints, meant that the weekly reports were riddled with errors, which took a great deal of time and effort to rectify.

The modern world moves at breakneck speeds. Compiling metrics, however, requires careful attention, and this takes time. Of course, this does not mean that the opposite situation – "analysis paralysis," where an inordinate amount of time is spent on every single figure on the sheet – is desirable either. Sometimes, the desire to make the right choice leads to this very state of analysis paralysis, where it becomes impossible to make any decision whatsoever. The uncertainty about what the decision will lead to is prohibitively high, or the framework for making the decision too rigid. An easy way to fall into analysis paralysis is to approach decision-making in a purely rational manner, guided by logic only.

Graeme Simsion's *The Rosie Project* (a favourite of Bill Gates and his wife) illustrates this idea perfectly. The novel tells the story of Don Tillman, a successful young genetics professor who is eager to find himself a wife but has never managed to get further than the first date. He thus concludes that the traditional way of finding a soulmate is inefficient and decides to take a scientific approach to the problem. The first stage of his so-called "Wife Project" is a detailed 30-page questionnaire designed to weed out unsuitable candidates and identify the perfect mate. Obviously, no one can satisfy such a list of requirements. Don is then introduced to a girl who does not demonstrate any of the traits of his perfect woman. No prizes for guessing who Don ends up with.

Another example is buying a car. The last time I bought a car, I drew up a massive spreadsheet in Excel listing all the technical parameters of the cars I had my eye on, even down to the size of the boot in centimetres! I spent a whole year pondering the decision, going to showrooms, checking out cars, yet I ended up buying one that wasn't even on my list – one that spoke to me. Well, I guess I didn't follow my heart entirely, because that year of searching and analysing helped me realize what was really important on that list and what wasn't.

I could give you an example from my professional life too, one that is connected with hypotheses or, more precisely, with tests. Imagine you've come up with a new recommendation algorithm that you think is better than the existing one and you want to test it out. So, you compare the two algorithms on ten websites. In four cases, your new algorithm proves to be superior, in two it fares worse, and in four there is nothing between the two. Do you phase out the old algorithm in favour of the new one? It all depends on the criteria you devised for making the decision before comparing the two algorithms. Was the new algorithm supposed to be better in all cases? Or just most of the time? In the first case, you are likely to bury yourself in endless iterations of the algorithm, honing it to perfection, especially given the fact that the tests will take several weeks to complete. This is a classic case of "analysis paralysis." As for the second case, the task would appear to be far more straightforward. But practice tells us otherwise.

I believe there should always be an element of conscious risk when it comes to making decisions; we should be able to make a decision even if we don't have all the information. These days, we can't afford to spend time mulling over our decisions. The world is moving too quickly to afford us that luxury. If you don't make a decision, then someone else – a competitor – will make it for you.

MISTAKES AND THE CALIPER RULE

The next thing I discovered was that the numbers don't lie. I spent years analysing marketing strategies, including advertising campaigns. I was the one who was tasked with judging, as accurately as I could, the extent to which these strategies impacted our business. My managers acted rather predictably – if the numbers were good, then they wouldn't even bother checking them. But if they were bad, they would immediately start looking for mistakes. And, of course, they would usually "find" something. It's kind of like physics lab work at school or university, when we would mindlessly search for errors in our work. Systemic errors, human errors... How much time did we waste adjusting our results so that they would fit in with our hypotheses?

You can't do this in business, or indeed science, especially if you want to be a good analyst and not have to resort to those "relatively honest ways" we talked about earlier to manipulate the numbers. The measurement error of web analytics (systems that measure website traffic) today is approximately 5%. That is roughly the same as the entire analytical system at Ozon.ru when I was working there (discrepancies with accounting data). One time, we had a mini-crisis when I discovered a bug in the commercial web analytics software we were using (Omniture SiteCatalyst, now known as Adobe Analytics) where it was not counting Opera web browser users in its figures. Around 10% of all orders in the system that we paid over $100,000 per year for were lost as a result. We kind of lost faith in the system, but, thankfully, once I discovered the error and reported it to Omniture, their developers fixed it.

My work with errors led me to develop what I call the "Caliper Rule." A caliper is a tool used to measure the dimensions of an object with an accuracy of tenths of a millimetre. However, we don't need that degree of accuracy when measuring, say, a brick. It's just not practical – we can just use a ruler or tape measure for that. The Caliper Rule reads as follows:

> All measurements contain errors. This is a fact, get over it. Errors themselves should be noted and not considered errors as such (I'll explain how we can monitor this in a later chapter).

The analyst's job is to reduce the number of errors to a manageable amount, find out why they are there in the first place and accept that they will always be there in one form or another. The pursuit of super-precision leads to systems becoming increasingly complex, computationally difficult and thus more expensive, because it costs money to make changes.

THE PARETO PRINCIPLE

In 1897, Italian economist Vilfredo Pareto discovered in the course of his research into the structure of household income in Italy that approximately 80% of the land in the country was owned by 20% of the population. The universal principle named in his honour was first proposed in 1951 and states that "80% of results are produced by 20% of causes."

Based on my own experience, I would formulate the Pareto principle as follows in relation to data:

- 80% of the information is produced by 20% of the data (data science).
- 80% of a model's accuracy is produced by 20% of its features or variables (machine learning).
- 80% of the cumulative positive effect is produced by 20% of the successful hypotheses (hypothesis testing).

I've been working with data for almost 20 years and every day I am convinced that this principle holds true. At first, it might seem like an excuse to cut corners. But the fact is that you've got to give 100% in order to learn exactly which 20% will produce the desired results. Back in 1998, Steve Jobs told *Business Week*, "Simple can be harder than complex: you have to work hard to get your thinking clean to make it simple. But it's worth it in the end because once you get there, you can move mountains."

Let me give you an example of how the Pareto principle can be applied in machine learning. For any given project, a number of features are typically readied to help test a model. There can be dozens of these features. Launching the model in this state will be problematic, as hundreds of lines of code will be required to maintain it. There's a way around this – to calculate the relative importance of each feature and discard those that do not pull their weight. This is a direct application of the Pareto principle – 80% of the model's accuracy is produced by 20% of its features. In most cases, it is better to simplify the model by sacrificing an almost imperceptible amount of its accuracy. The upside to this is that the resulting project will be several times smaller than the original one. In practice, you can save time by looking at the features used to tackle similar problems on kaggle.com, taking the best ones and implementing them in the alpha version of your own project.

CAN WE MAKE DECISIONS BASED ON DATA ALONE?

We can, but not all the time and not in every situation. Computer algorithms are typically used in areas where decisions based solely on data can be taken. Algorithms don't get tired and they are eminently scalable. This is the kind of technology used in the self-driving cars that will soon be everywhere – algorithms will make decisions based on the data being fed to them by sensors to control the vehicle.

Humans are multi-faceted creatures capable of solving all kinds of problems. However, algorithms are capable of performing narrowly defined tasks faster than a thousand people working together. And, unlike humans, algorithms do not deviate from their instructions and can be endlessly refined. This is essentially what automation is all about – making processes cheaper, faster and capable of running with minimal human intervention. This is why everyone is so obsessed with the idea of artificial intelligence.

A number of factors come into play when we make decisions. One of these is cognitive bias, or systemic errors in our perception or way of thinking. A good example of this is survival bias. During the Second World War, the New York-based mathematician Abraham Wald was tasked with examining the distribution of damage to bomber planes returning after flying missions in order to work out which areas of the aircraft needed increased armour. The first "logical" solution was to strengthen armour in those places that had been damaged by the enemy's anti-aircraft and machine guns. However, Wald understood that there was no way he could inspect the entire fleet of planes, including those that had been destroyed. Having analysed the problem as a mathematician, he suggested reinforcing the parts of the planes that remained intact, because the aircraft that had suffered damage to these areas never made it back to base. In other words, the undamaged areas were considered to be the most vulnerable spots.

It is quite easy to stumble into a survival bias. What does Wald's example teach us? That you have to take the entire population into account. Survival bias is just one form of cognitive distortion.

In data analysis, survival bias is taking the known into account while neglecting the unknown (which nevertheless exists). It is extremely easy to fall into this trap when we need to draw a conclusion on the basis of a specific set of data. Data is by its very nature merely a sample, a snapshot of a much bigger picture. And samples are taken from the general population. Sufficiently large random samples are thus fine, as patterns typically emerge and the conclusions drawn are objective. Non-random samples, however, tend to produce erroneous conclusions. This is exactly what we saw in the case of the fighter planes, where Wald was at first tempted not to take the downed aircraft into account when making his recommendations.

For example, on average, only 1% of visitors to online stores actually make a purchase. Who do we need to appeal to if we want to improve these figures? Designers and product specialists tend to focus on existing customers. This is because the channels of communication are already open, the store has their contact details and a wealth of statistics on them. The problem here is that the sample they are working with represents just 1% of the general population of visitors to their website. And there is no way of getting in touch with the remaining 99% – they are downed fighter jets. Any conclusions drawn on the basis of this sample will, of course, be skewed towards the "survivors," and the results of the analysis will not be applicable to the vast majority of visitors to the site.

Another form of cognitive distortion is outcome bias. Imagine that you're about to observe the simultaneous flip of a fair coin and roll of a fair six-sided die. Before it happens, you are offered the choice between two gambles:

- Gamble on the coin: get $100 if it's heads; or
- Gamble on the die: get $100 if it's a six.

Which would you choose? The first one, of course, as you've got a 1/2 chance of winning, compared to a 1/6 chance in the second case. So, you flip the coin, and it lands on tails. You get nothing. Then you roll the die and it lands on six. Annoying, right? But does that mean we made the wrong choice?

I took this example from the article "Focus on Decisions, not Outcomes!" by Cassie Kozyrkov [5], Head of Google's Decision Intelligence division [4]. In the article, Kozyrkov implores us to "always evaluate decision quality based only on what was known at the time the decision was made." Many people regret not quitting their jobs earlier as procrastinating on the decision. I was guilty of this myself. This is a perfect example of *outcome bias* – we realise that we should have quit our jobs earlier based on the information we have now. For example, your pay has stagnated, or that interesting project you were looking forward to never got off the ground. When looking back on our past decisions (especially the poor ones) in moments of soul-searching, we should always remember that we made those decisions in conditions of uncertainty.

[4]    [5]

Chapter 2

LET'S DO SOME DATA ANALYSIS

When I was working at Wikimart.ru, the founders of the project introduced me to DJ Patil, one of the biggest angel investors in the project who had previously led the analytics division at LinkedIn before serving as the Chief Data Scientist of the United States Office of Science and Technology Policy under the Barack Obama administration. I met with DJ a few times in Moscow, as well as in Silicon Valley, California. He was in Moscow to promote his eBook, *Building Data Science Teams* [9], published by O'Reilly Media Inc., which talks about the experience of leading companies in Silicon Valley. I highly recommend the book, as its thoughts are close to my own, and I tested them out in practice. This is how he defines data-driven organizations:

> "A data-driven organization acquires, processes, and leverages data in a timely fashion to create efficiencies, iterate on and develop new products, and navigate the competitive landscape."

Patil then points out that the strongest data-driven organizations all follow the principle "if you can't measure it, you can't fix it." This paves the way for a number of recommendations:

- Collect as much data as you can. Whether you're doing business intelligence or building products.
- Measure in a proactive and timely manner.
- Get as many people in the organization as possible to look at the data. Multiple eyes help you identify obvious problems quicker.
- Foster increased curiosity among employees about why the data has or has not changed.

I will return to this topic in the chapter on data. Right now, it is time to talk about what we get at the end of the data analysis process.

[9]

DATA ANALYSIS ARTIFACTS

In the context of this book, "artifacts" means tangible results, a physical or virtual object. They can be divided into three types (Fig. 2.1):

- Business intelligence artifacts
- Machine learning artifacts
- Data engineering artifacts.

Let's look at each of these in more detail.

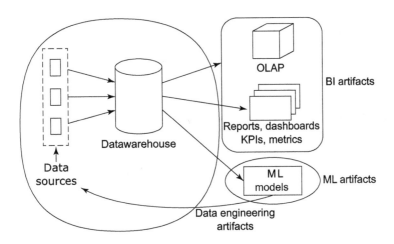

Fig. 2.1. Analysis Artifacts

BUSINESS INTELLIGENCE ARTIFACTS

Business Intelligence, or simply BI, is a well-established term. This is how Wikipedia defines it:

"Business intelligence (BI) comprises the strategies and technologies used by enterprises for the data analysis of business information."

By business intelligence, I mean the combination of business context and data, which allows businesses to ask questions about the data and search for answers. The first artifacts are so-called insights and hypotheses, followed by reports or dashboards, metrics and key performance indicators (KPIs). Let's look a bit closer at insights and hypotheses.

INSIGHTS AND HYPOTHESES

Insight means the capacity to gain an understanding of the reasons for something occurring. This is precisely what analysts want to achieve. Analytics and statistics help us to gain insight:

- The purpose of analytics [10] is to help us formulate hypotheses.

- The purpose of statistics [10] is to test and confirm these hypotheses.

Let me explain. In business, like in life, we look for the causes of a problem by asking the question "why"? We can't make a decision if we do not know the causes. This is where analytics comes into play – we formulate a list of possible causes (or hypotheses). And to do this, we need to ask a few questions:

- Has anything like this happened before? If it has, what were the causes? This gives us the first and most probable hypothesis.

- Has anything unusual happened from a business point of view? It is often the case that events going on at the same time have can bring about problems. This gives us a few more hypotheses.

- Exploratory data analysis: does an examination of the data in a given analytical system (for example, OLAP cubes) reveal any obvious anomalies? Perhaps some distributions have changed over time (types of customer, sales structure, etc.). If something looks iffy, then it should be added to the list.

Do we need to use more sophisticated search methods to find anomalies or identify changes, such as those described here? [11]

Our goal is to come up with as many hypotheses as possible, to let our imaginations run wild, and then sort these hypotheses into a list in decreasing order of probability in order to identify the correct one as quickly as possible. Or even use Occam's razor to sort hypotheses by how difficult they are to test out. Otherwise, you run the risk of analysis paralysis, testing each and every hypothesis without exception like a research scientist. This doesn't happen in real life, as we are always working within certain constraints – at the very least time. As soon as we have our hypotheses, it's time to subject them to statistical analysis. I'll talk about how to do this in the chapter on experiments in ML.

As Director of Analytics at Retail Rocket (a recommendation service for online stores), I was often tasked, along with my team of analysts, with carrying out investigations – it was a big company, after all, with over 1000 customers, and odd things are bound to crop up from time to time. We did a lot of so-called A/B testing, where visitors to the site are randomly divided into two groups: the first group sees one version of the website, while the second sees another. These tests are commonly used to assess the impact of changes on the business metrics of a company's website – the first (control) group is browsing the old site while the second is browsing the new version. If it is an online store, then we are most likely talking sales. We then apply certain statistical criteria to the test results in order to give us an idea of how successful the changes have been.

These tests are good at identifying problems. For example, the version of the website that contained updated Retail Rocket recommendations actually performed worse than the old version. As soon as these issues become known, it is time to look into the reasons why. The first thing to

[10]    [11]

be investigated is integration, and this brings us to our first hypothesis: Is the data from the online store transmitted to us correctly? Sixty to seventy percent of problems are typically dealt with at this stage. Next, we try to understand if this store is somehow different from other stores in the same category (for example, clothing stores). This is our second working hypothesis. As our third hypothesis, we look to see whether the new layout of the site relegated useful information to the bottom of the page. Fourth, we try to ascertain whether the test itself could have had a negative effect on certain categories of goods.

Once a list of hypotheses has been compiled, we then set about testing them in roughly the same sequence that I described above. Most of the time, we identify the cause of the problems. But not always. Sometimes fate plays cat and mouse with us, and the mouse is extremely elusive!

I remember one time we were involved in a kind of impromptu tender, when the baby store Dochki-Synochki decided to test our services against those of one of our competitors. And what a true crime story it turned out to be [12]! Worried about losing the tender, the other company fudged the results by moving users who were close to making a purchase (for example, those who had already added an item to their carts) to their own system. They weren't doing this all the time, only on certain days and at certain times. The main metric used to decide the tender winner was website conversion (hit rate) – that is, the percentage of users who actually made a purchase. Obviously, the competitor's fraudulent scheme produced a higher hit rate, as they were effectively stealing users from us. Meanwhile, Retail Rocket fought clean! So we started to dig around a bit. Two months later, we discovered what the other company had been up to and published our findings [12]. We had our day (well, days) in court and justice was done.

[12]

REPORTS, DASHBOARDS AND METRICS

The concept of *reporting* is extremely broad in its scope. Here, when I talk about reports and reporting, I mean a tabular or other kind of graphic representation of data. Reports can come in many different forms:

- A simple table with "raw" data – for example, a table listing customer orders.

- A document containing "aggregated" data. "Aggregated data" in this sense means numbers, quantities and other statistical information. For example, a table listing the names of customers and the number of orders each of them have placed.

- Dashboards containing key indicators and metrics.

The first two are relatively simple and are taken care of by dedicated systems that can generate reports on demand. I try to leave this task to the users as much as possible. Why? Because getting highly qualified employees to waste their time on such tasks is like using a sledgehammer to crack a nut. This is the kind of work that trainee analysts can do, as it is a great way to gain experience and learn about the inner workings of the business. How can we motivate users to do this themselves? First off, they will save time that is usually spent delegating and waiting for results. Second, they can make edits and changes (and thus be creative) themselves. I have noticed that it is usually ambitious employees who are not afraid to learn a skill in order to do their job better who take on such tasks. Everyone else will be stuck in the usual task-scheduling cycle, which eats up time (lasting for days or even weeks) and is very inflexible in terms of the scope of work. By the way, all the CEOs I worked with (at Ozon.ru, Wikimart.ru and Ostrovok) used OLAP cubes on their computers. OLAP cubes are very good at providing solutions to simple questions, and when they fail, you can always turn to your analytics team.

Now let's look at dashboards, starting with the definition from Wikipedia:

"A dashboard is a type of graphical user interface which often provides at-a-glance views of key performance indicators (KPIs) relevant to a particular objective or business process. In other usage, 'dashboard' is another name for 'progress report' or 'report' and considered a form of data visualization."

Dashboards typically consist of key performance indicators and metrics represented using visual tools (graphs, charts, etc.):

- Key performance indicators (KPI) – an indicator that tells us how far we are from our targets (plan implementation progress).

- Metrics – figures that describe a given process and which are usually used for reference purposes.

The main difference between metrics and key performance indicators is that the latter are geared towards the achievement of targets and goals. Metrics are not. As a rule, KPIs are used in company dashboards when both the product and the business process are "fixed." A great deal of data has already been accumulated and targets can be set. I typically use metrics in the absence of stable processes, when the goals are not yet clear. Looking at the ratio of KPIs to metrics gives us an idea of how "sophisticated" the dashboard is: more metrics means a less refined dashboard.

Dashboards usually describe some kind of business process (the word "process" is used interchangeably with "business process" from here on out), for example, advertising effectiveness, stock balance, sales, etc. The key features of dashboards:

- they are more than just a "sheet of numbers"; and

- tell you where a problem occurred, although they cannot tell you why.

It's often tempting to draw up a huge sheet of numbers covering all aspects of the business. And I understand business owners and managers who want as much information at the beginning of a project so that an in-house analytical system can be set up. I witnessed this first-hand at both Ozon.ru and Ostrovok.ru. In fact, these lines are based on a letter I wrote eight years ago to the COO of Ostrovok.ru, who was asking that his analysts produce one of those "sheets" full of numbers. I call this digital "micromanagement." It's easy to get lost in all the figures, and the most important indicators get buried among all the others. It is almost impossible to immediately see where a problem may have originated, which is the main function of dashboards. This is where OKRs (Objectives and Key Results) [13] or Balanced Scorecards can be useful. I'm not going to dwell on these methods here, but I would suggest that you learn about them in your own time. Frequent use of visual elements can also help – adding trend lines to charts (using a seven-day moving average to prevent boom periods from skewing the results), for example, makes it easier to spot trends.

Dashboards help you identify problems, but they tell you nothing about why they have occurred. It might be tempting to draw up a huge and detailed report in order to pinpoint the reasons, but all you'll end up with is a sheet full of figures, like I mentioned earlier. You can't interact with a mass of numbers, and the only way to analyse them is to immerse yourself fully in them, which requires a completely different set of tools. Next time you feel the urge to start wading through numbers, try and recall the last time you were able to find the cause of a problem with the help of a dashboard.

Dashboards are not a substitute for interactive analysis, which requires a specific analytical system (SQL, OLAP, Google Data Studio, Tableau) and an understanding of the context. Reports can only tell us so much – there's no magic formula that will tell us *why* certain things happened. What we can do is increase (within reason) the number of useful metrics based on the types of incident to be monitored.

This is why I always favour concise automatically generated reports that address two questions: 1) Is there a problem? 2) Where did it arise? If there is a problem, then we need to turn to interactive data analysis tools.

Dashboard development is one of the most loathed jobs among data analysts. I brought this up during one of my conversations with DJ Patil. Upon hearing that 50% of the analytical department's time was spent working on reporting, he told me that similar tasks often mounted up

[13]

at LinkedIn too. And this seemed to make him sad. But the fact of the matter is that dashboards are vital, as they help you monitor the overall health of the system. For systems administrators, this means the servers and networks entrusted to them. For CEOs, it means the entire company.

MACHINE LEARNING ARTIFACTS

For a long time, the only way to control computers was through direct commands or instructions: turn here, back up, set down, etc. This is what we call deterministic programming – the algorithm is made up of understandable instructions; we formulate the commands and the computer carries them out. Machine learning involves a completely different approach to programming, namely, learning by example. Here, we show the system something with the help of examples, thus eliminating the need to write these instructions in the form of code, which is by no means an easy task. It's just a matter of learning the ML algorithm.

For me, machine learning differs from programming in the same way that quantum physics differs from classical physics. Classical physics allows us to determine exactly where the planets of the solar system are. Quantum mechanics is different. It tells us that all potential outcomes are equally possible – we cannot predict the exact location of a particle in space, only the probability of finding it at different locations. Machine learning works with probabilities in much the same way. For example, an image recognition model can estimate the probability of a given image being the photo of a cat. When I say model here, I mean a computer program (or code) with a number of features:

- The ability to receive data (features, independent predictors, independent variables) for learning, and produce the correct answer (output). The result is then stored inside the model itself. This is called training the model.

- Predictive capacity, or the ability to predict the results for new examples.

Take the following example. We've got a bunch of photos of cats and dogs and we want to separate them into two files – one with pictures of cats and the other with pictures of dogs. When I say we've got a bunch of photos, I mean a lot, like millions. And we don't want to put them in the correct folders by hand! So, we create a training dataset of 1000 photos each labelled "cat" or "dog." All we have to do is select the correct model, "feed" the train function with the labelled dataset, and the model does the rest. The model itself looks like a black box to us, although we can, of course, look inside it (which is precisely what we will do in the chapter on machine learning). Once the model has "learnt" from the initial dataset, we can start feeding it the photos. The machine will calculate the probability of each photo containing a cat or a dog. We can then use this information to separate the photos.

I've seen this work in practice. It was around the time that neural networks (deep learning) were gaining in popularity, and Kaggle.com set up a competition with almost the exact same parameters as this problem [14]. I decided to enter, and I found some code on the internet that didn't use neural networks. Of course, nothing came of it. My algorithm was so bad that I may as well have been flipping a coin! The winning entrants developed code that gave the correct result in almost 99% of cases (predictive accuracy). Their model was based on convolutional neural networks. I was amazed at what they'd come up with. But this was back in 2013, before deep learning had become so popular. That's how quickly technology is changing!

The next postulate is that the data used to train the model is part of the code. This is another way in which machine learning differs from classical programming. The code itself can be replicated by publishing the lines on the internet. It will work exactly the same everywhere. But

[14]    [15]

if you want to share the trained model, then you'll have to send both the code and the resulting black box. That's how researchers share their trained models. For example, the Resnet 50 neural network model [15] was trained using millions of images. And it works without any additional preparation – feed it a photograph and it can name all the objects in it.

DATA ENGINEERING ARTIFACTS

Nothing is possible without data engineering. Even simple makeshift solutions demand answers to the following questions:

- Where can we get the data from? How often? And how can we get access to it?
- What output capacity of the data sources is required for the business to run smoothly and for data to be readily available for analysis?
- What storage architecture is needed? Can we do without it?
- What analytical system should we use?
- How can we use trained machine learning models (ML models) in processes?

I could go on here. These issues should be resolved and automated. Data engineering artifacts include:

- Analytical system architecture.
- Program code that ensures the operation of the system.

If everything is done perfectly, then these two artifacts are enough to deploy (prepare) the analytical system in the shortest possible time. In powerful iterations, this can be done automatically with the press of one button. This is important for the stable performance of the analytical system. Unfortunately, the work of the people who do this (systems administrators, engineers) is nearly invisible, especially when everything is working as it should. They are barely noticed and no one understands exactly what it is they do, which is why they are chronically underappreciated.

Analytical system architecture is made up of several levels:

- Physical – servers and the communication channels between them.
- Data – data warehouses.
- Application – programs that allow users to access data and publish ML models.

Systems administrators are responsible for the physical level. They take care of the hardware in order to make sure that the system is fault-tolerant. They also constantly monitor the health of the system. You know how to tell whether you've got a good system and a good administrator? You have no idea what the administrator does and the system works without any major issues.

Data engineers (also known as ETL engineers) are responsible for the data level of analytics architecture. Their main task is to make sure that data is delivered from data sources and stored in data warehouses. They often take care of data processing and BI system deployment (OLAP cubes and reporting systems) as well.

At the level of applications, we have ML engineers and data scientists. ML engineers create ML models and are sometimes involved in their deployment and implementation (although in large companies other engineers are usually involved in this work). Meanwhile, data scientists test and evaluate models. In smaller companies, roles of ML engineer and data scientist are often combined. I remember interviewing at the Quora.com office in Palo Alto, California, when I discovered that they have ML engineers who are responsible for developing ML models and data scientists who work on metrics, data analysis and other things – but not ML models.

WHO ANALYSES DATA?

The closer data analysis is to the decision node, the better. If a project manager runs into an issue but has a complete understanding of the business context (what events occurred, and so on) and is working with an analytical system that has a high level of interactivity, then most problems are easily resolved. Up to 80% (remember the Pareto principle), to be precise. What are the advantages of these kinds of solution? There's no middleman, so everything works faster! The user might not even have a clearly formulated question, something that most certainly is needed if the task if delegated to analysts. This is why it is vital to "sell" employees on the usefulness of the analytical approach and regularly train them in its use.

If the business context is fuzzy or goes beyond the manager's competencies, or if the client is asking a question that the manager simply cannot answer, then analysts need to be brought in. I usually recommend that departments have their own "in-house" analyst, who understands the workings of the department (its business context) and has highly developed analytical and technical skills. This is the second line of defence. An "in-house" analyst will be able to solve issues within the department faster than an analyst from the analytics department, for the simple reason that he or she has nothing else to do!

The third line of defence is when we transfer a task to the data analytics department. We resort to this when:

- the task requires changes to the system kernel
- the task is too technically complex for the given department's in-house
- large-scale collaboration between departments is required.

I wasn't able to fully implement such a system during my time at Ozon. ru. It was a different story at Wikimart.ru, however: interactive data analysis in OLAP cubes allowed users to resolve issues quickly, in-house analysts took care of departmental data, and the analytics department created the core of the entire analytical system. By the way, I've received countless letters over the years from former Ozon.ru employees who used OLAP cubes in their work lamenting the fact that other companies simply do not use these analytical tools. I guess it's easy to get used to a good thing!

THE PERFECT BUTTON

I didn't know any English at all when I went to university. Regrettably, I'd studied German at school. But I had to know English for my course, so I was placed in a beginners group at the start of my first year, along with just three other people! We had two classes a week every week for three years. It was one of my favourite subjects, and one that came in handy on more than one occasion. In my fourth year, I got a side gig translating a book about StatSoft's STATISTICA data analysis program from English into Russian. It was an intern position, and I was expected to translate 15,000 characters a day. My head would be spinning by the end of each day! I gradually got the hang of it and they started giving me more interesting things to do – teaching seminars, giving sales presentations, going on business trips, etc. I moved into consulting, where I realized one important thing: all clients want is a button, preferably right there on their chair, that they can sit on and all their work magically gets done.

More than that, they are often too lazy to go into details and are ready to pay crazy money for pretty wrapping. IT companies and consultants are very good at exploiting this phenomenon. And I witnessed it for myself when Ozon.ru was looking for a web analytics solution and couldn't choose between SiteCatalyst and Webtrends. The sales teams for both companies promised a "bright" future. As none of the decisionmakers (including myself) was particularly clued in about the subject, they went with the company that put on the best sales pitch. Omniture's presentation was simply better – they gave us radio-controlled cars and all kinds of gifts. So, we chose them, even though there was really nothing in it in terms of the solutions they offered and the price. By the time I was hired by Wikimart.ru, I had a much better understanding of what users need from web analytics. I drew up the technical requirements myself, got the developers to write the necessary code, and two months later we had our own web analytics system that was just as good as Omniture's, saving the company around $100,000 per year in the process.

I'm not trying to say that salespeople and consultants are bad, I'm simply urging you not to be lazy. Read a book on the subject, cover to cover. Better yet, read two. Search out independent experts whose opinions you can trust. Most importantly, dive into the details – this is where you'll find the problems, as well as their solutions. Learn to be sceptical of your emotions. Don't believe everything you hear at conferences; people only give you one side of the story, it's all just too perfect to be true. Not that you can't take positives away from such events, just that people conveniently forget to tell you the cost of this or that decision.

SELL ANALYTICS INTERNALLY

This is a complicated issue. In the previous section, I mentioned that it took me just two months to get the analytical system up and running (and that was when I was working two days a week). Actually "selling" it to the end user took much longer, and it was a good four months or so before they were using the system on a more or less regular basis. And I'd organized a kick-off presentation pretty much as soon as the system was ready for launch, inviting all the company's top execs, including its founders.

I find it easier to work with people on an individual level – chatting over lunch, shooting the breeze by the water cooler, taking an interest in other people's tasks, and generally digging deeper. Then I try to come up with a way to solve the task at hand, what we have and what is missing, and run it by the necessary people. You can't just drop a new system into people's laps and expect them to get it immediately. You've got to show them how it works, let them see for themselves how it can speed up the problem-solving process.

This is precisely how we went about implementing analytics at Retail Rocket using the ClickHouse system. Before we arrived on the scene, the company's data was only available in an SQL interface through a computer cluster based on Spark, Hadoop (we'll discuss these technologies in the chapter on storage) and Hive. Facebook uses a similar scheme to provide access to data internally. The problem with this technology is that it processes data slowly – requests took up to 30 minutes. What is more, no data beyond the previous day was available. The only people who had access to the system were the technical support staff. We decided to try out Yandex's ClickHouse analytical database on one of our projects and were immediately impressed: it processed the data quickly (most requests took seconds) and, with a little tweaking, we managed to get the system working in almost real time. Tech support, one of the biggest divisions at Retail Rocket, switched entirely to the new system. They soon fell in love with it and ended up abandoning Hive altogether. We then started offering it to other divisions within the company. We held a number of training presentations to familiarize employees with the system, and many of them signed up on the spot. The only problem was that they didn't actually start using it. So, we decided to take a different approach: incoming tasks that could be solved using the system were repeatedly "sent back" with a note essentially telling those employees who had sent the tasks to "take care of them" themselves. We wanted to show them exactly what the system was capable of. And it worked, as a number of employees started to work with the system on their own! There's still a lot that can be done, but I'm happy with what we've managed to achieve.

What typically happens if we separate analytics from sales, we see that the business often does not have a person in charge of the internal product, someone who could help employees perform their tasks more efficiently, better automate internal processes, and get rid of pointless functions. Businesses love implementing processes that increase the level of bureaucracy in the company, but hardly anyone thinks about the internal product in order to improve productivity among employees. I think this is because it is difficult to calculate how much a company could make from such work. But it is extremely important, nevertheless. And when it happens, you don't even have to spend time trying to convince the other divisions within the company to use the product – they'll come to you.

THE CONFLICT BETWEEN THE RESEARCHER AND BUSINESS

During my years in data analysis, I noticed a conflict of interests not unlike the generation gap: young and daring analysts and engineers are keen to create something that is – well, maybe not monumental, but at least meaningful and elegant, something they can brag about, use to bolster their self-esteem, or put on their resume. Many of them are obsessed with machine learning, trying to apply it to every task at hand, regardless of whether it's really fit for the purpose. Business, however, is not so romantic in its aspirations: it measures meaningfulness with money. It is literally obliged to do so: the charter of almost every limited liability company in Russia, for example, has a clause that says something like, "The purpose of the Company is to achieve maximum economic efficiency and profitability."

I have interviewed many job candidates, from graduates to seasoned professionals, and there is a clear trend: people today tend to look for jobs that are interesting. Those who are well into their career say, "I'm sick of all the routine and petty things, I want to work with machine learning models." Meanwhile, newcomers are all, "I want to do computer vision and NLP [natural language processing]." Machine learning is clearly very popular, but for me it sounds a lot like a construction worker who loves hammers and wants to build a house with nothing but a hammer.

Andrew Ng, who has done more to popularize ML than perhaps anybody else – and the author of my favourite course on Coursera – wrote this in his deeplearning.ai newsletter:

> "There's a huge difference between building a Jupyter notebook model in the lab and deploying a production system that generates business value. AI as a field sometimes seems crowded but, in fact, it's wide open to professionals who know what they're doing."

Data analysis and machine learning courses have a useful role to play, but they can be compared to model ships – they are as far from real ships as courses are from real-life ML applications.

Former Basecamp data scientist Noah Lorang wrote in his blog [16]:

> "The dirty little secret of the ongoing 'data science' boom is that most of what people talk about as being data science isn't what businesses actually need. Businesses need accurate and actionable information to help them make decisions about how they spend their time and resources. There is a very small subset of business problems that are best solved by machine learning; most of them just need good data and an understanding of what it means that is best gained using simple methods."

I can personally vouch for every single word here. Sadly, there's a lot of hype around our profession. YouTubers promote data science courses, presidents talk about AI, and Tesla's stock goes up every day. But young specialists who want to build spaceships eventually meet companies that want to make money. In the following chapters, I will discuss ways to reconcile their interests.

THE WEAKNESSES OF A STATISTICAL APPROACH IN DATA ANALYSIS

Data analysis turns people into averages. Answering the BBC's question about the fate of the individual in modern thought, Carl Jung, the founder of analytical psychology, said [17]:

> "Well, that is, of course, one of the consequences of our modern science, which is chiefly based upon the average, the statistical average. Now, the statistical average produces a picture of man which is utterly unimportant. It is a mere abstraction, it is not a real man.

Our Weltanschauung [world view] that is based upon the statistical average is an abstraction. It is not the real world. And therefore the individual is a sort of random phenomenon. But in reality the individual is the only reality.

And if you follow the idea of the statistical average, then you have only the idea of the so-called "normal man", and the normal man does not exist. He is a mere abstraction. We have to deal with individuals only. So, anything that can happen in the way of development or results or so on, happens to the individual, and not to an average man. And you cannot do it with masses, with numbers. It must be the concrete, individual man that has to do it."

The statistical approach, dealing with data as "aggregates" (sums, quantities, averages), removes "weak" signals of individuality. For an algorithm, a person is just a data point with several numbers and an ID. Everything else is superfluous, just irrelevant features that the model cannot extract any value from. Machine learning models tend to overgeneralize and oversimplify. They see things in black and white, without any shades in between. Their output is a banality – a score, a quantitative measure that informs the decision to approve a loan or not, etc. This is my general impression of ML models.

Another drawback of the statistical approach is that it is based on measuring things. Jerry Muller, scientist and contributor to *The New York Times* and *The Wall Street Journal*, writes about this in his book *The Tyranny of Metrics* [18]:

"There are things that can be measured. There are things that are worth measuring. But what can be measured is not always what is worth measuring; what gets measured may have no relationship to what we really want to know. The costs of measuring may be greater than the benefits. The things that get measured may draw effort away from the things we really care about."

Mindlessly adopting quantitative metrics for every single purpose is wrong. I remember when I was at school, they made us do fitness tests in gym class. One of the things we had to do was run 100 metres for time and then do the long jump. But no one seemed to want to teach us the benefits of regular exercise. Everything took a backseat to the standards they had set for us. They didn't care about our personal progress (we're all different, and you can't hold everyone to the same standard) or how much we may have liked a given sport. This is deeply wrong. I remember reading a social media post by a graduate of the Moscow Institute of Physics and Technology (MIPT/Phystech): "It was 1987. We had already passed the entrance exams… And then we were given a sort of a physical education test, which was to swim across the 25m university pool. Everyone had to do it, and then the results were put up on a stand for all to see. I remember looking at those numbers: 30 seconds, 35 seconds, 1 minute, 2 minutes, 5 minutes… Down at the bottom it read, 'Did not finish.' What on earth could that mean?"

Quantitative scores may indeed be bad, but no one has come up with anything better. And we have to admit that the methodologies used for coming up with these scores are evolving and becoming more complex. Ten years ago, when assessing a site's effectiveness, I (and likely most of my colleagues) would focus on conversion; only later did we start using other metrics as well, such as average revenue per visitor, average order value, average items per order and even margin. Those indicators would then be broken down by top-level product categories and user groups (if enough data was available). In other words, a single metric (conversion) was not sufficient: ecommerce economics is more complex.

[16]   [17]    [18]

Chapter 3

BUILDING ANALYTICS FROM SCRATCH

In this chapter, I will outline my approach to building a company's analytics framework from the ground up. I have done this twice as an employee (at Ozon.ru and Wikimart.ru) and once as a co-founder (at Retail Rocket). I have also consulted several companies while also helping them hire people.

STEP ONE

When I need to create or significantly improve an analytics system, I always take a two-pronged approach: on the one hand, I determine what tasks and issues we are facing, and on the other, I find out what data is available.

To compile a list of tasks, we need to conduct interviews with all potential information consumers who may be affected. When designing the system for its users, you need to know the answers to the following questions:

- What metrics do you need to calculate?
- What dashboards do you need to develop?
- What information do you need to feed to interactive systems?
- Will there be any ML (machine learning) tasks?

What makes this step hard is that consumers (customers) don't always know what kind of information they will need. And in order to build an effective system, the analyst must have at least some expertise in the business he or she is analysing. After working in ecommerce, I found the transition to Ostrovok.ru (a hotel booking system) somewhat jarring. Sure, we did online sales, but I needed very specific knowledge of the hotel business. When you understand the business, you know what questions to ask the customer. You can then use their answers to build a data structure that will help solve the client's problems.

Then I go to the developers and start exploring what they actually have – what data they collect and where this data is located. First, I am looking for data that will help solve the client's tasks (and I make a point of looking not only at flowcharts, but also at examples of such data – the actual table rows and files). Second, an important thing for me is finding data that exists but has not yet been used from the point of view of the tasks that they could solve? By the end of this stage, I already have:

- A list of issues that are covered by current data
- A list of questions that do not have data, and an understanding of how much effort it will take to obtain them
- Data that does not yet solve any urgent problems
- Data sources and their approximate volumes.

This is just the first iteration. I take this list to the customers. I talk to the same people, explain whether it is possible to answer their questions and whether additional data is needed, and then I go back to the developers. It looks like shuttle diplomacy, but that's how I plan the project.

In the end, I have a list of system requirements and a list of available data and tasks that need to be completed in order to get the missing numbers. It looks simple, but sometimes these steps can take weeks. I don't just go and download all the data from the data warehouse and immediately start trying to make metrics and dashboards. Instead, I try to solve the problem in my head. This saves me a lot of energy, and the customers a lot of worry. They will know in advance what will work out right away and what will not.

CHOOSING THE TECH

This is my second step. The right technology stack will save you years of headaches. I will discuss technologies in detail in the following chapters, so I will just outline the general picture here. An indicative list of questions about technologies looks like this:

- Own storage or cloud storage?
- Should open-source technologies be used?

- What programming language should be used for engineering arti-facts?
- Can we outsource the development of analytics to a third party?
- Which reporting system should we use?
- Are near-real-time analytics required anywhere?

These are the most basic questions, but a lot depends on them – includ-ing what kind of employees to hire, how much investment is needed, and how quickly we can start the project.

My rule of thumb when it comes to data storage is that if a company is going to make a significant portion of its revenue from data, then it is better to have its own storage. If analytics is just a supporting project, then it is better to use cloud storage.

The goal of any business is to make profit. Profit is revenue minus costs, which include the cost of storing data. And this cost can be quite large if the data is stored in the cloud. Setting up our own storage can be a solution. Yes, this will entail administration costs, and the system will require more attention. But you will obviously have more ways to reduce costs, and the system will be far more flexible. If analytics do not have such a direct impact on P&L, then cloud storage will be much easier. You won't have to think about failed servers – "the cloud" will do that job for you.

Open-source technologies are very important in analytics. I first encoun-tered them when I was studying at Phystech. In my second year, I got a computer. It wasn't particularly powerful even by those days' standards, so I installed Linux on it. I spent hours compiling the kernel to fit my needs, learning to work in the console. This experience would come in handy exactly ten years later, when I visited the Netflix office in Los Gatos, California, and met Eric Colson, who was Head of Analytics. He talked about the tools his employees use in their work, and even wrote them out on a board with a marker. He was also big on open-source software for data analysis, such as Python, Hadoop and R. Before that, I had only used commercial software. I remember sitting alone in the empty Wikimart.ru offices one night that summer (everyone had gone to a staff party) writing the first nine lines of code in Pig for the Hadoop platform (my Linux skills came in handy here). It took four hours. What I didn't know then was that just a few years later, this language and this platform would be used to write the "brain" of the Retail Rocket recommendation system. By the way, the entire Retail Rocket analytics system – both the internal system for making decisions and the system that generates recommendations – was written using only open-source technologies.

Now, looking back, I can say that Retail Rocket is the coolest thing I have ever done in my career: the company quickly broke even and is now successfully competing with Western counterparts, employing more than a hundred people around the world with main offices in Moscow, Togliatti (Russia), The Hague, Santiago, Madrid and Barcelona. A Russian company, developing and creating jobs abroad! The development vector has changed: in addition to the Retail Rocket recommendation system, the company is selling many related services for online stores. The big data analysis and ML technologies that we created back in 2013 are still relevant today, and I am very proud that we managed to rise head and shoulders above our competitors in terms of technology.

When is using proprietary software a good idea? The answer is, when you have the money. Almost any proprietary software has an open-source counterpart, although it is true that they are generally worse, especially in certain areas. For example, I've never found a decent open-source analogue for OLAP cubes. Open-source reporting systems also look half-baked. However, when it comes to engineering technologies such as Hadoop, Spark or Kafka, they are very reliable and powerful developer tools that have proven their excellence in commercial applications.

Let's discuss the programming languages that will be used in the development of the system. My motto is, the fewer the better. Before Retail Rocket, I was able to get by with just SQL – although I did have to use commercial tools from Microsoft to move data (ETL) from the source to the warehouse. Retail Rocket's recommendation engine used to be implemented using four programming languages: Pig, Hive, Java and

Python. Then we replaced all of them with Scala, since it belongs to the JVM family that Hadoop is written in. This makes Scala very easy to use on the Hadoop/Spark platform, with the latter supporting it natively. But a couple of years ago, we started using Python and SQL – we had to move away from Scala, as it was inconvenient for some things.

Scala is a beautiful and elegant programming language, but we ran into two problems. First, it would be very difficult for users to use it as an interface to data. SQL is much better for this. Second, all modern ML libraries are written in Python. So we decided to use Scala for the central core of the system, data aggregation and delivery, SQL for reports, and Python for developing ML models and simple prototypes. The choice of a programming language usually depends on several things:

- the system it will be used for (for example, SQL is ideal for databases)
- whether or not there are people who work with this language in your company or on the market as a whole.

For example, forcing the users of your system to learn difficult programming languages to obtain data access is a bad idea. For users, it is just an auxiliary tool, and they don't want to spend too much time learning it.

The skills market is a source of constant headaches. Scala is a very rare language, and it is quite difficult to learn. There are very few people on the market who know it, and those who do are expensive. Python, on the contrary, is very popular. But I'd happily give three Python programmers for one Scala developer. Here we made a conscious decision – the quality of our work is more important to us, so we chose Scala. It was almost impossible to hire people trained in Scala people, so we devised our own crash course [19], teaching beginners to program in it in six months.

[19]

LET'S TALK ABOUT OUTSOURCING

Now let's look at bringing in external contractors to set up an analytical system. Various aspects can be outsourced:

- the creation and maintenance of the technical part of the system
- the analytical part of the system
- specific parts of the system.

Good contractors are needed when we need to reduce the set-up time of the technical part of the project and achieve high-quality results. Good luck on that one! Contractors generally do not have a deep enough knowledge of the task at hand and, on top of that, the customer rarely knows what they want.

I remember being put on a project team once at one of the places I worked. It wasn't an analytical project, and in theory it looked great. Better still, the team leader taught systems design at one of the best universities in the country. We chose the most "up-to-date" technologies to implement the project. Three or four developers spent an entire year writing the system. When it was finally ready, they wasted a whole day trying to get it to work... with absolutely no success, so we ended up throwing the entire system onto the scrapheap. The same thing can happen with analytics. Theory and practice are two wildly different things, especially in today's rapidly changing world.

The risk is reduced if you have an experienced analyst on your team who has personally implemented a number of similar projects in the past. He or she can be an independent advisor on your project, or even a moderator of sorts. This is necessary, on the one hand, to keep the customer "grounded," and, on the other, to keep a rein on the contractor. I believe that, to begin with, it is better to produce a stripped-down version of the project that we can get up and running as soon as possible. There are a few reasons for this. First off, after you (the client) have spent some time with the program, you will have a much better idea of what you actually want. It's hard to get a clear picture of the project when it is still on paper – it's like a spherical cow in a vacuum. The second reason is motivation, which is extremely important for me personally. When the time starts to drag, the team, as well as the customers, gradually lose interest in the project. The result is a laboured project that we don't really want to be a part of anymore.

If you can't find someone who can act as an advisor on the project, try to get an understanding of the problem yourself – read a book, watch video recordings of conferences, etc. Otherwise, you're running the risk of the project never making it off the ground, which would be a huge waste of time and resources.

It's all well and good outsourcing the technological part of projects, but can you outsource analytics too? The short answer is, "no, you can't." Third-party analysts will never be able to fully grasp the complete business context. That said, some areas of analytics – advertising, for example – can indeed be outsourced.

Another option is to outsource an entire part of the project: you give them the data and end up with a finished product.

One example of this kind of cooperation is Retail Rocket, where we started out with product recommendations. Online stores provided us with data and a product base, and in the end, they got readymade recommendations. The idea for this kind of business came to me when I was working at Wikimart.ru. I was making recommendations for the company's website and thought to myself, "why not launch a retail solution?" This way, the online store would not need to hire machine learning engineers and re-invent the wheel. The result was obtained much faster, literally within a week. And our recommendation system was better than the in-house one. If an online store was to hire me today, then I would probably contract a third-party recommendation service instead of developing one in-house.

Let me tell you a little about my own personal experience with outsourcing. I left Ozon.ru in 2009. I'd be running my own blog, KPIs.ru, for a few years by that time and it was proving to be rather popular. People had even started to look to me for consulting services in all kinds of areas: game development, ecommerce, venture capital, etc. Slowly, I started to build up my consulting activities, working for three companies at the same time. I helped the first company choose the right technology and hire personnel for the project team, which included conducting interviews. The second company was looking for assistance in growing startups. My job with the third company was more hands-on, as I helped set up the analytical system from scratch. I took a lot away from this experience. First of all, I was able to help companies without being bogged down in corporate details and politics, something that certainly would not have been possible if I had been hired as a full-time member of staff there. My work also allowed the companies to launch projects quickly. I ended up staying on at the third company (Wikimart.ru) full time, as its founder offered me the job of head of analytics. I agreed because, at the time, I wanted to be working directly with data and "get my hands dirty," as it were. And that was the end of my little outsourcing adventure.

HIRING AND FIRING (OR RESIGNING)

So, let's say the technologies have been chosen, the tasks clearly set out, and the information on the available data is in our hands. Maybe we've got the analytical system up and running and there to be used. Now let's talk about hiring employees.

I described the many roles in the previous chapter. Ideally, there should be one person per function. However, it is not uncommon at the initial stages to combine roles: the analyst can retrieve the data and set up the ML model, for instance. I never hire anyone we don't need, as I am a proponent of the lean startup theory. It's better to hire new people as and when you need them and expand the department in a consistent manner than mindlessly hire a bunch of people and then not know what to do with them.

We'll assume that you've settled on a list of who you need. Now I'd like to share a little about my experience of hiring people. I've interviewed hundreds of experts over the years, and I've got a pretty clear picture in my head of what I am looking for in terms of professional qualities (the HR Department can sift through candidates at this stage). What I look for in employees is clear-headedness, a desire for professional development and similar values to my own. On occasion, I've managed to find junior analysts/developers and part-time trainees through group interviews. This is essentially how it works, start to finish. First, we advertise vacancies, which includes posting listings around universities. The recruiter gets in touch with all the applicants and invites them to the recruitment day, which is typically divided into a number of stages:

1. Welcome address. This involves introducing the company, what it does etc. Fifteen minutes is sufficient for this.

2. Group work. The candidates are then randomly split into groups of three to four. They are given a simple analytical task and 30 or so minutes to discuss it within their groups. I suggest walking around and listening to what the candidates are saying here. One person from each group then stands up and explains what their group came up with.

3. Individual task. Offer an approach or solution to a given task. Written tasks are fine here. This part should not take longer than 30 minutes.

So, in just two hours, you get a reasonably good picture of all the candidates. You'll have an idea of who might be a good fit and who won't. You'll see all this because you are able to compare the candidates with each other in real time, which is very convenient. A certain number of candidates will make it to the next round. This is where they are all interviewed individually. I used this simple process on a number of occasions to hire interns at two companies. I ended up working with them for a long time, and almost every one of them has grown into a top-rate specialist. Putting time and effort into the hiring process really paid off.

It's a little trickier when it comes to hiring specialists. You can't use recruitment days here. We expect more from candidates in terms of their qualifications. Plus, there's a staggering imbalance in the market. Recently, I was looking to hire two people – a data engineer and a data scientist. Which vacancy do you think most people applied for? Okay, let me ask you another question: Are there more guitarists or drummers in Russia? I played the #ROCKNMOB show three times. For those who don't know, #ROCKNMOB is a kind of large-scale flash mob for amateur musicians – hundreds of singers, bass players, guitarists and drummers from all over the country get together and play rock hits, from Queen to Rammstein. One time 27 drummers and 151 guitarists showed up. These numbers reflect what we see in real life: the guitarist is always the "sexy" archetype (I play guitar, by the way), and guitarists just look cooler than drummers! Plus, guitars are cheaper than drum kits. Data engineers are on the wrong end of an even bigger beating, with 95% of candidates applying for the data scientist position. They're the guitarists of the analytics world! The problem is that the majority of them are not sufficiently qualified and have spotty resumes at best. Yet they act like they know everything. That's what hype will do for you!

This is what I do when I interview data scientists: first I schedule a 15-minute call and ask them some basic questions to gauge their understanding of machine learning. If they seem relatively knowledgeable, I invite them for the interview proper. The first interview is divided into two parts: first, we chat for half an hour about machine learning, covering the basics and more complex aspects; then I ask questions about engineering, such as how certain things are done in SQL. We'll then set up a second interview where the candidates are given a simple machine learning task to solve. We literally sit down together at a computer and the candidate completes the task. I'll ask various questions while they are doing this to make sure that they understand what they are doing and why they are doing it. What I really want to gauge is whether or not the candidate has practical experience. You can usually tell right away from how fast they code. These interviews are generally enough to see if a candidate has what it takes and offer them the job.

Firing is typically a taboo subject, but I would say that it is even more important than hiring. I don't subscribe to such populist sentiments as "hire slowly, fire quickly!" You've got to treat your employees like people. And this extends to letting them go as well. This is an important part of corporate culture. There are generally two ways an employee can leave a company: they can resign, or they can be fired. I've seen more of the first in my field. The main reason for this is "not enough machine learning," even though they were told they would be doing loads of it at university.

This is one of those cases where scientific theory and real-life practice diverge significantly. I never grow tired of repeating that real machine learning takes up just 5–10% of the time spent on machine learning projects. Once I'd figured this out, I started to weed out those candidates who were clearly living in a dream world at the interview stage. The second reason why people quit their jobs is that they have outgrown their current position or are sick of working on one and the same project all the time. In these cases, I usually try to pull a few strings to help them land a job elsewhere.

There are many reasons to let an employee go – they make glaring errors, do not fit into our analytical culture, etc. But I never make rash decisions. I mean, we all mess up from time to time. First, I talk to every member of the team individually to get their feedback. If the general feeling is negative, it almost always means we need to let the person go. We can try chatting to them, give them some projects to work on, but that rarely helps. In my experience, these people tend to go off and find "normal" jobs where they are much happier. They weren't "bad" employees or anything like that, they were just a bad fit for us.

WHO DO ANALYSTS ANSWER TO?

Ideally, analysts should have no connections whatsoever with the managers they are evaluating. The basic principle that rules here is "he who pays the piper calls the tune." What if an analyst can't evaluate his manager's work objectively? Solve issues in the department? No problem (recall the case of decentralization we talked about in the previous chapter)! But evaluate the manager's work? Nope! This is where operational independence is vital. I would recommend that the central analytics department report to the CEO, or to the finance or IT departments (in order of priority). I've reported to CEOs, CMOs and IT directors in the past. By far the best experience was reporting to CEOs, as there is minimal pressure from the outside. But there's a caveat here: as a rule, managers have no idea how to manage analytics, while the CEO simply doesn't have the time.

The head of analytics will have to display remarkable independence. I've been given assignments that have essentially amounted to "find something interesting." I started writing this book in the hope, among other things, that top managers who are responsible for analytics teams would read it. I'd consider it a small victory if they do!

SHOULD THE HEAD OF ANALYTICS WRITE CODE?

I've always loved the role of "player-manager" – managing a small team of people, teaching interns, and getting my hands dirty as well. I can say with no hint of false modesty that my teams are always like a special forces detachment that has to perform complex tasks in a limited amount of time. At the initial stages, I would be heavily involved alongside everyone else in designing the analytical system and writing the basic code. Just like in a startup! But at some point, I'd realise that the other members of the team were better than me, so I could delegate both individual tasks and entire areas to them. Of course, I would continue to do certain tasks myself, as I just couldn't entrust the coding entirely to someone else. Plus, I didn't want my own skills to atrophy. But then circumstances forced me to look at the responsibilities of Head of Analytics in a different light.

I was interviewing for the position of manager at Quora when the Director of Analytics Xavier Amatriain, upon listening to what I was doing in my current job, said quite bluntly, "you're neither this nor that – you're not a manager, and you're not a developer." And they didn't hire me. This made me take a step back and think: if you chase two rabbits, you will lose them both. In other words, it's almost impossible to be a player-manager and do a good job at both.

Then, I stumbled across the answer on Quora, courtesy of a post by Eric Colson (who was Head of Analytics for Netflix at the time) [20]:

"In most cases, the manager's primary activity becomes recruiting (it is such a challenge to find great data scientists!). Next, is figuring out how to organize teams – not just the data science team... but also define how data science will work with other teams in the organization (Product, Eng, Marketing... etc.). Then, there's communication, coordination, guiding, directing... etc. For the manager, there is really not much time left for problem-solving and hence it gets delegated off... The leader's technical skills atrophy."

And he's absolutely right! First, you're drawn in by the magic of the black boxes. Then you want more. You become a manager and that's where things end – what was once magical becomes routine. You only see the metrics, and the code becomes less and less comprehensible. That pretty much sums up my story. The role of player-manager is necessary and useful, but only at the initial stages. At some point, you need to start delegating everything, otherwise you'll do a poor job at both player and manager. Moreover, any coding or other tasks that the manager performs are far more expensive. Once I had put my first team together at Retail Rocket, I transitioned from programming to checking (testing) all the tasks. Then, one of the partners talked me into going back to coding, a decision I would later regret. I agree with Colson – at some point, the manager's got to abandon programming and problem-solving.

Another important aspect is how motivated the manager is. I often like to quote Richard Hamming's lecture "You and Your Research." [21] Richard worked at Bell Labs alongside Claude Shannon (the "father of information theory"). Like many prominent scientists of the time, Hamming was involved in the Manhattan Project to produce the first atomic bomb. Bell Labs itself has an impressive track record: the first transistor was developed there, and seven Nobel Prizes have been awarded for work conducted there. During the lecture, Hamming was asked to compare research and management, to which he replied:

"If you want to be a great researcher, you won't make it being president of the company. If you want to be president of the company, that's another thing. I'm not against being president of the company. I just don't want to be.

I think Ian Ross does a good job as President of Bell Labs. I'm not against it; but you have to be clear on what you want. Furthermore, when you're young, you may have picked wanting to be a great scientist, but as you live longer, you may change your mind. For instance, I went to my boss, Bode, one day and said, 'Why did you ever become department head? Why didn't you just be a good scientist?' He said, 'Hamming, I had a vision of what mathematics should be in Bell Laboratories. And I saw if that vision was going to be realized, I had to make it happen; I had to be department head.' When your vision of what you want to do is what you can do single-handedly, then you should pursue it. The day your vision, what you think needs to be done, is bigger than what you can do single-handedly, then you have to move toward management. And the bigger the vision is, the farther in management you have to go. If you have a vision of what the whole laboratory should be, or the whole Bell System, you have to get there to make it happen. You can't make it happen from the bottom very easily.

It depends upon what goals and what desires you have. And as they change in life, you have to be prepared to change. I chose to avoid management because I preferred to do what I could do single-handedly. But that's the choice that I made, and it is biased. Each person is entitled to their choice. Keep an open mind. But when you do choose a path, for heaven's sake be aware of what you have done and the choice you have made. Don't try to do both sides."

The main downside to moving into management completely is that your technical skills will start to atrophy. It's difficult for a manager to go back to hands-on work. And we see this from time to time in startups. Colson talks about this too [20], "For the very passionate data science leader those elusive activities don't completely slip away... time is found. It hides in the late evenings or perhaps weekend mornings. With access to the data, and not-fully-atrophied skills, the leader is compelled by

[20]   [21]

insatiable curiosity to tinker. The code is clumsy and the graphs are basic. But, this hands-on tinkering provides context that is unattainable by any other means." This gives you a much-needed confidence boost and helps motivate your team to be curious and love what they do. I love my craft. Even when I'm managing a project, I'm always interested in seeing the code, how it works inside the black box.

TASK MANAGEMENT

Analytics tasks can generally be broken down into various areas, each of which requires a specific approach:

* Engineering tasks
* Investigating the causes of a given phenomenon (insight)
* Hypothesis testing or research.

Engineering tasks include developing dashboards, metrics, adding data sources, optimizing calculations and solving technical debt issues. All these tasks are united by the fact that they have a clear and understandable result and, as a rule, are easy to plan out in terms of how much work is required. They have clearly defined stages (Fig. 3.1):

* The task comes in from the client (New).
* The task is given a priority level, its complexity is assessed, and it is put in the queue for execution (To Do).
* Work on the task commences (In Progress).
* The task implementation is tested (Review).
* The task is tested by the client (Test).
* The task is completed (For Done).

This is a rather typical scheme and is based on common sense. Tasks can be accepted or rejected for various reasons (for example, we may be unable to proceed without the manager's signoff). When a given task has been accepted, the analytics team discusses it directly with the client and then estimates its size and the amount of work required to complete it. One of the methods used to do this is planning poker [22]. The task is then queued for execution according to its level of priority. And we had a rule: do whichever task is at the top of the pile. The categories of tasks are thus randomized and the analysts develop a rounded skillset.

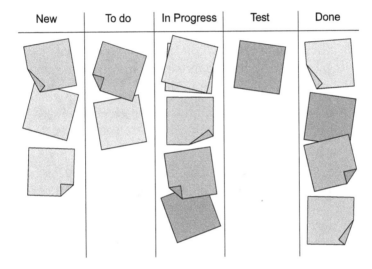

Fig. 3.1. Kanban board

What are the benefits of this kind of randomization? To begin with, all the members of the team are able to get an understanding of how the system as a whole works, which means that they can cover for each other if one of them goes on vacation, is ill or dismissed. This partly solves the "bus factor" (the number of team members a company can afford to lose

[22]

while still functioning). I never thought about such issues before I was hired by Retail Rocket. If someone quit, we would put their project on hold until we found someone to replace them. However, analytics plays a far more important role at my current company (which I co-founded), and the level of responsibility is greater too.

Randomization also has its downsides:

- Every member of the team has his or her strengths and weaknesses. Some are good at the engineering side, others are good at building models, etc. It naturally follows that an engineer with have problems with ML models, while data scientists will struggle with engineering tasks.

- Team members also have a professional and personal interest in taking on certain kinds of tasks. Random tasks can prove to be disruptive for them.

- Initiative gets suppressed. Team members stop putting forward interesting tasks – one person makes a suggestion, another doesn't think it's worthwhile, etc. If the latter gets that task, then there's a chance they will sabotage it. At the very least, they will not put the same kind of effort into it as the person who proposed it.

Thus, this system is not a fix-all solution.

When a task is complete, another employee in the department checks to see whether it has been implemented correctly from an engineering point of view. This could involve a code review, an analysis of the architectural decisions that were made, a check for software tests, etc. Once this has been done, the task is handed over to the client for further checks. If there are no issues, the task is considered complete, and no sooner. In our case, we use a combination of Scrum and Kanban methodologies. But that doesn't mean you should create a cargo cult out of them. They depend on the size of the teams, the ins and outs of the tasks at hand and, most importantly, the technological knowhow of the team members. I started out with the most basic columns with simple statuses for managing tasks in Trello and eventually worked my way to the scheme I outlined above, although I don't think that's perfect either. There's no single methodology that will make you completely happy. You've just got to use a bit of common sense.

The next class of tasks relates to data analysis: the search for insights. Usually these are tasks set by managers or clients. They typically describe a problem, and you need to find the cause. Such tasks typically go through the same statuses as engineering tasks, but with one difference – we have no idea whether or not we will actually find the cause. The end result is unknown, which means that, in theory, we can waste countless hours on the task without producing anything.

The third class of tasks concerns research, which includes testing hypotheses and conducting experiments. These are the most difficult (and at the same time interesting) tasks, and they can have unpredictable results. They are perfect for those who like to learn and experiment. These tasks are characterized by their unpredictable results and the long waiting times.

Hypothesis management is not as easy as it would first appear. For example, at Retail Rocket, only 3 out of every 10 hypotheses for improving recommendations produced positive results. It takes at least six weeks to test a single hypothesis. That's not cheap by any stretch. By "hypothesis," we mean any change that will improve something. This is typically a streamlining proposal aimed at improving a specific metric. Metrics are mandatory attributes. The most important metric to begin with was website conversion (the percentage of visitors who made a purchase). Then we took it one step further: we wanted to increase revenue per visitor, average order value, average items per order, and even the visual appeal of recommended items. Streamlining proposals can vary: from correcting an error in an algorithm to implementing a machine learning algorithm based on neural networks. We tried to run all the changes in the algorithms through hypotheses, because even fixing a simple mistake in real life can adversely impact the metric.

Just like tasks, hypotheses have their own life cycle. First, hypotheses need to be clearly prioritized, as they are extremely labour-intensive and do not produce immediate results. Making a mistake at this prioritization stage can be very costly. I believe that hypotheses should be prioritized from the outside, that is, the goals should be determined by the business. This is typically done by the product team. They talk to customers and know what is best for them. One of the mistakes I made at Retail Rocket was prioritizing hypotheses myself. The analysts would come up with hypotheses on their own and then prioritize and test them. While we did optimize the algorithms, and the groundwork we laid would later prove useful against our competition, we could have achieved so much more if we had only given more thought to what the client wanted. I put that down to the analysts becoming overqualified and the business itself just couldn't keep up. Evaluating a hypothesis, understanding its potential benefits and finding a balance between the work put in and the end result is a fine art.

Interestingly, these problems persist in the West too. In 2016, I submitted a paper entitled "Hypothesis Testing: How to Eliminate Ideas as Soon as Possible" [23] for the ACM RecSys international Conference on Recommender Systems. It's extremely difficult to get accepted, as all submissions are reviewed by several researchers. We had submitted a paper once before [24], which was rejected. This time, however, the topic turned out to be a good fit for the conference programme. I presented the paper – a talk on how we test hypotheses – at MIT in Boston. I remember being incredibly nervous beforehand, and I learnt the text almost by heart. But everything went well in the end. Xavier Amatriain, ex-head of analytics at Netflix and one of the organizers of the conference, even gave me a proverbial pat on the back. He then invited me for an interview at the Quora office, where he had a management position at the time – apparently, my story about hypothesis testing had made quite the impression.

[23]    [24]

HOW TO GET THE BEST OUT OF DAYDREAMERS

For me, the perfect manager:

- incessantly works towards goals
- treats people fairly
- can turn chaos (including the creative process) into the "everyday"
- gives employees leeway to pursue interesting tasks on their own.

Let's look a bit closer at this last point. In the previous chapter, I talked about the conflict between the researcher and the business: the researcher wants to do something meaningful using the latest ML developments, while the business is often uninterested in this. So what do we do? In our line of work, analysts and machine learning engineers spend 5–10% of their time creating an algorithm and the remaining 90% making sure the new algorithm is profitable. This conflict is the main reason why I have lost employees over the years.

A conservative business doesn't want to pay for expensive research that produces unclear results. Bigger companies, however, are more inclined to do this. Large companies often have employ "research scientists," for example. But then another problem emerges, where everything becomes theoretical – researchers never see the real-life, practical implementation of their ideas, and this demotivates them. This is why it is important to find a balance. How do analytics managers achieve this balance?

As you know, companies have to account for the risk of losing key staff. This is achieved by automation, a decent "bus factor," and established processes – when everything that is creative and chaotic is turned into a process and becomes routine. As I write these lines, I am imagining a soulless assembly line with people coming up and turning different screws at different stages. All the tasks are as mundane as possible. Only when all the kinks have been worked out and everything is running like a well-oiled machine can you introduce more compelling tasks into the equation for your employees. This is something that I often have difficulties with. I would suggest that these tasks meet the following requirements:

- the result should bring some benefit in the long term
- tech support should be able to work without the person who developed the solution.

Otherwise, the researcher will glue together a huge spaceship that won't fly. He or she will be fired, only to be replaced by another researcher who will set about building the ship from scratch. In any case, it's best to treat projects like this as venture capital investments. And the result is usually only achieved when the whole company gets in on the project, at which point the entire enterprise is more serious than just research.

Let me give you an example. One of Retail Rocket's internal analytics products uses deep learning to carry out NLP tasks (semantic analysis). The project, which started out as something of a "plaything," turned out to be rather complex and interesting from a development point of view. In the course of our work, we were able to prove its effectiveness, and now the product is in full service. We've had some not-so-successful projects too. For example, we tried to make a "related products" ("people often buy x with this product") section for clothing stores that relied on style compatibility [25]. We were able to make the algorithm do what we want using Siamese neural networks, and the result was visually compelling. When we tested it on commercial sites, however, we saw no improvement. So we had to concede that the project had failed.

[25]

Chapter 4

HOW ABOUT SOME ANALYTICAL TASKS?

Box & Plots

This chapter is made up of two parts: first, I will talk about how to break down the process of data analysis into tasks, and then I will talk about data analysis specifically.

PART I
HOW TO SET TASKS FOR DATA SCIENTISTS

In the last chapter, I talked about the task status board. Now, let's look at tasks themselves. Ideally, the wording of the task should include the following (before it has been scheduled):

- originator
- why the task has appeared
- expected result
- the time needed and level of priority.

The originator is the person who needs the task performed in order to make a decision. It is vital that this person is not an intermediary. Managers typically like to set such tasks on behalf of their team, or, in the best case scenario, their assistants. But it is the manager who makes the final decision. Task planning (in terms of labour intensity, timeframes and expected result) is essentially a negotiation, during which the task often changes dramatically or is even cancelled altogether if simpler ways to solve the problem present themselves. It often happens that the person charged with setting the task does not have the authority to make a decision themselves. What do you think, is it possible to come to an agreement with them immediately? Nope! They've got to run it by their manager first. This whole process takes up a lot of time. Is the originator needed at the negotiation and planning stage? Absolutely! Because any professional communication essentially amounts to the signing of a contract, and a contract implies negotiations. The originator wants analysts to commit to a task that will take up a lot of their time – hours or even days. So, why can't the originator take ten minutes to agree this with the analysts personally? If this does not happen, this is a red flag that suggests this is not an important task, and the analysts would be better off devoting their time to other, higher-priority tasks.

The reason why the task has appeared must be clearly stated. This will be useful for everyone involved: the originator is aware of it and the analysts understand the context, meaning that they will find ways to solve it faster. Moreover, it ensures that no one will forget it. And when it is finally time to talk about the results of the task, it will make life so much easier if a description of the reason for the task being implemented is included.

The expected result should be worded in such a way that pleases the person who came up with the task in the first place. Results can come in various forms: a few sentences with explanations; a table with data and graphs; data to be uploaded to an external system, etc. At the planning meeting, the originator must explain why he needs the results in a given form and what he or she plans to do with them later. Or at least explain that this is simply the way they prefer to make decisions. It's one thing to write a short message with a few figures, and it's quite another to produce a lengthy report with all kinds of graphs and calculations. Tasks for internal use typically look simpler than reports for clients, for example.

Deciding on the time needed and level of priority allow you to carefully set a task queue. No one likes tasks that have to be completed yesterday, especially those that were set today! This is one of the qualities that managers have to possess: the ability to set tasks in advance. This is actually a good way of judging how effective a management team is. In my experience, these tasks often "burn out" and are no longer interesting to the client after completion.

Let's take a look at two examples of task-setting, one good and one bad. We'll start with the good one. You get an email with a well-formulated task:

- *Originator*: Sales Director I. Ivanov
- *Reason*: Toy sales have fallen behind the plan. This could be because we have not been spending enough on advertising.

- *Expected result*: Discover the reason for the fall in sales – a written comment with some explanatory figures.

- *Timeframe*: We can wait five business days, any longer will cut into our decision-making time.

Everything here is clear – the originator is kept in the loop, the problem is laid out and a possible reason for it given, and the employee knows why the task has been set. He or she is trusted, a person who knows how to do their job.

An example of a poorly formulated task:

- *Originator*: A. Sidorov, on the instruction of I. Ivanov

- Send me the sales breakdown for the Toys category by advertising channel as soon as possible.

This is bad from start to finish. The task is set through an intermediary, and there's no deadline – it's needed "yesterday." The originator is convinced that they know the reason for the problem and does not see any reason to let the employee in on the details. As a result, the employee charged with carrying out the task is cut off from the context and has no idea why they should do it. A good analyst will, of course, complete the task, but it will likely be sent back to them, as the reason – and thus the hypothesis – turned out to be wrong. Setting tasks this way leaves no room for creativity, and I know from personal experience that this can be extremely demotivating – you feel like you're nothing more than a calculator. Of course, there are people who like this kind of approach. But this is no way to hold on to the best employees. Eventually, they'll start looking for something else – something that gives them a better chance of reaching their potential.

Task scheduling [22] is an important process that comes in many different forms: it can be handled by a manager, or by the team as a whole. It can be done in real time, with tasks being scheduled as they come up, or periodically, after a number of tasks have been accumulated. Having tried out all these methods, I am convinced that it is better when everyone is involved in planning. This is how we do it at Retail Rocket [22], and we do it at specific times. I personally find it difficult to argue with my employees about options and deadlines, and I often want to make decisions myself. But there's a formula to this – the stronger you are, the better employees you will hire and the greater freedom you will give them in decision making. This is how you build a strong team, where everyone has the opportunity to speak their minds.

At Retail Rocket, we always record the audio of our scheduling meetings. Not only does this keep us disciplined, but we can always go back to the recordings if we disagree about something later on. That said, it is still better to write everything down in the wording of the task itself, as this ensures that everyone has understood everything correctly, especially if there were some heated discussions before the task was agreed upon.

HOW TO CHECK TASKS

To check a task, you need to remember the artifacts we can get:

- insight, an answer to the question "why"
- automated response (dashboard)
- ML models
- code of the data analysis system.

Almost all of these tasks are united by the fact that they all contain code. The only exception is possible insight, for which an ordinary Excel file can often be enough and programming might not be required.

Checking the code involves carrying out a code review. At this stage, an employee (not the person carrying out the task) will study the code in

[22]

order to gauge how correct the chosen method is and whether or not it corresponds to the stylistic approach adopted by the team. This practice is common in software development.

You should write a program as if it were a document for other people to read. This was not as important in the past, when code was often written and checked by one and the same person. Today, software development is carried out by a team, and quality is a must. The computer doesn't care how beautifully written your code is. People do. Those who will be working with your code later – checking it, optimizing the workflow, porting it to another platform – should be able to understand it without any extra effort. If the code raises questions, the programmer will be asked to make changes to it so that it is more easily readable and unambiguous. This is one of the objectives of checking the code in the first place. Similar work standards apply to analytics as well, although it differs in a number of ways to normal software development. Let's look at these.

Software development uses version control systems such as Git, which allow developers to make changes to the company's analytical system and review the code. I recommend keeping all code in the version control system. The advantages of doing this are:

- All changes will be transparent.
- If a developer or data scientist leaves, you will still have all the code.
- If a problem arises, it's easy to roll back changes and revert to the previous version.

Code review is relatively easy to do in terms of all data analysis artifacts except insights. Insights are slightly trickier. Various tools are used to search for and calculate them: Excel or similar programs, the analytical system's GUI, SQL, Python or other notebooks (for example, Jupyter Notebooks). These tasks typically involve several stages:

- data acquisition
- data cleaning
- data analysis
- data output.

Review needs to be carried out at every stage. Data acquisition (often written in a code such as SQL) is relatively easy to inspect – all you have to do is see if the data you want has been used. Incidentally, it is extremely useful during the scheduling stage to discuss how the task will be solved, what to look for and what data may be needed. It could be useful here to take similar tasks that you have carried out in the past as a basis. During the review, it is easier to correlate the solution with the option that was agreed upon at the planning stage. I suggest that you limit the time spent on such tasks, otherwise you could be endlessly searching for insight. Data cleaning and analysis are more difficult to check, although having code in there makes things somewhat easier. One problem with notebooks (for example, Jupyter Notebooks) is error hiding. Notebooks are used to perform one-time (ad-hoc) tasks, meaning that analysts disregard development standards in terms of code review and other tests. What can we do about this? There are several ways to inspect code and data output.

First, the person carrying out the review can check the solution as a whole for errors. This is time-consuming, as it essentially involves building a solution from scratch inside the reviewer's head. Second, other data sources can be used that could at least indirectly confirm the conclusion. Third, you can do what Cassie Kozyrkov, Head of Google's Decision Intelligence division, suggests in her article "The Most Powerful Idea in Data Science" [26]: to randomly split the data into two datasets. The analyst will search for the reason in the first dataset, while the person reviewing the data will check the analyst's conclusions by looking at the second dataset. This approach is used all the time in machine learning and is called validation.

I'd like to make an important point here about solutions that don't use code. What problems present themselves when checking them? Imagine

[26]

that you are working in Excel and have already received the data as a file. You have to open it in Excel, check it, clean it up, write formulas, create tables or pivot tables (which makes it easier to check). Now imagine you're the person reviewing the end solution. Some of the Excel operations are carried out using a mouse, data can be copied and pasted in blocks, and there is no log of actions taken. If you want to see a formula, you have to click on the correct cell. But what if there are loads of these formulas? Some of them may have been filled in by dragging. What if you made a mistake, fixed it and forgot to update all the formulas? It's a little easier with interfaces where blocks are lined up graphically and connected by arrows. You have to click on every one of them and check that everything is correct.

It's so much easier to check things that have code, as all data operations are written in text! You don't need to click anywhere because everything's immediately visible. Another advantage of code is that you can recalculate a task extremely quickly – just run the code. With codeless solutions, the data scientist has to write a log detailing what they did step by step. This makes it easier to check and allows you to repeat the task in the future without much pain. Of course, Excel and other visual tools speed up workflow. I use them myself and have no intention of trying to convince you not to. I'm simply outlining the pros and cons of each approach. You can decide for yourself which works best for you.

It was only when I got to Retail Rocket that I started to understand these nuances. I put this down to the quality requirements being so much higher than they had been at my previous jobs. Before that, I'd only checked the result, and not the entire solution.

HOW TO TEST AND INTRODUCE CHANGES INTO A WORKING SYSTEM

If the task introduces changes to the working system, then the next verification step is to deploy those changes. There is nothing non-standard that needs to be done here in terms of development, and you can use the practices adopted by your developers. We used CI/CD (continuous integration and continuous delivery) based on GitLab at Retail Rocket analytics, which allows changes to be laid out at the click of a button. We thought about who should do it and, after various experiments, agreed that it should be the person who performs the task. As we don't have test engineers as such, the person who performs the task is responsible for transferring it to the Testing status. He or she then performs the deployment, makes sure that all the tests are carried out and the changes are reflected in the operation of the system. For example, they check that the reports are working and that the information is provided in the required form. The purpose of deployment is to reflect the changes in the working system, check that everything is working according to the requirements of the task.

JUSTIFYING THE TASK FOR THE ORIGINATOR

Each and every task has an originator, and only they can give permission for a given task to be marked "complete." During testing, once all the necessary calculations have been completed, the person performing the task asks the originator the check the results, whether it be an insight, a software change to the system or whatever. The originator can either agree or disagree with the results. In the latter case, I would recommend comparing what the originator requires now on the basis of the results that have been obtained with the task as it was originally set. There is often a big difference between what they want from you now and what they wanted when they first set the task. What should we do in such cases, especially when the person who set the task is higher up on the corporate ladder than you? First, the rules of the game must be clearly set out so that everyone is aware of them. Second, as I mentioned earlier, you should always record the audio of your planning meetings. Third, if the conditions of the task have changed considerably, then the sides should concede that the results are not relevant and that time has been wasted. A new task thus has to be formulated, the complexity of which must be decided upon separately.

Another problem entirely is when the person who set the task does not follow up with the person charged with carrying it out and does nothing with the results. This could suggest that the task has "burned out" and is no longer of any interest to the person who set it – unless, of course, there were no force majeure circumstances at play. It would be nice if someone told us before resources were spent on the task. But what are you going to do? I find that not giving high priority to subsequent tasks set by these people tends to work, although, to be fair, I've only managed to do this in my role as co-founder of my own company.

DO YOU NEED TO KNOW HOW TO CODE?

Yes, you do! We're living in the 21st century, where everyone should ideally understand how to use programming in their work. Coding used to be something that only a small number of engineers would, or could, do. However, over time, applied programming became more accessible, open to the layman and convenient.

I learned how to program myself when I was a kid. My dad bought a Partner 01.01 (a Soviet PC) in the late 80s when I was around eleven and I started to get into programming big time. I started out with BASIC and, when I was comfortable with that, soon moved on to the assembler language. I learned from books, as there was no one I could ask back then. The groundwork I had laid during my childhood proved to be extremely useful later on in my life. My main "weapon" back then was a blinking white cursor on a black screen, and you had to save your programs on a cassette tape – we've come a million miles since those days. The basics of programming are quite easy to learn. When my daughter was five and a half years old, I enrolled her on a simple programming course in Scratch.

I gave her a few pointers along the way, and she ended up earning an entry-level MIT certificate.

Applied programming allows you to automate certain employee functions – primarily actions that need to be repeated.

Analytics comes in two flavours. The first is using ready-made tools (Excel, Tableau, SAS, SPSS, etc.), where a mouse is all you need to perform any given action and the most programming you will be expected to do is to enter a formula. The second is coding in Python, R or SQL. These are two fundamentally different approaches, and someone who is good at their job must be proficient in both. When carrying out a task, you need to find a balance between speed and quality. This is particularly true when you are looking for insights. I've come across both diehard supporters of programming and stubborn so-and-sos who can only use a mouse and are proficient in one program only. A competent data scientist will know which tool is right for the task at hand. Sometimes they will write a program, other times they will use Excel. They may even have occasion to combine these approaches: unpacking data in SQL, processing the resulting dataset in Python and analysing it in an Excel or Google Docs pivot table. The point is that they can work much faster than if they were using a single tool. Knowledge is freedom.

By the time I was at university, I was already fluent in several programming languages and even managed to score a gig as a software developer, where I spent a year and a half. Those were difficult times. I started at the Moscow Institute of Physics and Technology in June 1998, and two months later, Russia was hit by a devastating financial crisis. There was no way I'd be able to survive on my scholarship and I didn't want to ask my parents for money. I caught a break in my second year when I was hired to be a developer at one of the companies owned by the university. That's where I really deepened my knowledge of assembler language and C. I was later hired by StatSoft Russia to work in technical support, where I improved my statistical analysis skills. At Ozon.ru, I completed a number of training courses and became SAS certified. I also wrote a lot in SQL when I was there. My programming experience proved extremely useful. I wasn't afraid of taking on new things, I just got on with it. I would even say that most of the interesting things that have happened to me in my life have happened because I learned how to program. This includes founding Retail Rocket with my partners.

PART II
DATASETS

Datasets most often come in the form of a table, unloaded from a data warehouse (for example, via SQL) or obtained in another way. A table is made up of columns and rows (rows are usually referred to as records). In machine learning, the columns themselves are independent variables or predictors, or more commonly features and dependent variables (outcomes). This is how you will find them described in the literature. Machine learning involves training a model that can use independent variables (features) to correctly predict the value of dependent variable (as a rule, there is only one dependent variable in a dataset).

There are two main kinds of variables – categorical and quantitative. A categorical variable contains the text or digital encoding of "categories." This can be:

- Binary – which can only be one of two values (for example: yes/no, 0/1)

- Nominal – which can have more than two values (for example: yes/no/don't know)

- Ordinal – when order matters (for example, athlete ranking).

A quantitative variable may be:

- Discrete – a countable value (for example: the number of people in a room)

- Continuous – any value from an interval (for example: box weight, product price).

Let's look at an example. We've got a table of apartment prices (the dependent variable) with one row (record) for each apartment. Each apartment has a set of attributes (independent variables) with the following columns:

- Price of the apartment – continuous, dependent
- Size of the apartment – continuous
- The number of rooms – discrete (1, 2, 3, etc.)
- En suite bathroom (yes/no) – binary
- Floor number – ordinal or nominal (depending on the task at hand)
- Distance to the city centre – continuous.

DESCRIPTIVE STATISTICS

The very first thing you should do after unloading the data from the data warehouse is to do exploratory data analysis, which includes descriptive statistics and data visualization, and possibly data cleaning by removing outliers.

Descriptive statistics typically include different statistics for each of the variables in the input datasets:

- The number of non-missing values
- The number of unique values
- Minimum–maximum
- The average (mean) value
- The median value
- The standard deviation
- Percentiles – 25%, 50% (median), 75%, 95%.

Not all variable types can be calculated. For example, the average can only be calculated for quantitative variables. Statistical packages and data analysis libraries already have ready-made functions that calculate descriptive statistics. For example, the pandas Python Data Analysis Library has a describe function that immediately displays several statistics for one or all of the variables in the dataset:

```
s = pd.Series([4-1, 2, 3])
s.describe()
count 3.0
mean 2.0
std 1.0
min 1.0
25% 1.5
50% 2.0
75% 2.5
max 3.0
```

While this book is not intended to be a textbook on statistics, I will give you some helpful tips. In theory, we often assume that we are working with normally distributed data, which has a bell-shaped histogram (Fig. 4.1).

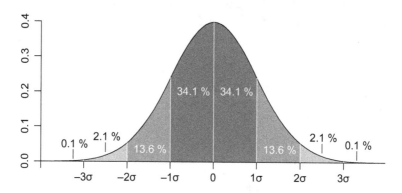

Fig. 4.1. Normal Distribution and Six Sigma

I highly recommend testing this assumption, at the very least an eyeball test. The median is the value that separates the higher half from the lower half of a given data sample. For example, if the 25th and 75th percentiles are different distances from the median, this already suggests a shifted distribution. Another factor is the big difference between the mean and the median – in a normal distribution, they are practically the same. When analysing customer behaviour, you'll often be dealing with exponential distribution. For example, in Ozon.ru, the time between successive customer orders will have an exponential distribution. Here, the mean and median differ significantly. This is why the figure to go with here is the median – the figure that halves the sample. Sticking with the Ozon.ru example, this would be the time during which 50% of users place their next order. The median is also more resilient to outliers in the data. If you want to work with averages because, say, the statistical package you are using is limited, and because it takes less time to calculate the mean than the median, then, in the case of exponential distribution, you can process it with a natural logarithm. To return to the original data scale, you need to process the resulting average using the usual exponential curve.

A percentile is a value that a given random variable does not exceed with a fixed probability. For example, the phrase "the 25th percentile of the price of goods is equal to $150" means that 25% of goods cost less than or equal to $150, and the remaining 75% of goods cost more than $150.

For a normal distribution, if you know the mean and standard deviation, there are some useful theoretically derived patterns – 95% of all values are within two standard deviations of the mean in either direction. That is, the interval width is four sigma. You may have heard the term Six Sigma (Fig. 4.1) – a measure of variation from the expected or optimal result (a product that is free of defects). The general rule of thumb here is that 99.99966% of the results produced fall within six standard deviations around the mean (three in each direction), meaning that they are of ideal quality. Percentiles are useful for identifying and removing outliers. For example, when analysing experimental data, you can assume that all the information outside the 99th percentile is an outlier and can thus be removed.

DIAGRAMS

A good diagram is worth a thousand words. I typically use the following types of diagram:

- histograms
- scatterplots
- time series charts with trend lines
- box plot, box and whiskers plot.

Histograms (Fig. 4.2) are the most useful analysis tool. They allow you to visualize the frequency distribution of a given value (for categorical variables) or break a continuous variable into ranges (bins). The second is used more frequently, and if you provide additional descriptive statistics to such a diagram, then you will have a complete picture of the variable you are interested in. The histogram is a simple and intuitive tool.

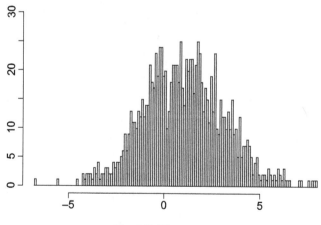

Fig. 4.2. Histogram

Scatterplots (Fig. 4.2) allow you to see the dependent relationship between two variables. They are easy to plot: the independent variable is plotted along the horizontal axis, while the dependent variable is plotted along the vertical axis. Values (records) are displayed as a series of dots. A trend line can also be added. Advanced statistical analysis software allows you to mark outliers interactively.

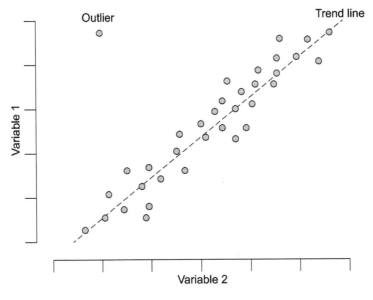

Fig. 4.3. Scatterplot

Time series charts (Fig. 4.4) are similar to scatterplots, with the independent variable (on the horizontal axis) representing time. Two components can typically be distinguished from a time series graph – cyclical components and trend components. A trend can be built when you know how long the cycle is. For example, grocery stores generally use a seven-day cycle, meaning that a repeating picture can be seen on the time series every seven days. A moving average with a window length equal to the cycle is then superimposed on the chart to give you a trend line. Most statistical packages (Excel, Google Sheets, etc.) are capable of doing this. If you need a cyclical component, just subtract the trend line from the time series. These simple calculations are used to build basic algorithms for time series forecasting.

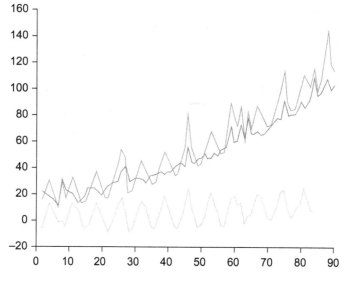

Fig. 4.4. Time series

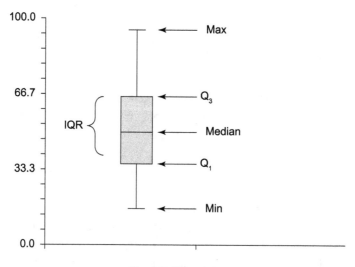

Fig. 4.5. Box plots

Box plots (Fig. 4.5) are interesting: to some extent, they do the same thing as histograms, as they show an estimate of the distribution.

Box plots consist of several elements: whiskers denoting the minimum and maximum data values feasible; and a box whose upper edge represents the 75th percentile and whose lower edge represents the 25th percentile. The line in the box is the median – the "middle" value that divides the sample into halves. This type of graph is useful for comparing experimental results or variables with each other. An example is given below (Fig. 4.6). For me, this is the best way to visualize the results of hypothesis testing.

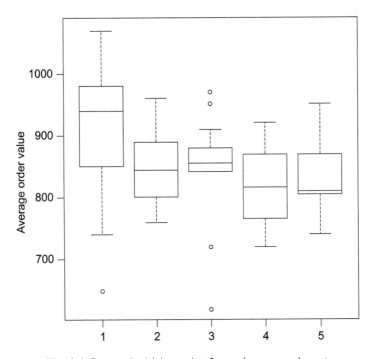

Fig. 4.6. Box and whiskers plot for various experiments

A GENERAL APPROACH TO DATA VISUALIZATION

Data visualization is needed for two things: 1) for data discovery; and 2) as an aid when explaining findings to clients. Several methods are typically used to present results: a simple comment with a few numbers; a spreadsheet in Excel or another program; or a presentation with slides. Each of these methods provides a conclusion and evidence supporting that conclusion (an explanation of how it was reached). Graphs are an easy way of expressing this evidence. In 90% of cases, the types of graph we talked about above are sufficient. Exploratory graphs and presentation graphs serve different purposes. Exploratory graphs are used to find a pattern or cause. There are many types of exploratory graph, and they are sometimes made up on the spot. Presentation graphs are used to help make decisions. Everything is important here, from the name of the slide to the sequence in which they are presented (designed to lead to the desired conclusion). The goal is to explain your conclusions to the client succinctly in order to get their approval. Presentations are not always necessary for this. Personally, I prefer to write a few lines summing up my conclusions, accompanied by a graph or two are some numbers – and that's it.

In his book *Say It With Charts*, Director of Visual Communications for McKinsey & Company Gene Zelazny notes [28]:

> "It is not the data – be they dollars, percentages, liters, yen, etc. – that determine the chart. It is not the measure – be it profits, return on investment, compensation, etc. – that determines the chart. Rather, it is your message, what you want to show, the specific point you want to make."

I recommend that you pay attention to graphs in presentations and articles. Do they back up the author's conclusions? Do you like everything about them? Could they be more convincing?

As the publisher's preface to Zelazny's book (Russian edition) says [28]:

> "With digital technologies at our disposal, we can achieve in minutes what used to take hours of painstaking work – and now slides are being produced like hot cakes ... bland and flavourless hot cakes."

I've given plenty of presentations in my time, from short 5–10 minute summaries to hour-long reports. Sometimes, I'd use slides, other times I wouldn't. I can assure you that it is far more difficult to write a convincing text for a short report without slides than it is to put together an entire PowerPoint presentation. Just look at politicians when they speak. Their job is to convince the people they are addressing. How many of them use slides to do this? Words are more convincing; slides are nothing but additional visual material. Pulling up slides is far easier than talking convincingly. When I'm preparing a PowerPoint presentation, I find myself thinking about how the presentation looks. But when I'm writing a report, I am far more concerned about how convincing my arguments are, I work on my intonation and try to make sure that I am presenting my arguments clearly. Ask yourself this: Is a presentation really necessary? Do you want to turn your meeting into a boring slide show? Or do you want decisions to be made?

"Meetings should center on concisely written reports on paper, not fragmented bulleted talking points projected up on the wall," says data visualization expert Edward Tufte in his book *The Cognitive Style of PowerPoint* [29].

[28]   [29]

PAIR DATA ANALYSIS

I learned about pair programming from the developers at Retail Rocket [30]. Pair programming is a software development technique where the source code is created by two programmers working on the same task at the same workstation. One programmer writes the code, while the other reviews each line in real time. The two periodically switch roles.

We adapted this technique for use in analytics. Analytics, like programming, is a creative process. Imagine you need to build a wall. You've got one guy working on the job. Get a second one in there and they'll work at roughly twice the speed. Well, that's not how it works when you're doing something creative. The project won't get finished two times faster. Sure, you can decompose the project, but I'm talking about tasks that can't be decomposed that are assigned to a single person. The paired approach allows you to speed up this process many times over. One programmer at the keyboard, and the other sits next to them. Two brains working on the same problem. When I'm in the thick of a task, I often talk to myself. Two people can come up with a better solution. We use pair programming:

- When we need to transfer knowledge of one project from one employee to another (for example, a new recruit). The "head" in this case is the person who is imparting the knowledge, while the "hands" at the keyboard are the person receiving it.

- When a problem is proving to be complex and difficult to understand. In this case, two seasoned employees working on the same task are able to find a solution far more efficiently than one. This also prevents one-dimensional solutions.

We typically work out which tasks would be better tackled in pairs at the planning stage.

The advantages of the pair approach are that time is used far more efficiently, as the setup promotes focus and discipline among the two analysts. In addition, more creative solutions are found to complex tasks, and far quicker. The disadvantage is that you can't work for more than a few hours at a time, as it is extremely taxing.

TECHNICAL DEBT

Another important thing I learned from the engineers at Retail Rocket was how to work with technical debt [31]. Technical debt is working with old projects, optimizing the speed of operations, switching to new versions of libraries, removing old code from hypothesis testing, and simplifying projects from an engineering standpoint. All these tasks take up a good third of analysts' development time.

I've seen software "swamps," where old stuff gets in the way of creating new stuff. The whole idea of technical debt is that you have to service everything you've done before. It's like car maintenance – you need to have your car serviced regularly, otherwise it will break down when you least expect it. Code that hasn't been changed or updated for a long time is bad code. Although the mantra "if it ain't broke, don't fix it" usually reigns supreme. I remember talking to a Bing developer four years ago. He told me that the search engine's architecture contained a compiled library, the code of which had been lost. What's more, no one knows how to restore it. The longer this situation persists, the worse things will get.

This is how Retail Rocket analysts serve technical debt:

- Whenever we carry out hypothesis testing, we delete the code for the hypothesis wherever possible once we are done. This way, we don't have to deal with unnecessary junk that doesn't work.

- If any versions of the libraries have been updated, we wait a while to perform the update ourselves, although we do update regularly. For example, we update the Spark platform regularly, staring at version 1.0.0.

[30]   [31]

- If any components of data processing are slow, we set a task and carry it out.

- If there are any potentially dangerous risks (for example, cluster disk overflow), we set the necessary task to eliminate the problem.

My work at Retail Rocket convinced me that dealing with technical debt is the key to ensuring quality. From an engineering point of view, the project is built to the best Silicon Valley standards.

Chapter 5

DATA

Data is a representation of facts, concepts, or instructions in a manner suitable for communication, interpretation, or processing by humans or by automatic means

ISO/IEC/IEEE 24765-2010

Before moving on to data analysis itself, I think we should meditate for a while on what data actually is. The quotation above is the definition of data given by the ISO/IEC/IEEE international standard. It's dry, yet comprehensive. I've deliberately narrowed this definition in this book: data here will refer to digital data that can be read and processed by software.

Data comes in various forms: medical test results, photographs, maps, descriptions of goods, browsing history, customer lists, and much more. In our line of work, data has one purpose – to help people make decisions and to create systems that facilitate this.

- *Medical analysis* – making decisions about bringing a given medicine to market
- *Photographs* – searching for specific objects, facial recognition
- *Goods* – ordering the necessary products for the warehouse
- *Browsing history* – developing recommendation systems
- *Customer lists* – separating customers into groups in order to offer them targeted discounts
- *Maps* – creating routes based on real-time traffic data.

HOW WE COLLECT DATA

Let's do a simple experiment. Open your favourite web browser and go to a news site. Open the developer tools section and click on "Network Requests." Now refresh the page. You'll see all of your browser's network interactions. There could easily be over 1000 network requests on a single page. Most of them will be downloading pictures and scripts that render the page on your screen. But there are also requests from trackers and ad networks whose task is to put together your "customer profile" on one or several sites. Additionally, your internet service provider will record all your requests on their servers, which the security agencies have access to.

Another example is driving a car. It's no secret that satnavs use data about our movements to build live traffic maps. They get this data from an app, as well as from sensors installed on the roads.

One more example is geolocation. Our movements, or, more precisely, the movements of our phones, are recorded by mobile operators and stored in a data warehouse. Various services are then created based on this data. One of them is to work out the best place to open a new sales outlet.

BIG DATA

"Big Data" is all over the news these days. I'm fortunate enough to have been working in this area for the past eight years, so I know what I'm talking about. Let me try and give my own definition: Big Data is such a massive amount of data that it cannot be processed in the required time on a single machine (server)

Usually, when people talk about Big Data, they are only referring to the size of the data. But time is extremely important in commercial and scientific applications. Researchers can't wait forever. The quicker the result, the better. Especially when we don't know what the result will be and the data query needs to be refined iteratively, typically starting with the simplest steps. Modern technology, particularly the speed of mobile phone apps, has taught us react quickly to our actions. And we subconsciously expect the same from data processing systems.

It's actually fairly easy to obtain a large amount of data. Let's say you save your GPS coordinates every millisecond, for example: 1000 milliseconds × 60 seconds × 60 minutes × 24 hours = 86,400,000 events. This number is even more impressive when you scale it up to all the people on Earth. I'll talk about Big Data in greater detail in the chapter on data warehouses.

DATA CONNECTIVITY

One of the most important features of data is its ability to link different sources of data. For example, data can be used to link the cost of online advertising to sales, thus giving you an efficiency tool. Next, we add data on completed orders, as the bounce rate can be extremely high in some online businesses. The output gives us efficiency adjusted for the number of visitors who did not make a purchase. Further, we can add product categories to the data, which shows how effective advertising has been for different product categories. We could continue this process of linking sources of data indefinitely. This is an illustration of what we call "end-to-end analytics."

The above example shows that, by adding a new source of data, we can improve accuracy and increase the number of "degrees of freedom" in terms of what we can do with the data itself. As far as I am concerned, this increases the value of data exponentially. The only snag is how to link the data. This requires a "key," which must be present in both sources. But the key is not always as accurate as we need. Let me give you an example. You want to link online advertising costs with purchases, but you need a key – a user ID. The problem is that the advertising systems likely don't provide information about how much you have spent on a specific user. Because of this, you have to use a set of link keys that characterize the ad. This negatively affects accuracy, but such is the nature of data – it's better to have something than nothing at all.

THERE'S NO SUCH THING AS TOO MUCH DATA

I used to say this all the time when I was working at Ostrovok.ru. I don't remember what exactly it was in connection with, maybe it was to do with the need to expand the server farm. I believe that, in the era of cloud computing, cheap data storage and good compression algorithms, it is important to save as much as you can and in as much detail as you can. Believe me, there's nothing worse than searching for a solution to a problem only to find that there's no data on it, even though there could have been. It will need to be collected sooner or later, so why not do it now?

IMPORTANT! There's just one problem here: developers always ignore analysts. I've seen this at every company I've worked for. When developing any kind of software system or product, analysing its functionality through data is always an afterthought. In the best-case scenario, the developer will collect the most basic of metrics. Then project or product managers, as well as the owners of the business, typically start to take an interest in its fate. "What about the figures?" Then they go running to the analysts and ask them to dig up whatever data they can. What can analysts do if there isn't enough data for statistical tests and accuracy suffers as a result? Pull some data out of thin air? In my experience, analysts are put in this situation all the time. I can literally count on one hand the number of times that things have been done properly.

We've got to push back against this. On the one hand, you can understand the position that developers are in. They need to roll out new, high-quality features as quickly as possible. They're not concerned with analysing metrics. As far as they are concerned, these are useless lines of code that data scientists need to worry about. So, what can we do? That's where the project or product manager comes in, as he or she is the person who set the development task in the first place. When such a task is set, the developers should ask the analysts to draw up a list of project requirements. This should work as follows:

1. The developers explain the technical requirements of the project to the analysts along with a list of questions about its effectiveness from managers.

2. The analysts, in turn, provide the developers with a list of metrics they will need, as well as technical requirements of their own regarding the logging of project data (collecting of metrics): what to collect and in what format.

This process isn't a straightforward as it would seem. It is often the case that all the nuances and restrictions have to be negotiated in an iterative format, including with developers. It's kind of like bargaining, but it's worth it. A well-planned solution will never be 100% perfect, but if management has 80% of their questions answered within a few days of the feature's launch, it can be considered a success. Time is always our biggest enemy! And it's better to take the time before launch to get things right, rather than waste time and money afterwards on a product that doesn't work the way it is supposed to.

DATA ACCESS

Who exactly in a company has access to its data?

Let's look at Netflix, one of the biggest streaming services in the world (I'm a big fan of *House of Cards* myself). Netflix has an interesting corporate culture [32]. One of its principles is: "Share information openly, broadly, and deliberately."

There is one exception to this rule, however: the company has a zero-tolerance policy when it comes to trading insider information and customer payment details. Access to this information is restricted. How can this principle be applied in practice? Don't restrict access to information for your employees, rather, restrict access to the personal data of your customers. I usually go even further and try to remove the barrier between non-analysts and data. The point is, I believe in the freedom of access to data. More than that, I believe that the number of intermediaries between the person seeking data and the data itself should be kept to a minimum. This is important because we are always in a race against

[32]

time. The data requests themselves are often rather simple, you can do them yourself. "Upload such and such data for me, will you!" That's not a task for an analyst. The manager knows exactly what he or she needs, so wouldn't it be easier to get it themselves through a simple interface. To do this, you need to train your team to work with data by themselves. Having intermediaries only creates delays. The only time an intermediary should be used is when the person seeking information is incapable of getting the information on their own, or simply does not want to. This way, you will kill two birds with one stone – your data scientists won't be demotivated by the mundane task of uploading data, and your managers will get the data they need almost instantaneously, which in turn will keep them incentivized.

Of course, customers' personal data must be anonymized. This can be done by encrypting their personal information. It's better not to delete it completely so that you can solve certain customer support issues using your data analysis system.

I try to use this approach wherever I go. You've got no idea how grateful the users of you analytical systems will be when they can access their data on their own. The brightest and most proactive employees devour information to help them make decisions, and it would be a crime to put obstacles in their way.

DATA QUALITY

Data can be dirty, filthy even. If you ever come across "clean" data, it's likely not clean at all. But you never know, you might get lucky. Data scientists spend the majority of their time removing outliers and other artifacts that can prevent them from getting the right solution from data. We work in conditions of uncertainty, and we don't want to increase the likelihood of error due to dirt in the data.

For me, quality data is data that can be used to solve a specific task without having to go through any preliminary cleaning. I deliberately wrote "specific task" here because I believe that different tasks require different degrees of accuracy. As such, they carry different consequences and risks for the company. And we walk on the razor's edge, trying to solve the problem as quickly as possible with minimum effort. We have to balance labour intensity against the cost of making a mistake. If we're talking about an accounting problem, then accuracy is of utmost importance, as tax penalties can be rather painful. If it's a managerial task and the stakes are not quite as high, then accuracy is not as critical. It's up to the head of analytics to make the call.

Poor data quality is usually the result of one of the following:

- the human factor
- technical data loss
- errors integrating and uploading data to the data warehouse
- data latency.

Let's look at these in greater detail.

Some data comes from people directly – we receive numbers from them through various channels. For the sake of simplicity, let's assume that they occasionally fill out a form and send it to us. Our physics teacher at school taught us about scale-reading errors, which are equal to half the division value for any given measurement. If you've got a ruler that measures in millimetres, for example, then the reading error would be half a millimetre. This is due to the fact that we may be looking from the wrong angle – move the ruler only slightly and our reading could be wrong. What can you expect from people using tools that are far more complicated than a ruler?

And then we've got the deliberate falsification of data. Let's call it like it is: whenever someone alters data, even if they do it with the best of intentions, it is a deliberate falsification. One glaring example of this is elections! It is thanks to the work of independent researchers who analyse the polls and look for anomalies, outliers and other "non-random" patterns that such falsifications are identified. Businesses too have their own techniques for finding anomalies – for example, using statistical process control charts.

Technical data loss is a big issue in web analytics (the analysis of website traffic). Not all data from your computer or smartphone reaches the analytic server. There may be a dozen routers between the server and the client, some of the network packets may get lost, the user might close his or her browser while sending information, etc. As a rule, approximately 5% of data is lost, and it is almost impossible to reduce this number without complex tweaks. One way to do it is to place the block with the code for calling the analytic system at the very top of the web page. This will ensure that the data is sent before the page is fully loaded, thus decreasing losses somewhat.

Data integration errors are extremely unpleasant. They always crop up when you least expect them and are difficult to diagnose. When I say integration error, I mean the loss of data due to a malfunction in the data collection process. Sometimes, the error can be reversed, others it can't. Errors can be reversed if the data can be found at the source and subsequently re-read. This is impossible if the data "disappears" after it has been sent to us – that is, it if it flows in a stream and is not saved at any point on its journey. I've already written about the time I discovered that one of the most advanced web analytics systems in the world was not transmitting data via the Opera browser. After the problem was fixed, the data started to flow once again. But there is no way of restoring the old data. It sometimes happens that the developers of a complex solution lose sight of the fact that statistical information about the use of a product needs to be collected, or make a mistake in implementing this function. In this case, you will only get the statistics after the problem has been fixed, and you can say goodbye to the old data forever.

Data latency can also be a problem. At the very least, it's something you need to think about when working with this data. There are many different ways to update data warehouses, and we'll talk about them in the relevant chapter. The most important thing to remember is that the customer (and sometimes you as the data scientist) expect the system to correspond perfectly with the real picture of this world. But this is not the case. There is always a lag from the moment an event occurs to the moment that information about this event reaches your data warehouse. It could take seconds, but it could just as well take days. This is not necessarily down to an error, but you've always got to keep in mind which data source is being updated and when and keep an eye on the schedule to avoid any unpleasant surprises.

CHECKING AND MONITORING DATA QUALITY

I see this as an artform. That said, there are a number of useful practices that, according to the Pareto principle, give us 80% of the result with just 20% of the effort:

- monitoring data uploads to the warehouse
- having a healthy amount of scepticism about the analysis results
- carrying out a statistical analysis of outliers
- paying special attention to non-duplicated data sources.

The first step for any analytics system is monitoring – namely, monitoring data uploads to the warehouse. This is both easy to do and extremely effective in terms of identifying problems as quickly as possible. Monitoring of this kind can be divided into two parts: 1) making sure that the data arrives in the system on time; and 2) making sure that the data is correct. The first part is simple and is typically carried out using a special program or scheduler. The main thing here is to stay on top of error notifications. It's like replacing lightbulbs immediately after they break. It is also worth drawing up instructions for staff to respond to accidents.

The second part is considerably more difficult. Reliable data validation tests cost a lot of money. If you've got access to the source and a way to run simple queries on it, then you can compare simple statistics on the data in the warehouse to that in the source. You can also check the integrity of the data by comparing it in the warehouse itself: Do all the directories contain information? And so forth.

It is useful to be sceptical about the results that data analysis produces. What I mean here is that you can try different methods or run the analysis through a different data source. If the results match, then this is a sign that everything is correct. Another way is to test the data at every step – check its distribution and whether or not it "looks" right (follows common sense). I do this to avoid many of the mistakes I make when I want to get a certain result as quickly as possible.

Outliers are data points that do not fit into our picture of the world, or rather, into the distribution that we normally observe: an unusually large purchase in an online store; strange data coming in from a polling station; an excessively large deposit in a bank account, etc. These are all outliers, but you can't just remove them from the analysis. Removing an outlier can often lead to conclusions and decisions that are the exact opposite of what you need. Working with outliers is an artform. We will look at this in greater detail in the chapter on hypotheses.

Now let's talk about data that can't be recovered by re-reading it from the source. Earlier, I wrote about how this can happen: due to an integration error in the system, or because the developers did not collect and send the necessary data. Such data sources need to be closely monitored, for example, by running special tests designed to detect problems as early as possible. Developers can be careless, so it's better to address such issues at the management level, or try to bring about a change of culture among the developers. I talked about this in the section entitled "There's No Such Thing as Too Much Data."

DATA TYPES

These are the main types of data that you will have to work with:

1. Point-in-time data (data snapshot)
2. Data change logs
3. Reference data.

Let's look at each of these separately. Imagine you've got a current account where your salary is paid on the first of every month. You've got a card linked to that account that you use to make purchases. Your current balance reflects the state of your account at a certain point in time. The movement of funds on the account is what we call the log of changes in the state of the account (data change logs). The reference data might be categories of purchases listed in the bank's online app, for example: groceries, air tickets, cinema, restaurant, etc. Now let's look at each data type in more detail.

Point-in-time data. We all deal with different objects, both physical and virtual. These objects have properties or attributes that can change over time. For example, the coordinates of your current location on a map, your bank account balance, the colour of your hair after a trip to the hair salon, your height and weight over time, the status of your order in an online store, your position at work, etc. These are all objects with a given property. To track changes in these properties, you need to "remember" them at certain points in time, for example, by taking a "snapshot" of all customer accounts (Table 5.1). Two snapshots allow to you calculate any changes with ease. There is, however, another way to track changes.

Table 5.1. Example of a "snapshot" of customer accounts

Account ID	Amount of Funds
234	2000
245	5000
857	2000

If we remember the point in time that a given property or attribute of an object changes, including information about its new value, then we have a data change log. When it comes to this type of data, I usually think of a table (Table 5.2) with the following indispensable attributes:

- The date and time on which the property or attribute changed (down to the nanosecond, if such accuracy is needed).

- The name of the object that has changed. For example, bank account number.

- The new value of (or change in) the property or attribute. For example, you can put the new account balance here, but it is more common to list the amount debited or credited to the account with a plus or minus sign.

The table can sometimes include a number of optional fields: the name of the property or attribute if there are several of them (for example, height, weight, etc.); the old value of the property or attribute, and so on. You may need to check the integrity of the data here (Table 5.2).

Table 5.2. Changes to customer accounts

Date, time	Account ID	Change
20.06.2018 13:24:05.001	123	+1000
23.07.2018 12:20:23.034	245	−2000
10.08.2018 10:34:20.300	678	+4000

As for reference data, they usually contain information that does not change frequently, which allows you to "decipher" or generalize the data in front of you. For example, the point-in-time or data change log table may not store the client's name, but rather his or her number or ID. The directory will then remember that the ID is linked to the client's name. Generalization may be needed to aggregate the data, for example, by type of consumer – legal entity or individual. For an online store, this could be a category of goods or even a category tree with a special structure. The reference data itself can also change, and can be represented in either a point-in-time table or a change log, depending on what is needed.

Most data in the world belongs to one of these three types, as they are sufficient to perform the vast majority of data analysis tasks.

FILE STORAGE FORMATS

Analysts generally work with two forms of data: files and databases.

Files are the most common form of data in data analysis. Virtually all data you can find in open sources is published as files. Big data systems such as Hadoop also use files for storage. A file is basically a way of transmitting information. When your software "saves" something, it "serializes" the data into a sequence of zeroes and ones (bits) to be stored on the drive. When you open a file to load it into memory, it is "deserialized," that is, the sequence of zeroes and ones (bits) is translated into data structures that the program can understand. Try to remember these terms, as they will come in handy when reading literature and articles on data processing.

File formats can be either text or binary. Text files, which you can view with any text editor, are used for simple data. If your data can be represented as text – letters and digits – then a text format is all you need. For data types that cannot be reduced to text, such as images and sound, you will need binary. Of course, you can convert binary data to text by using special codecs, such as Base64. That way, you can store your binary data in a text file. The catch is, this will inflate the file size by about 36%, which can take up quite a bit of storage if you're working with big data.

The three most common text file formats are:

- CSV (comma-separated values) or TSV (tab-separated values)
- JSON (JavaScript Object Notation)
- XML (eXtensible Markup Language).

CSV files are the simplest and most convenient to use. A CSV file is essentially a table where the columns are separated by commas (even though another symbol, such as a tab or a semicolon, may be used) and rows (records) are separated by line breaks. Parsing such files (making your software read the file and separate the values from each other) is a piece of cake. They can be viewed in any text editor or console. There are only two drawbacks. First, if any of your values contain the symbol that serves as the field separator (e.g., a comma), it needs to be "escaped," for example by wrapping the whole value in quotation marks. However, there may be values that happen to contain quotation marks as well. This will have to be supported by the parser (the program or piece of code that reads this file) in some way. This complicates work with CSV files and may lead to broken records that fail to be parsed. The second drawback is that the table is flat, so it cannot store complex data structures, unless you want to pack them into a complex format like JSON and place the data in fields like you would with regular text.

```
Year,Make,Model,Description,Price
1997,Ford,E350,"ac, abs, moon",3000.00
1999,Chevy,"Venture ""Extended Edition""","",4900.00
1999,Chevy,"Venture ""Extended Edition, Very Large""",,5000.00
1996,Jeep,Grand Cherokee,"MUST SELL! air, moon roof,
loaded",4799.00
```

JSON is a much more complex format; it is the *de facto* standard for exchanging data between services on the internet. Its main feature is that each cell has a name. This is both an advantage and a disadvantage. The advantage is that it allows JSON to house complex structures and hierarchies, and is very easy to parse and can be opened in a text editor or web browser. The main disadvantage is that you are left with heaps of unnecessary information: whereas a table only has column titles, in JSON you've got names for each value in the table, which increases the file size significantly.

```
{
 "firstName": "Ivan",
 "lastName": "Ivanov",
 "address": {
 "streetAddress": "101 Moskovskoye Highway, apartment 101",
 "city": "St. Petersburg",
 "postalCode": 101101
 },
 "phoneNumbers": [5-
 "812 123-1234",
 "916 123-4567"
 ]
}
```

XML is less common than JSON, its main competitor. It is often used for configuration data in various systems. I prefer JSON for data storage, as it is the lighter and easier option. As for XML, online stores use it to transmit product information: catalogue structure, prices, and product names and attributes.

```
<person>
 <firstName>Ivan</firstName>
 <lastName>Ivanov</lastName>
 <address>
 <streetAddress>101 Moskovskoye Highway, apartment 101</
streetAddress>
 <city>St. Petersburg</city>
 <postalCode>101101</postalCode>
 </address>
 <phoneNumbers>
 <phoneNumber>812 123-1234</phoneNumber>
 <phoneNumber>916 123-4567</phoneNumber>
 </phoneNumbers>
</person>
```

Some of the more exotic formats you can encounter in your practice include:

- pkl ("pickle") is a binary Python object. If you read it using Python, you will get the necessary data structure in your memory without any parsing.

- hdf is a hierarchical data structure format. It may contain various types of data, for example, a store's product catalogue, sales, etc. The file contains metainformation: product names, data types, etc. I've never worked with such files myself, but they may be useful for transferring data from a complex project to another team or publish them on the internet.

- parquet and avro are formats designed for big data. They generally contain a data schema (metainformation) that defines field types and names and are optimized for use in systems such as Hadoop. Both of these formats are binary, though avro can be based on JSON.

What else is there to know about storage files? They have a different approach to storing metainformation. If someone sends you data in a CSV file, then the first line will likely contain field names, but you won't get information about the data type (whether a value is a number, text, date, etc.). Field descriptions will have to be sent separately, otherwise you will have to make assumptions. If you get a JSON or XML file, they have a way of describing data types, which makes them more convenient in this regard.

As for databases, we will discuss them in the chapter on data warehouses.

WAYS TO RETRIEVE DATA

There are three main ways to retrieve data:

- Read a file (as we just discussed)
- Make an API call
- Query a database.

Reading a file is the easiest way: if it's a CSV file, you can open it in Microsoft Excel, Google Sheets, OpenOffice, etc. All data analysis packages and all programming libraries support this format. It is very simple and easy to use. With JSON and XML, you will have to tinker around and, most likely, even write a little piece of code (small program) to extract the data you need.

The second way is to send a request to the network API (Application Programming Interface). The request is sent in the format required by the API and, as a rule, you receive a JSON as the output, which you can process, save to a file, etc. This takes a bit of coding, but working with such interfaces can be very interesting.

The third method is to query a database using the SQL programming language. Different database systems have their own dialects of this language, usually due to some specific optimizations and extensions they use. To retrieve data from the database, you need to connect to it via the API driver over the network, send an SQL query and, if all goes well, get the output data. In all the companies I worked for, I used SQL. I strongly recommend that you familiarize yourself with this programming language, or at least with its basics.

Chapter 6

DATA WAREHOUSES

WHY DO WE NEED DATA WAREHOUSES?

A data warehouse contains a copy of all data required for the analytics system to function. In recent years, the term "data lakes" has become rather popular. A data lake is a system or repository of data stored in its natural form, that is, in a format that assumes the simultaneous storage of data in various schemes and formats. Data is stored in the form in which it was created: video files, images, documents, table dumps from databases, CSV files, etc. The definition of storage that I offered earlier overlaps in many significant respects with the definition of data lakes. We also keep downloaded images and raw and processed data on the cluster. You don't need to pay too much attention to all these terms – no one will give you clear instructions on how to store your data anyway. You are the one making decisions based on the tasks that you have set.

These days, data warehouses do far more than just storing data for reports. For example, they can be used as a data source for training ML models. Data does not have to be stored exclusively in a database; you can also store it as files, which is what Hadoop does.

The way I see it, a data warehouse should have the following attributes:

1. It must serve as a digital archive of the company.

2. It must be a copy of the data found at the source.

3. It must be non-alterable.

4. It must be stored in a form that it as close as possible to the data at the source.

5. It must be able to combine data from different sources.

The data warehouse should be treated as a company archive [34] – all the company's data from its very inception is stored there. Some of the data you won't find anywhere else, as the sources are cleaned periodically. At Retail Rocket, for example, we routinely archive all our data: the product bases of online stores (which change over time), their catalogue structures, the recommendations themselves, and so on. They no longer appear in any sources, but they are in the data warehouse and they help us perform important tasks, such as searching for the causes of problems and simulating new recommendation algorithms.

You shouldn't work directly with the data source. There are two main reasons for this. First, read requests place a heavy load on disks and increase the response time of the working machines. Consequently, clients receive responses from your systems with a time delay. Second, the confidentiality of the data stored in the sources can be violated. Not all data needs to be taken from there in its original form, and it is better not to touch the sensitive information of clients or encrypt it when uploading it into the data warehouse. The data warehouse itself draws an invisible line between your working system, which needs to work reliably, and the data that will be used for analysis. I once had a case at Ozon.ru where one of my team went right to the source and damaged the client's data. The developers were livid!

The inalterability of the data that has already been uploaded to the warehouse does not mean that your analytical reports will never change. It would be disingenuous of me to suggest otherwise. But this is usually down to technical errors or the fact that the list of stored data has been expanded. We need to keep such incidents to a minimum, however, for two reasons. First, it can take forever to reload data, and the analytics system can't function while this is happening. At Retail Rocket, for example, it was not unheard of for Hadoop and ClickHouse to take days or even weeks to reload the data. Secondly, your users will lose confidence in your system due to the changes in the data, and, consequently, the reports and decisions made on the basis of those changes. After all, how can you trust data that changes after the fact?

[34]

I always try to store data in the same form that it is stored at the source. Another approach is to convert the data when it is copied to the data warehouse. This approach, in my opinion, has one big drawback: there is no guarantee that the conversion or filtering process will run smoothly without errors. At the very least, the data in the source will change so the converted data will not be up to date. Sooner or later, you'll notice that the data doesn't match. Then you'll have to go digging into the source, download the data (which can be huge) and compare it line by line with what's in the data warehouse. It's incredibly difficult to find errors this way. It's so much easier when the source data is stored in its raw form. This, of course, does not mean that converting data is not important or not necessary, only that it is better to store data that has been changed in separate tables or files (in a separate layer in the data warehouse). This way, checking it against the source is simply a matter of comparing the number of rows between tables. Any conversion errors can easily be detected in the data warehouse itself, as you have all the sources. The various data correction incidents that I have had to deal with in my career have led me to this conclusion. While it is true that this method can almost double the amount of data in the warehouse, the low cost of storage these days and the principle of "there's no such thing as too much data" make it worthwhile.

In the chapter on data, I discussed the idea of data connectivity – that the most interesting insights are found at the where different data sources meet. Data is merged through the use of keys. The process itself is called data joining and it is extremely resource intensive. Database developers are always looking for ways to speed it up. I was once at a Microsoft lecture where they said that the number of such operations needs to be kept to a minimum when you are dealing with big data. To do this, you need to join the data in the data warehouse and store it in this form. That was around ten years ago. Nowadays, we have systems that can do this better than traditional databases. But I'll come back to that later in this chapter.

I was chatting with a Netflix developer some time ago when I got on to the subject of data warehouses. He stopped me in my tracks and said, "Why don't you just restore the database from your backup and work with that?" First off, if you don't use cloud services (and Netflix does), it's incredibly difficult to restore data from a backup. Second, data warehouses often contain their own aggregates (I'll talk about them later) that need to be maintained. Third, if you've got lots of sources and they're different databases or file stores, then it will be impossible to execute queries that connect these sources.

DATA WAREHOUSE LAYERS

Data warehouses can be made up of several layers (Fig. 6.1) [34]:

- Data from sources "as is" (primary data layer), otherwise known as raw data. As I noted earlier, it is better to store such data in a form that matches the source as much as possible.

- Data that has been brought into a holistic form that is independent of the source (core data layer). This means that we are already able to work with a logical scheme and human-readable terms. The analyst does not have to think about how the terms in different sources relate as everything has already been done in this layer.

- Data presented in the form of marts for a specific set of users (data mart layer). The division is made according to subject area: marketing, sales, warehousing, etc. The best example of this would be preparing data for OLAP cubes. Data for OLAP cubes has to be prepared in a specific manner, but we'll talk about that in greater detail in the next chapter on data analysis tools.

These layers are logical and, in many ways, arbitrary. Physically, they can be located either in different systems, or in a single system.

At Retail Rocket, I worked a lot with user activity data. Data arrives in the cluster in real time in JavaScript Object Notation (JSON) format and

[34]

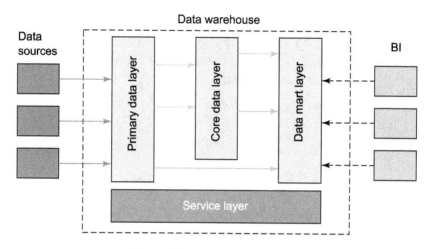

Fig. 6.1. Data warehouse layers

is stored in one folder. This is the first layer, raw data. We immediately convert the data so that we can work with it in the CSV format. We store it in a second folder. This the second layer. Data from the second layer is then sent to the ClickHouse analytical database, where special tables have been built for whatever task you want – for example, to track the effectiveness of recommendation algorithms. This is the third layer, data marts.

WHAT KINDS OF DATA WAREHOUSE EXIST?

If I had to list all the kinds of data warehouse by popularity, it would probably look like this:

1. Relational databases – Postgre, Oracle, MS SQL Server, etc.

2. Columnar databases – Vertica, Greenplum, ClickHouse; cloud-based – Google BigQuery, Amazon Redshift.

3. Files – Hadoop.

I didn't include large enterprise systems from IBM, Teradata and other vendors in the list, as they have their own niches that I have never worked in.

I worked with Microsoft SQL Server at Ozon.ru and Wikimart.ru, Postgres at Ostrovok.ru, Hadoop at Wikimart.ru and Retail Rocket, and ClickHouse at Retail Rocket. I've not nothing but good things to say about these technologies. But these days I prefer to save money and use open-source technologies.

Relational databases (Fig. 6.2) are the workhorses of many businesses. They continue to be hugely popular, despite the advance of NoSQL technologies. Data in relational databases is stored in tables with columns and rows. There are "relations" between the tables, you can set the logic for operations with fields, etc. Performance can be optimized through index tuning and various hacks (all vendors have their own way of doing things). The popularity of relational databases can be put down to the fact that most specialists know how to work with them. Their biggest contribution to data analysis is the SQL (Structured Query Language) programming language, which can be used to make changes to and retrieve data. The main disadvantage of relational databases is their poor performance when working with big data. At Ozon.ru and Wikimart.ru, I kept website

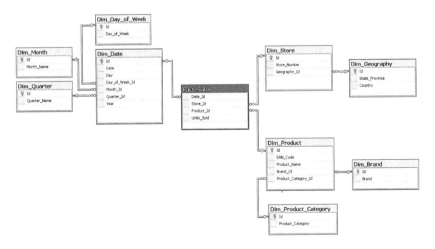

Fig. 6.2. Relational database tables

usage statistics in an ordinary table, which is billions of rows. I'd often enter a query and then go to lunch while it was being dealt with.

Columnar databases store data by columns and thus became a huge help to relational databases [35]. They were a true revelation! Here's an example of a relational database (Table 6.1):

Table 6.1. Relational database: Data example

ID	Name	Type	Color
1	Chair	Kitchen furniture	White
2	Chair	Kitchen furniture	Red
3	Chair	Living room	Blue

If you want to find all products that belong to the "Living room" type (in the Type column), you will have to read all data rows (if there is no index for this column). This is an exceedingly depressing task if you have billions, or even trillions, of rows. Columnar databases store data separately by columns (hence the term "columnar databases"):

```
ID: 1 (1), 2 (2), 3 (3)
Name: Chair (1), Chair (2), Chair (3)
Type: Kitchen furniture (1), Kitchen furniture (2), Living room (3)
Color: White (1), Red (2), Blue (3)
```

Now if you select products by "Living room" type, only the data in the relevant column needs to be read. So, how do we find the records we need? No problem: each column value contains the number of the record to which it refers. What's more, column values can be sorted and even compressed, which makes the database even faster. The downside of such a system is that you are limited by the power of the machines

[35]

on the server that the database is running on. Columnar databases are perfect for analytical tasks that involve a large number of filtering and aggregate queries.

If you need a "thresher" for extremely large amounts of data, then look no further than Yahoo's Hadoop, which runs on a proprietary distributed file system (HDFS) and does not place excessive loads on hardware. Facebook developed the Hive SQL engine for Hadoop, which allows users to write data queries in SQL. The main advantage of Hadoop is its reliability, although this comes at the expense of speed. That said, Hadoop is able to complete tasks that a regular database simply cannot cope with – sure, it might do it at an agonizingly slow pace, but it gets the job done! I've used Hive in the past and been extremely impressed with it. I've even managed to write some basic recommendation algorithms for it.

So, the main question here is: Which technologies should we use and when?

I've got a kind of cheat sheet to help me out on such occasions:

- If there's a relatively small amount of data (i.e. not tables with billions of rows), then it is easier to use a regular relational database.

- If you've got several billion rows of data, or speed is a big concern for dealing with analytical queries (aggregation and selection), then a columnar database is the way to go.

- If you need to store a massive amount of data with hundreds of billions of rows and are willing to put up with low speeds, or if you want an archive of raw data, then Hadoop is what you need.

At Retail Rocket, I used Hive on top of Hadoop for technical support; requests could take more than half an hour to process. The required data was thus transferred to ClickHouse (a columnar database), which increased query processing speeds by several hundred times. Speed is extremely important for interactive analytical tasks. Retail Rocket employees immediately fell in love with the new solution thanks to its speed. Hadoop was still our workhorse for calculating recommendations, though.

HOW DATA MAKES IT INTO THE WAREHOUSE

Data needs to be updated periodically to make sure that it does not become redundant. We can do this with full or incremental updates.

A full update is applied to reference data and states at a certain point in time (we covered point-in-time data in the previous chapter). This is how it works: data is downloaded from the source to a staging table or folder; if this operation is successful, the old data is replaced with fresh data. Updating in this manner ensures that the data is fully consistent with the source data at the time of the download. The main problem here is that it takes a relatively long time to update the tables, as they are exactly the same size as the original data. Another drawback is that you lose any changes made before the update was carried out. Imagine you've got a directory of store goods. The reference data is always up to date in the source system, and the information in the data warehouse is updated at midnight every day. If a product is added or removed from the reference data, this will not show up in the data warehouse. As far as the data scientist is concerned, the product never existed. But it can still be ordered from the site. We are thus left with a data integrity violation: the order appears in the table, but not the product catalogue.

Incremental updates are used for the change log (we talked about this in the chapter on data). You can, of course, reboot the system completely, but this is not practical given the large amount of data and the slow update speed. This is how incremental updates work: the system scans the warehouse to see which data was loaded most recently (it can search by time or another identifier). A request is then submitted to the source: "Give me all the data that was uploaded after X." Once the relevant data has been sent, it is added to the old data in the warehouse. The advantage of incremental updates is their speed. The disadvantage is that the data may be out of sync – records may be duplicated or, conversely, lost altogether.

There are essentially two types of incremental update: batch and stream.

In a batch update, data is uploaded in large blocks. For example, you've got a spreadsheet with customer orders that is updated once a day between midnight and 1 am with data from the previous day. This data is added to the warehouse. There are several options for how you want the update to be carried out – from specialized software to proprietary systems. I've personally used both approaches. At Ozon.ru and Wiki-market.ru, I used Microsoft Integration Services, which is part of the MS SQL Server package. All you do is move your mouse to move the data flows between the source and the warehouse, barely any programming is needed. Retail Rocket used a proprietary utility without a GUI that downloaded data from Hadoop to ClickHouse.

Stream data is data that is uploaded one record at a time or in small packets as they arrive. This is usually done for data that needs to be maintained in real time. Returning to the example above, new orders will be added to the spreadsheet as they are placed. In this case, there will be a slight delay between the order being placed and its appearance in the data warehouse. This delay can vary from milliseconds to hours, and it must be constantly monitored.

HADOOP AND MAPREDUCE

The history of Hadoop is intricately connected with Google. The company has come up with two great inventions – PageRank and MapReduce. In 2003, Jeffrey Dean and Sanjay Ghemawat spent four months developing MapReduce [38]. The idea came to them when they were rewriting (for the third time) Google's engine for downloading and indexing pages. They managed to overcome an important problem in that they found a way to coordinate the work of a huge number of unreliable computers in different data centres around the world. Before this, if one or multiple computers failed, the calculations would have to be started again, which is extremely problematic when we are dealing with a thousand machines. Even more remarkably, Dean and Ghemawat did more than simply come up with a solution to a particular problem – they created a philosophy. MapReduce allowed Google developers to access their data centre servers as if it were one huge computer.

Before MapReduce, developers had to come up with a diagram of how to divide and distribute data, run the calculation and deal with any equipment failures that may come up themselves. MapReduce introduced a new principle for solving problems. The algorithm required the task to be split into two stages: the "Map" (preprocessing) stage, during which the programmer tells each machine what kind of data preprocessing it needs to perform – for example, counting how many times the word "cat" appears on a webpage. Then you need to write instructions for the "Reduce" (folding) stage, for example, getting the machines to calculate the total number of "cats" on all web pages in existence.

In 2004, Google's indexing engine was migrated to MapReduce. The technology was then used for video processing and rendering Google Maps. It turned out to be so simple that it was used for a wide range of problems. That same year, Google filed a patent for MapReduce [36]. Dean and Ghemawat later realized that astronomers, geneticists and other researchers who deal with large amounts of data could get a lot from MapReduce. They went on to publish a paper called "MapReduce: Simplified Data Processing on Large Clusters" [37] that sent waves through the data analysis community. Cheap hardware and a surge in the number of web services and devices connected to the web led to a "deluge" of data. Only a few software companies were equipped to deal with this.

Mike Cafarella and Doug Cutting were working on scaling their Nutch search engine at the time. They were so impressed with Dean and Ghemawat's paper that they set about writing the Hadoop project from scratch. This led to Yahoo inviting Cutting to continue work on

[36]   [37]

the project for them. In 2008, tech companies across the world starting to adopt Hadoop. Apache Hadoop is currently available under a free license [39].

Most big data tech companies use Hadoop – if not an Apache distribution, then a commercial version from Map, Cloudera or another vendor. Some companies (Yandex, for example) chose to develop their own version.

The following is an illustration of how MapReduce works (Fig. 6.3).

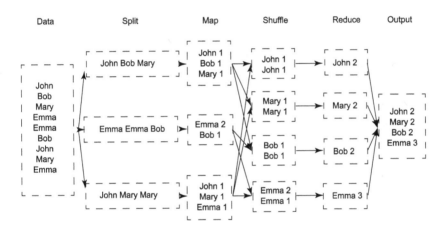

Fig. 6.3. Counting the number of words in a text

On the left, we have the source text, each line of which contains the names of people. The first operation (Split) splits the text line by line, with each line being independently processed. The second operation (Map) counts the number of times each name appears in the line. Because the lines are independent of each other, we can run the operation in parallel on dif-

[38]  [39]

ferent machines. The third operation (Shuffle) then separates the names into groups, and the fourth operation (Reduce) calculates the number of times each name is mentioned in different lines. At the output, we get the number of times each name is mentioned in the text. The example we have here consists of three lines, but the exact same operations would be carried out for a trillion lines of text.

MapReduce is a concept. Hadoop is a piece of software than implements this concept. Hadoop itself consists of two main components: the HDFS distributed file system and the YARN resource scheduler.

To users, the HDFS (Hadoop Distributed File System) looks just like a regular file system with the usual folders and files. The system itself is located on a least one computer and has two main functions – a name node and a data node. When the user wants to write a file to the HDFS, the file is split into blocks (the size of which depends on the system settings) and the name node returns the data node where the block needs to be saved. The client sends data to the data node. The data is recorded and then copied to other nodes (replicated). The default replication factor is 3, which means than one chunk of data will exist across three data nodes. Once the process is complete and all the blocks have been written, the name node makes the relevant entry in its tables (where, which block has been stored, and which file it belongs to). This protects us against errors, for example, when the server goes down. With a replication factor of 3, we can lose two nodes without it being a problem. And if this does happen, the HDFS will automatically start to replicate the data and send it to other "live" nodes to make sure the required replication factor is achieved once again. This is how we get data sustainability.

The YARN resource scheduler allocates computer power on Hadoop clusters. This allows us to carry out several tasks in a single cluster simultaneously. The calculations are typically carried out in the same place where the data is located – on the same nodes and with the same data. This saves a lot of time, since data is read from the disk far quicker that it is copied over the network. When running a task through YARN, it lists the resources you will need to perform the calculation: how many machines (executors) from the cluster; how many processor cores; and how much RAM. YARN also provides real-time reports on the task's progress.

I first heard about Hadoop when I visited the Netflix offices in 2011. I immediately set about learning as much as I could about the service and watched conferences on YouTube about how to work with it. I decided to try an experiment and launch Hadoop on my work laptop using Cloudera as the distribution. The good thing about Hadoop is that it can even be installed on a laptop – all services will run on it. As your data grows, you can easily add servers, even cheap ones. That's exactly what I did when I started writing the Retail Rocket recommendation engine. I started with a couple of servers and now, five years later, the Hadoop cluster has grown to 50 machines and holds around 2 petabytes of compressed data.

We wrote the first version of the recommendation in two Hadoop programming languages – Pig and Hive – before switching to Spark and then Scala.

Don't overlook MapReduce principles. They came in handy for me once in a Kaggle competition. I was dealing with a dataset so large that it didn't all fit into the computer's memory, so I had to write a preprocess operation in pure Python using the MapReduce approach. It took forever! If I were to do it today, I would install the Spark framework locally rather than try to reinvent the wheel. This would work, as MapReduce operations can be performed both in parallel on different machines and sequentially. The calculations will still take a lot of time, but at least they'll get done, and you won't be worrying about whether you've got enough memory for it.

SPARK

I was introduced to the Spark framework in 2012, when I got hold of some video recordings of the Strata Data Conference for the Ostrovok.ru corporate library. The conferences are organized by O'Reilly Media in the United States. In one of the lectures, I saw Matei Zaharia (the brain behind Spark) talk about the advantages of Spark over a pure implementation of MapReduce in Hadoop. The biggest advantage of Spark is that it loads data into so-called resilient distributed datasets (RDDs) and allows you to work with it iteratively in memory. Pure Hadoop relies on disk storage – for each pair of MapReduce operations, data is read from the disk and then stored. If the algorithm requires more operations, then data will have to be read from the disk and then saved back every time. What Spark does after having completed the first operation is save the data into memory. Subsequent MapReduce operations will work with this array until the program explicitly commands it to the saved to disk. This is crucial for machine learning problems, where iterative algorithms are used to find the optimal solution. This method provides a massive performance boost, sometimes up to 100 times faster than Hadoop.

The ideas that Matei Zaharia had introduced me to came in handy a few years later when we set about writing the second version of the Retail Rocket recommendation engine. Version 1.0.0 had just come out. It was summer 2014 when we tried to run Spark on top of Hadoop, and everything went swimmingly. We managed to boost speed by three to four times during testing, although we did run into performance issues when dealing with large numbers of small files. So we wrote a small library that glued them all together when booting up and that fixed the problem [41]. We've been using Spark on our Hadoop cluster ever since and have absolutely no regrets.

When we switched from pure Hadoop to "Spark on top of Hadoop," we had to get rid of much of our code that had been written in Pig, Hive, Java and Python – a veritable zoo that was the cause of endless headaches because we had to be fluent in all of them. And we used a bunch of Python tools when prototyping machine learning tasks, including IPython + Pyhs2 (Python hive driver) + Pandas + Sklearn. Using Spark

[19]    [41]

meant that we were able to use a single programming language for prototyping experimental versions and developing a working version. This was a massive achievement for our modestly sized team.

Spark supports four programming languages out of the box – Python, Scala, Java and R via an API. Spark itself is written in Scala, which is why we chose it. This would allow us to read the Spark source code and even fix any bugs in it (although we never had to). What's more, Scala belongs to the JVM family of programming languages, which is handy when you're working with the Hadoop file system directly via an API, since it is written in Java.

Below is a comparison of programming languages for Spark, where + and – represent the pros and cons of each language, respectively.

Scala:

+ functional and thus convenient for processing data of any volume

+ native to Spark, which is important if you need to understand how Spark works from the inside

+ based on JVM, which makes it compatible with Hadoop

+ static type system; the compiler will help you find some of your errors

– difficult to learn; we had do develop our own training programme for beginners [19]

– Scala developers are generally more expensive than Java and Python developers

– the language is not as widespread as Java and Python.

Python:

+ popular

+ simple

– dynamic type system; the compiler may not be able to detect certain errors

– poor performance compared to Scala

– no pure functionality, unlike Scala.

Java:

+ popular

+ native to Hadoop

+ static type system

– not functional (although things were much better after the release of Java 8).

The decision to use Scala as the main programming language for the second version of the Retail Rocket recommendation engine was not taken lightly, as no one knew the language. If I could go back, I would likely give Java 8 and later versions some serious consideration, as Java developers are easier to find.

Spark is moving towards dataframes and datasets, a trend started by the pandas library for Python [42], which just so happens to be the most popular library for data analysis. It's easier to write in pandas, but there's a catch – the compiler can't check your work with internal variables, which is far from ideal for large projects.

OPTIMIZING WORK SPEED

If the user isn't happy with the response speed of the analytics system, then it's time to optimize the data warehouse speed. There are simple and not-so-simple ways to do this. The first thing you need to under-

[42]

stand is how to do it as painlessly as possible. When you're working with relational databases, you can add indexes. Databases have so-called profilers for this very purpose that will suggest which indexes to add on the basis of the queries you have typed in. The ClickHouse columnar database allows you to change the partitioning scheme or carry out sampling when the query only uses part of the data. In Hadoop, you can allocate more resources or even optimize your code. I've done it both ways.

There's also another method that works just about everywhere. Joining data across tables always slows down query speeds. Imagine we've got two tables, one for customers and one for orders. These tables are connected via customer ID (which is present in both tables). Why not just perform the data connection during certain periods, for example at night, and save the result back to the data warehouse? This is called the materialized view. In this case, customers won't be seeing the data itself, but rather a representation of that data. Speed will have increased exponentially, which is a good thing. The problem, however, is that this way of dealing with the issue complicates the entire structure. If something goes wrong and the donor tables contain incorrect data, then these views will have to be recalculated. You've got to keep this in mind at all times.

A more radical approach would be to switch technology to something that is better suited to the tasks at hand. I gave an example of this earlier, when working with Hadoop we transferred users to the ClickHouse columnar database and boosted performance by up to 100 times.

Another inexpensive way to speed up your analytics system is to upgrade to a hardware server. This is easy to do in Hadoop and ClickHouse systems, as all you need to do is add more machines. This is called horizontal positioning or sharding – where data is split into records and distributed across servers. Data queries are executed in parallel on multiple servers and the results are then merged. This type of setup can theoretically provide you with linear acceleration: two servers will work twice as fast as one server, and so on.

DATA ARCHIVING AND OBSOLESCENCE

Another common problem with data warehouses is the sheer size of the data they need to store, which leads to a lack of free space. This will be a constant headache. There's no such thing as too much data, only small budgets. What strategies can we employ to deal with this?

The first and most straightforward approach is to get rid of obsolete data – all data that is older than two or five years, say, depending on your current tasks. Hadoop allows you to take a different approach, however, and that is to change the replication factor. The default setting is 3, meaning that three terabytes of disk space are required to store one terabyte of data. This is the price of reliability: this ensures that you will not lose any data if two data nodes crash at the same time. The replication factor can be set for individual files – we can thus reduce it for older files. For example, we can set the replication factor for files created within the last two years to 3; to 2 for files created within the last two to four years; and delete files that are older than four years. Facebook uses this approach. Some companies archive old data on cheap storage devices to ensure that it can be retrieved if necessary. I'm not a fan of this approach. It's like hoarding things in a closet – you end up forgetting about them, and when you do remember, you can't be bothered looking for them anyway.

The second method is to use compression codecs (Table 6.2) [43]. This works extremely well in Hadoop and Spark. Compressing data kills two birds with one stone. First, we reduce the amount of disk space the data is taking up. Second, we speed up the work with data – read times are greatly reduced, and the data races across the network between cluster servers many times faster. But this isn't a miracle solution either. The harder the codec presses, the greater CPU resources it requires.

[43]

We use codecs on our cluster, namely gzip, bzip2 and lzma. Lzma provides the highest compression and is used to archive data. Gzip is used for all other data arriving in the cluster. Whether or not a file can be split for a Map operation without being decompressed depends on the specific compression codec used. Like I said earlier, for Map operations, data is "sliced" into blocks whose size is specified in the Hadoop settings (block size). If the compressed file is larger than the block size, then it can be split and unpacked into parts in different nodes of the cluster in parallel – assuming it a splittable codec, that is. Otherwise, you'll have to unpack the huge file completely, which will take far longer.

Table 6.2. Comparison of compression codecs

Codec	File extension	Splittable?	Data compression ratio	Compression speed
Gzip	.gz	No	Average	Average
Bzip2	.bz2	Yes	High	Slow
Snappy	.snappy	No	Average	Fast
LZO	.lzo	No, without indexing	Average	Fast
LZMA	.xz	Yes	High	Very slow

MONITORING DATA WAREHOUSES

Users of your analytics systems often have to make important data-driven decisions, so it is vital that you provide them with reliable data.

Here's a horror story for you. One Friday evening, I decided to make changes to the data replenishment system in the Ozon.ru data warehouse. Then I left for my vacation. Wouldn't you know it, that was the weekend that the entire system crashed. The following Monday, our data scientists got a letter from the CEO in English that started, "I'm fed up..."

They, of course, managed to identify the cause of the problem and fix it. What do you think I should have done? Well, first off, I shouldn't have made changes on a Friday, especially the Friday before my vacation. If I'd have done it on the Thursday, then the changes would have crashed the system on Friday morning and I would've been able to fix everything. Second, if we'd had a proper monitoring system up and running, then the developers would have received messages about the problem before anyone else. And they would have been able to warn users before they even had a chance to notice it.

Whenever I checked data analysis tasks or did them myself, I'd often torment myself with the question: "Is the data really right?" Sometimes my doubts were justified and there was a problem. So, the first thing we do is check. But this isn't always easy and can take time. The other option is to automate data validation and monitoring. So, let's talk about that.

There are two parameters that we need to check:

- whether or not all the data that is in the source is available
- the integrity of the data.

It's easy enough to check whether or not the data is available. First, you check when the last update (a file or table, for example) was made. Better still, use a date/time field – for example, the date and time an order was placed. Second, count and compare the number of records in the data warehouse and the source. If you've included a field with the date and time, you can make day-to-day comparisons. Of course, when you are checking, the data at the source will differ from that in the data warehouse because of the delta time between the data in the source changing and these changes being reflected in the warehouse. Once you are confident that the data is okay, you can establish acceptable thresholds for the percentage difference through trial and error. For some data, the acceptable threshold may be half a percent, for others it may be five. This type of data validation is good for 80% of the data storage problems you will encounter. And, as the Pareto principle tells us, it takes just 20% of the effort to get 80% of the result. This method is inexpensive and can be performed by anyone. I love how simple it is!

Checking the second parameter (data integrity) is trickier. When I say integrity, I mean that all the data in one table is also present in the second. For example, you've got two tables – one with customers, and one with orders. The table with the orders will have a "customer" field. The integrity of the table containing the orders depends on whether or not all the customers listed in this table can also be found in the customer reference table. If there are discrepancies, then "broken" data will appear when joining the two tables (if a "left join," "right join" or "full outer join" command was issued), or disappear altogether and the relevant sales data will drop out of reports (if only an "inner join" command was issued). Both of these outcomes may potentially lead to bad decisions. It would be nice to monitor this through independent tests, for example, by checking the relative volume of purchases made by customers who do not appear in the "customers" table.

MY PERSONAL EXPERIENCE

Don't be afraid! I set about creating my first data warehouse back in 2004 when I was working at Ozon.ru. My experience working with MS SQL Server in Softline when I was at StatSoft came in handy here. I've still got my MS SQL Server certificate! I knew almost nothing about creating data warehouses, but my knowledge of MS SQL Server and a healthy dose of common sense got me through! I managed to create my first "spider" that downloaded data into a hastily assembled data warehouse. I didn't get any help, but no one bothered me either, which is extremely important. The data warehouse has evolved since then, but the basic concept I laid down at the very beginning remains the same. At Wikimart.ru, I put together the first version of an analytics system with full internal web analytics in just two months – and I was only working two days a week there. If you want to better understand the principles of data warehousing, I suggest getting your hands on Ralph Kimball's books. They helped me out a lot!

Now let's talk about some of the difficulties you might run into. By the time I left Ozon.ru, the discrepancy between the sales data in the warehouse and the accounting department was around 4–5%. The accounting department would close the accounting period at some point during the month, while the data in the cubes of the analytics system would be there since the first of the month. After leaving Ozon.ru, I had a meeting with the COO of Svyaznoy – a small team came to talk to me about "building cubes." They were shocked that I had created the entire main engine on my own. I'm not a genius or anything, we were simply talking about the system's margin of error. You always want the discrepancy with the accounting department to be as low as possible, but the lower you go, the more difficult it becomes. Say you want to reduce the discrepancy from 4% to 3%. This will take up a great deal of my time, and we would probably need to hire one or two other people, thus complicating the system and increasing management entropy. If we want to reduce it even further, to 2%, say, then this will take exponentially more effort still. Every reduction will entail an exponential increase in complexity and cost. And, as a result, we lose flexibility and maneuverability. There's no point praying for a system that has zero errors, because that will never happen. Remember the Pareto principle – 80% of results are produced by 20% of causes. And that does not mean that the remaining 80% is worth spending. You'll probably be better served spending it on something else that will move us closer to our goal, rather than striving for perfect numbers.

Chapter 7

DATA ANALYSIS TOOLS

As you will recall from previous chapters, classical data analytics is divided into two stages: 1) searching for hypotheses; and 2) statistical testing of these hypotheses. In order to formulate hypotheses, we need descriptive statistics, data visualization and domain knowledge (for example, the company's history).

There are a number of software packages that make the analyst's work with descriptive statistics and data visualization easier and faster. Let's look at some diametrically opposite approaches here. You can only take one of them, but it is always useful to broaden your horizons – you never know, maybe an alternative approach will suit you better.

I categorize these tools according to how they interact with the user. This is somewhat provisional, as certain categories may overlap with one another.

- Spreadsheets – Microsoft Excel, Open Office Calc, Google Docs Sheets.
- Notebooks – Jupyter Notebook, Netflix Polynote, Google Colab, R studio, etc.
- Visual analysis tools – Tableau, Google Data Studio, Yandex Data Lens, Microsoft Power BI, Amazon QuickSight.
- Statistical software – SAS, SPSS, Statistica, Knime, Orange Data Mining.

SPREADSHEETS

Spreadsheets are one of the most widely used data analysis tools. My first experience with a spreadsheet was back in 1997 when I drew up some tables in Quattro Pro for a geography assignment at school. The teacher was most impressed! I went to my dad's work (he was an IT engineer at the time), typed out the text on a keyboard and scaled country maps on a copier. In the end, I had a fully printed report, which I guess was something of a novelty back then, especially in Tver (a town near Moscow). After that, I worked in Microsoft Excel, and then Google Sheets, both of which made it easy to collaborate in the cloud. The advantages of spreadsheets are:

- Low entry threshold.
- Everything is clear and intuitive, such as adding columns or formulas.
- You can analyse pivot tables (the most important tool for generating hypotheses).
- It's easy to create tables.

The biggest disadvantage of spreadsheets is that they are not designed to automate tasks through programming. Projects like this can get complicated fast, and it becomes hell for developers to maintain it. There's a lot of code inside spreadsheets that is outside the version control system, which makes it impossible to track its changes. I used to "prepare" complex reports for weekly directors' meetings at Ozon.ru and Wikimart.ru using spreadsheets. The Ozon.ru reports included data entered manually by managers, as well as OLAP cubes and SQL scripts. At some point, the report was updated using a program written especially for the purpose, saved to a folder and dated. At Wikimart.ru, the analysts also made manual corrections to the report and converted it into a PDF file for presentations. Looking back, I would ditch this practice in favour of more manageable solutions, even if they are less flexible than spreadsheets. And I would talk to management about changing the report template to reduce the amount of manual work.

NOTEBOOKS

Notebooks (Fig. 7.1) can be a powerful and flexible tool in the right hands. They have gained popularity thanks to the widespread use of R programming languages, particularly Python, for data analysis. A notebook runs as a web service on a server or your computer and consists of cells of text with program code. The cells can be launched at random, and all data output (graphs, statistics, error messages) appears under the cell. You can write text and titles in the cells. You can produce complete research projects in notebooks if you want. The two most well-known public notebook services are Google Colab and Kaggle Notebook (which offers a free trial). They also have powerful GPU cards, which allow you to perform tasks using deep learning. Personally, I quite liked the simplicity and power of the Google Colab service when I was experimenting with creating deepfake videos.

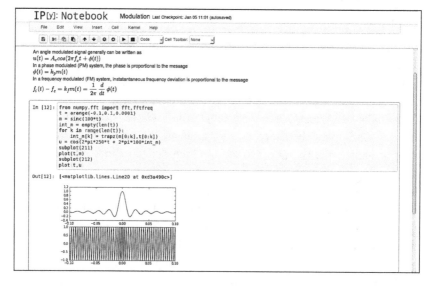

Fig. 7.1. Jupyter Notebook

Advantages:

- Flexibility. There are software libraries for every taste.

- Notebooks are easy to run in the cloud, so you don't have to waste your computer's resources.

- It's easy to share and publish your results.

- There is support for various programming languages. At Retail Rocket, I used Jupyter Notebook in Scala.

- You can work with any data source that has a driver.
- To repeat the result, the notebook just needs to restart and run all the cells. Not all tools can do this with such ease. For example, formulas in spreadsheets have a habit of jumping around or disappearing altogether. You don't have this problem with notebooks.

Disadvantages:

I don't think it's a good idea to use notebooks as a component of a working system, although I hear that many companies (even Netflix [49]) do just this. Notebooks are built for research, not creating workflows.

The entry threshold is higher than it is for spreadsheets. At least a basic knowledge of the chosen programming language is required.

VISUAL ANALYSIS TOOLS

I also call these personal dashboard services. This approach differs from the previous two in that you don't really have to do any programming whatsoever, as you can work through a so-called "thin client" (web browser) and publish the resulting dashboards on portals. The simplest of these is Google Data Studio, which allows you to work with data sources in the Google Cloud, including Google Sheets. These are more than just visualization tools. Power BI and Tableau (Fig. 7.2) have gone further, implementing ETL (Extract, Transform, Load) tools, where data is downloaded from sources to the user's computer or the cloud. Power BI does this using the Power Query programming language, while Tableau uses a visual interface (blocks with arrows connecting them).

[49]

Advantages:

- The entry threshold is lower than with notebooks.
- Visualization (especially in Tableau) is far better than alternative tools.
- They offer powerful interactive tools such as correlated analysis.
- Most, but not all, vendors offer "fat clients" (applications).
- You can build a simple BI system.

Disadvantages:

- Free versions are tied to the vendor's cloud. For example, Google Dashboard is tied to Google.
- The sets of data connectors available are incomplete. For example, Google Dashboard does not have a connector to ClickHouse. However, even the idea of making connectors is moot due to security issues. The Google client works from the cloud, which means you have to provide access to your internal databases from the internet, which is never a good idea.

Fig. 7.2. Tableau

STATISTICAL SOFTWARE

My introduction to data analysis came through statistical software when I was hired an intern at StatSoft. Spreadsheets and visual analysis tools are not good at statistical analysis, which is a key part of data analysis. Let's say you observe a difference in the indicators. How do we know that difference is real or an accident? We need to calculate its statistical significance.

Statistical analysis software usually come in the form of desktop applications (Fig. 7.3) that perform calculations locally. Data is loaded as spreadsheets. The software typically has a simple visual ETL (like in Tableau), as well as a built-in programming language for automating actions.

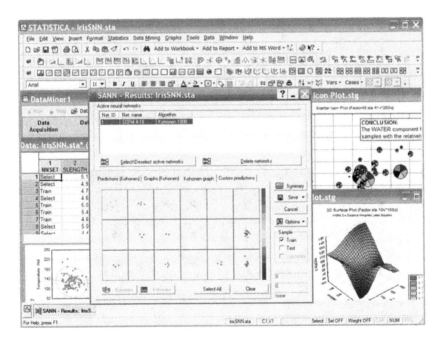

Fig. 7.3. STATISTICA

Advantages:

- Extensive statistical analysis possibilities. The manuals for these packages are just as good as data analysis textbooks. The statistical functions themselves are rigorously tested, unlike the statistical software that is freely available on the internet.

- Good for creating graphs.

- Attention to detail, which is important in scientific research.

- You can work with data offline.

Disadvantages:

- High entry threshold. You need to know what you're doing and which statistical criterion to use. Basic knowledge of mathematical statistics is a must.

- Commercial software packages are expensive.

WORKING WITH DATA IN THE CLOUD

We are living in a time where more and more people are working from home. Accordingly, an increasing number of tools are moving to the cloud. I think this has to do with the fact that businesses, and thus data sources, are starting to put everything on cloud servers. This makes transferring large amounts of data over the internet a pleasure. According to Gartner [46], public cloud services will cover 90% of all data analysis needs by 2022.

Almost all cloud vendors have already developed visual analysis tools: Google Data Studio, Microsoft Power BI, Amazon Quick Sight, Yandex DataLens, etc.

[46]

Advantages:

- Data and analytics are located within the same security perimeter. It is easy to manage data access. You don't need to expose yourself to risks by opening access to your data over the internet.

- Data is available within a single cloud network, which speeds up work.

- You can collaborate natively. I assume you have worked with services such as Google Docs. It's so much more convenient to collaborate than it is to work with a standard office suite.

- Thin client – everything is done in the browser. You don't need to install any programs.

- Flexible pricing – the price depends on how often you use the service and the amount of data.

- Maintenance costs are lower.

Disadvantages:

- Price. Even if the cloud provides visualization services for free, you still have to pay for the calculations and data aggregation. It's similar to car rental – if you are an active user, sooner or later it will make better financial sense for you to buy your own car. It's the same with cloud services.

- All your data is with a single vendor, meaning you will be tied to that vendor. If we're talking petabytes of data, it can be extremely difficult to transfer it all to your servers or another vendor's cloud.

I mostly like this trend of migrating data and data analysis to cloud services, as it makes developing analytics systems easier – and often cheaper – than buying corporate systems.

WHAT MAKES A GOOD REPORTING SYSTEM?

Let me describe a typical situation that arises when setting up an analytics system. Company X has a data warehouse and an analytics system connected to it. The analysts hold their first general meeting, show the system to management and demonstrate the data that is available. The most intellectually curious employees (hold onto them!) start working with the new data warehouse and analytics system. Comments soon start pouring in from them: the system's clunky; it's running too slow; there's not enough data. Let's talk about the minimum requirements for a reporting system at one of the places I worked.

First, let's look at two of the functions that these systems are expected to perform: dashboards and service reports. I covered dashboards in earlier chapters. Service reports are used to automate and simplify employee tasks. For example, service reports could include the contact details of problem customers who need to be called, customer ratings of the site's recommendation system, search terms that produce zero results, etc. These reports are even built into existing business processes.

Reports (and dashboards) always consist of blocks: tables and graphs. Blocks are often independent of one another but related by common parameters. Time and date are a perfect example. One attribute that is present in almost every report is the reporting period. In a good reporting system, this parameter is easy to transfer to all blocks. This is what it looks like for the user: the user opens the report they need in the browser, enters the reporting period (start and end date), waits a short while and gets the results. This is what it looks like for the developer: the developer collates several blocks into a single report, specifies the names of the general parameters in each block and in the general report, and then publishes it. It looks simple, but it's actually quite difficult to do in some reporting systems. Here's a recent example from Retail Rocket. We originally chose SuperSet for storage on ClickHouse. However, we kept running into issues in the parameters. So, we ended up switching to Metabase, where drawing up parametric reports is not nearly as tricky. Both systems are entirely free and open source.

Fat or thin clients: that is the question. A fat client is where there is a special program for viewing reports installed on the computer, while a thin client is where all the work is done on a browser. Most prefer to work using a thin client because of the low entry threshold – all you need to do is log in via a web browser and start using the system. There are far more options with fat clients, but it takes time to learn then all. Fat clients are important when you are working from a mobile phone; they adapt interfaces, albeit in a truncated fashion.

User administration is easy when there is a unified accounting system. In this case, users don't need to remember loads of passwords, and administrators can regulate access with ease. I can tell you from experience that if a company uses, say, Google Workspace (formerly G Suite) for business, then it saves a lot of headaches if you work with a reporting system that can use the same access authorization. For example, Metabase [47] allows you to log in through Google, while SuperSet [48] does not.

Reports can be generated and distributed periodically (hourly or on certain days, for example), or "triggered" in response to a specific event or change in a given indicator. Triggered reports (emails) are frequently used in IT – for example, to capture the moment when a system crashes or the load on the system reaches a critical level. This is done by establishing a threshold value for a given indicator in the system. A message will then be sent out every time this threshold is exceeded.

This is more difficult to do in business, as indicators do not change so quickly. In an online store, for example, you can set thresholds for the number of orders placed within the last hour or per number of visitors to the site in order to identify problems as soon as possible and avoid losing money. Reports can be sent in the body of the email, which is more convenient (you can see the result straight away), as an attachment (in and Excel file, for example), or as a summary in an email with a link to the full report. The convenience of email reports really depends on what you need to do with the information: if you need to quickly check some charts on your phone, then it is better to have the report in the body of the letter; if you need to work with numbers, then you'll greatly appreciate the report being sent as an attachment with a spreadsheet.

[47]   [48]

What should you do if you have to send the report many times in succession? For example, if several users ask for the same report at one-minute intervals. Wait five minutes while the report is generated? It depends on what cache scheme you have in place (all good systems use caching). When the report is published, the period for caching or saving past results is set. If you set a period of 30 minutes, for instance, then the report data will be saved for precisely 30 minutes. All subsequent reports sent within this 30-minute window will use this data. This is particularly useful when it comes to complex calculations, even if the data in the report lags behind that in the warehouse when cached. There was a time at Ozon.ru where we had a report in the back-office system containing the day's results. Employees would often update the report out of sheer excitement. This led to a Denial of Service (DoS) attack that caused performance to deteriorate. Caching reports for a designated period of time cooled the fervor of these number lovers and reduced the load on the ordering system.

Interactive analysis is when you dive a deep into numbers and metrics. It is *de facto* seen as the standard of any analytics system. You've got graphical analysis. A good example of this would be Google Analytics, where you can do just about everything with a mouse. And then you've got pivot tables, which I prefer. I select a data sample, copy it into a spreadsheet, run a pivot table analysis and then work with the data in the interface. We almost always use pivot tables when carrying out interactive data analysis.

In short, my minimum reporting system requirements are:

- User authorization that is preferably tied to the corporate access system.
- A thin client, via a web browser.
- The ability to view reports sent via immediately on the computer screen.
- Easy parameterization of large reports consisting of many blocks.
- Result caching.

PIVOT TABLES

Pivot tables are the best thing to ever happen to exploratory data analysis! Data scientists that know how to use pivot tables properly will never be out of a job. Pivot tables save us from having to perform a huge number of useless data queries when all we need is a tiny shred of data. I've already talked about my own personal interactive data analysis template: select the data, copy it into spreadsheets, build a pivot table and work with it. This method has literally saved me years compared to the time I would have spent if I had used the direct methods of calculating descriptive statistics and building simple graphs – the bread-and-butter data analysis operations for any analytical tool. Now, let's take a step-by-step look at how to work with pivot tables.

First, you've got to get the data ready. The data should be arranged into a fact table based on point-in-time tables or data change logs (we talked about these in the chapter on the types of data). If the table uses identifiers that are incomprehensible to any ordinary person, then this field should be decrypted by "joining" the reference data to (or "merging" it with) the fact table. Take the following example. Sales have dropped off and we want to understand why. Let's suppose we have plotted a point-in-time table for orders with the following fields:

- The time and date of the order (for example, 10 November 2020, 12:35:02).
- Customer type ID (1,2).
- Customer status ID in the loyalty programme (1,2,3).
- Order ID (2134, 2135, ...).
- Customer ID (1,2,3,4, ...).
- Order amount in roubles (102, 1012, ...).

The resulting table is a fact table – it records the fact of orders being placed. The data scientist wants to look at the buying habits of different types of customers and loyalty card holders. The working hypothesis is that this is where the main reason for the drop in sales can be found.

The ID fields are not readable and are used to normalize the tables in the accounting database. But we do have reference tables (tables 7.1 and 7.2) that we can use to decrypt them.

Table 7.1. Client type reference table

ID	Name
1	Individual
2	Business

Table 7.2. Customer status in the loyalty programme

ID	Name
1	VIP client
2	Loyalty card
3	No loyalty card

After joining (or merging) the fact and reference tables, we are left with an updated table of facts (Table 7.3):

- datetime – the time and date of the order (for example, 10 November 2020, 12:35:02).

- client_type – the type of customer that placed the order (an individual or a business).

- client_status – the customer's status in the loyalty programme (VIP, card holder or non-card holder).

- order_id – order ID (2134, 2135, ...).

- client_id – customer ID (1,2, ...).

- amount – order amount in roubles (102, 1012, ...).

What's good about this fact table is that the only ID fields are Order ID and Customer ID. These are useful fields, as they may be needed to view orders in greater detail in the internal accounting system. The analyst receives a sample of the data in this format, loads it into a spreadsheet (say, Microsoft Excel or Google Sheets), and builds a pivot table. So, let's analyse the pivot table.

Table 7.3. An example of data merging

datetime	client_type	client_status	order_id	client_id	amount
10-22-2020 12:35:02	Individual	VIP	2134	1	102 roubles
10-22-2020 12:35:02	Business	No loyalty card	2135	2	1012 roubles

Pivot tables contain two types of data: dimensions and measures. Dimensions are represented as a system of coordinates. When I hear the word "dimensions," I think of three axes of coordinates emanating from a single point perpendicular to each other, just like we were taught in geometry class at school. But there can be more than three dimensions (axes). Many, many more. You can use them as columns, rows, or pivot table filters, but they can never be placed in cells. Examples of dimensions:

▪ Date and time

▪ Client type

▪ Client status.

Measures are statistics that will be calculated in the pivot table when you "rotate" or change dimensions. They are, as a rule, aggregate figures: sums, averages, distinct count, count, etc. Measures for our task include:

▪ Order amount

▪ Average purchase size

- Number of orders (one line per order, no duplicate orders)
- Number of unique customers (the number of unique IDs should be counted here, as a single customer can place several orders, which will be counted several times).

Order IDs and Customer IDs can be both dimensions (where you can find statistics on specific orders or customers) and measures (where you can simply count the number of orders or customers). It depends on the specific task at hand, both methods work.

For each column, the analyst determines whether the data contained in it is a dimension or a measure, and what statistics on the measure are needed.

This is all the preparatory work that is needed. The next step is to formulate hypotheses and identify one or several slices that will either confirm or refute these hypotheses. We use the term "slice" because of the multidimensional nature of pivot tables. Imagine a three-dimensional object with a length, width and height. A knob of butter, for example. You take a knife and cut the butter to get a slice whose plane is perpendicular to the axis you are looking at. It's exactly the same principle with pivot tables, only you are slicing multidimensional data. There can be several axes depending on the number of dimensions there are – this is where the multidimensionality comes from. The location of the axis (dimension) perpendicular to which you make the cut is included in the report filter as a value that you record. The dimensions that lie in the plane of the slice will make up the columns and rows of our table. If the report filter is not used, all the data will be projected onto our slice through aggregation, which is selected individually for each indicator (sums, averages, and number).

The analyst formulates two hypotheses regarding the drop in sales:

- The change in consumer behaviour has been caused by one of the client types. Client type is one of the dimensions needed to make this hypothesis.
- The change in consumer behaviour has been caused by one of the loyalty programme groups. Client status is one of the dimensions needed to make this hypothesis.

As we are dealing with temporal changes, we need another dimension, namely time. So, we have formulated a hypothesis and carved out the required data slice. The rest is done by the technology: drag and drop the required dimensions with the mouse, for example, put the date into columns and client type into rows. Complete the table with the necessary measures and check whether the numbers confirm or refute the hypothesis being tested. Strictly speaking, a suitable statistical criterion should be used to test the correctness of the hypothesis, although this is rarely done in practice.

Hypotheses can be formulated and tested sequentially. And once you've got enough experience, you'll be able to formulate them at the subconscious level. Data scientists will play around with them in order to find the most probable cause of the problem or reason for the success: make the first slice, add the dimensions (cross-referencing them with existing ones) and change the measures.

This type of analysis would take ten times longer without spreadsheets and visual analysis tools on pivot tables. The analyst would have to program each slice, for example using the GROUP BY operator in SQL or pivot in the Python pandas library. Pivot tables allow data scientists to work as fast as their thoughts allow.

OLAP CUBES

Pivot tables do not reside in spreadsheets only. In fact, they run rather sluggishly, if at all, in spreadsheets containing massive amounts of data. But our goal is for everything to work at the speed of the analyst's thoughts, right? Software developers try all sorts of tricks to help make this happen. For example, they place data in a columnar database directly on the user's computer (we've already talked about the advantages of columnar databases in the chapter on data warehouses). The second method is to do all the calculations on servers and give the user access to these servers through the interface (fat or thin client).

This is how OLAP (On-Line Analytical Processing) cubes were invented.

The history of how OLAP cubes came to be is quite interesting, if only because our former compatriot Mikhail (Mosha) Pasumansky had a hand in it. Mosha moved to Israel form St. Petersburg in 1990. It was there that he wrote the Panorama analytical app, the first version of which came out in 1995. The following year, his company was bought out by Microsoft, which needed a similar solution for a new version of SQL Server. After integrating the system in Microsoft software, Mosha started developing a programming language for working with OLAP cubes called Multidimensional Expressions (MDX). MDX has become the standard for working with OLAP cubes and is supported by numerous vendors. OLAP cube services are now called Analysis Services.

We've already looked at how pivot tables work. Now let's delve into how the performance problem is solved in OLAP cubes, which pivot tables can calculate extremely quickly. I've worked a lot with Microsoft OLAP cube technologies, so I will draw on my experience here. The central link of any OLAP cube is the fact table, which we looked at through examples of building pivot tables earlier. There is a small but important difference here: as a rule, fact tables are not linked to directories; they are loaded into cubes separately from them.

To do this, the data in the warehouse needs to be prepared according to the so-called "star" schemas (Fig. 7.4): the fact table is connected by fields containing IDs (keys) with dimensional tables (reference data), as shown in the figure.

For this, the data in the warehouse is prepared according to the "star" scheme (Fig. 7.4): the fact table is connected by fields containing ID (keys) with reference books, as shown in the figure. The general rule here is to keep all dimensions in separate directories. This is so that they can be updated independently of the fact table. After preparing the necessary data in the design program, you need to make a note of which tables are dimension tables and which are fact tables. You also need to indicate in the settings which measures need to be calculated. The cube's preprocessing involves reading all the data from the warehouse and placing it in special structures that work quickly in terms of calculating pivot tables. The dimensions are read and processed first, then the fact table.

But it is when we start adding new data to the cube that things start to get really interesting.

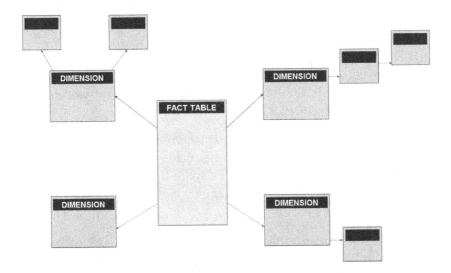

Fig. 7.4. Combining tables using a "star" schema

But what if new data appears? New data is entered into our "star" (the data warehouse) and the cube is updated accordingly. All the dimensions (directories) are read: if new elements have appeared or have been renamed, everything is updated. Dimension directories for OLAP cubes thus need to be saved and updated in their original form, you can't delete data from there. Updating fact tables is more interesting – you can either update and recalculate the cube entirely, or erase the old data from the fact table, fill it with completely new data and then update it. It is better to use incremental refresh here for quicker cube processing times. At Ozon.ru, full cube processing could take me four days, while incremental updates would take just 20 minutes.

There are a number of popular options for storing and processing data in OLAP cubes:

- MOLAP – the storage scheme I described above. Data is stored in special structures which calculate pivot tables extremely quickly.

- ROLAP – data is not placed anywhere, rather it is stored in the data warehouse. The OLAP cubes translate queries from pivot tables into data warehouse queries and return the results.

- HOLAP – data is partly stored in MOLAP, and partly in ROLAP schemes. This can help reduce any time lags in the cube's operation. The cube is updated daily in accordance with the MOLAP scheme, while new data is held in the ROLAP scheme.

I have always preferred MOLAP for its superior speed. Although the development of columnar databases has made ROLAP easier. This is because the ROLAP scheme does not require the cube to be carefully designed (unlike MOLAP), which makes it far easier to provide technical support for the OLAP cube.

Microsoft Excel spreadsheets are the perfect client for OLAP cubes, as working with Microsoft cubes is a breeze. Thin clients just don't provide the convenience and flexibility that Excel offers: the ability to use MDX, flexible formulas, and build reports from other reports. Unfortunately, this functionality is only supported on the Windows operating system; the OS X (Apple) version of Excel does not support it. You can't imagine how many team leaders and IT specialists curse MS developers for this! It means they've got to have separate Windows laptops or remote machines in the cloud just so they can work with Microsoft cubes. If you ask me, that's the biggest disadvantage that Microsoft could have in our field.

ENTERPRISE AND SELF-SERVICE BI SYSTEMS

There are two approaches to building analytics in a company – enterprise (corporate) and personal (self-service) BI. We've already talked about ways to use the self-service approach. Now, let's take a look at corporate-level systems.

An enterprise-wide decision-making system typically includes a number of components, all of which we have already mentioned:

- data warehouses
- a system for updating the data in the warehouse (ETL)
- an interactive analysis and reporting system.

Microsoft SQL Server is a good example of such a system: the SQL server itself acts as the data warehouse; Integration Services performs ETL; Analysis Services provides OLAP cubes for interactive and static reports; and Reporting Services is a thin client reporting system. Many BI systems vendors, including cloud-based ones, have a similar product range.

As far as I see it, the main difference between enterprise and self-service systems is that enterprise systems are developed centrally. For example, if you need to make changes to a report or other component, you can't do it yourself and have to contact the developer. The rather absurd situation often arises where it becomes impossible to change anything in the system without the participation of the developer.

Full self-service systems are automated: data is taken directly from data sources and stored as local files on the analyst's computer. No developer is needed, as the analyst can do everything themselves. This is the other extreme. Let's compare these two approaches:

- *The speed at which changes are made.* Self-service systems are better here. Any changes in the corporate system will be reflected on the systems of all end users. These kinds of changes need to be green-lit and properly coordinated, and they take time to implement. With a self-service system, the user simply makes the necessary changes and that is all.
- *Data quality.* Enterprise systems win. The conservative nature of corporate systems is a definite plus here: the development and design practices of the system allow us to monitor the quality of the data produced. Self-service systems are weak in this department, as they depend very much on the skills and attentiveness of the user, which increases the likelihood of errors.

- *Performance.* Enterprise systems are designed with the required load in mind, and if they struggle, there are technologies for scaling them. Self-service systems are more likely to experience poor performance.

- *Adapting the vendor's solution.* Corporate systems are like trees with strong roots which are extremely difficult to remove. Self-service systems don't have this problem.

I believe that both systems have their place. You'll probably get the best results by combining these approaches. There's nothing stopping you from building a data warehouse (or data lake) and then using flexible self-service tools for the "last mile." This eliminates some of the issues described above. The probability of user error remains, although it is mitigated somewhat.

MY EXPERIENCE

I've worked with a variety of systems in my time, from spreadsheets to Hadoop/Spark distributed systems with petabytes of data. All I can say is there's a time for everything. Analytics architecture is an artform that requires remarkable talent. I've talked a lot in this chapter about my own best practices, which have been tested through years of experience in the field. No matter what solution you come up with, there's bound to be pros and cons. And it's better to know what they are before you create a system, rather than after.

You're constantly performing a balancing act between speed and quality, between the costs now and the costs later. But it's always helpful to thinks about the user. The faster and more intuitively the user is able to work with data, the fewer errors he or she will make, which in turn will enable them to make decisions more efficiently. I believe it is speed that ensures the success of a company, even if the quality guarantees are so-so. The one who has made the most decisions wins.

Analytics systems allow you to navigate the data, but they don't make decisions. Humans do. So, why not improve the quality of their lives by making it easier for them to make decisions?

Chapter 8

MACHINE LEARNING ALGORITHMS

As I mentioned earlier, the main difference between machine learning and conventional programming is that the program learns by example, rather than by direct instructions. A model trained on data (examples) is thus an integral part of any solution. It's like a black box: you have code that serves as an interface for a trained model (the black box) to interact with the outside world. The box itself contains a set of coefficients and parameters that only the code can understand.

The advantage of machine learning is that it makes decisions automatically, meaning that data is processed much faster. Humans have what we would call "universal intelligence." However, this versatility means that the number of tasks that we can solve is a given unit of time is extremely limited. The same cannot be said of ML, which is focused on narrow tasks, yet can be infinitely scaled. You need one million predictions per second? Not a problem, just give us the resources.

This is not a machine learning textbook. We will only look at the basics of ML in this chapter, the stuff we will need later on. However, the basics cover 80% of what you need to know when working with structured data – the Pareto principle applies here too.

I chose algorithms that I have used many times in the past: linear regression, logistic regression, decision trees and ensembles (random forest, xgboost, catboost). These are the most popular algorithms for working with structured data issues. *Kaggle's State of Data Science and Machine Learning 2019* bears this out [53]. Page 18 of the Kaggle report presents a chart of the most popular machine learning methods (Fig. 8.1). The researchers thus concluded that "Respondents are big fans of keeping it simple. The most common methods are linear or logistic regression, followed by decision trees. While not as powerful as more complex techniques, they can still be quite effective and are easier to interpret."

[52]   [53]

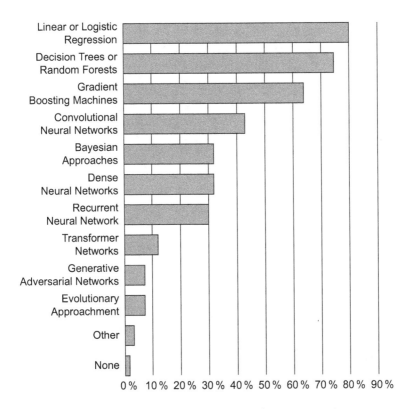

Fig. 8.1. Simple linear methods are the most popular

My first experience with neural networks was in 2002, when I started working at StatSoft. I wasn't particularly impressed at the time. Sure, the algorithm is beautiful and truly fascinating, but the problems they were tasked with solving could be solved using far simpler methods. It was around ten years ago that convolutional neural networks started to appear on a large scale, marking the dawn of the golden age of neural networks. They have since become an ideal tool for working with images, sound and other unstructured information. Attempts have been made to use them in recommendation services, albeit to no avail [52]. We tried using them at Retail Rocket too. While we saw no tangible benefits when it came to clothing recommendations [25], they did come in handy for removing "bad" recommendations, and they are still used today. The field itself is relatively young, and the GPU chips that are designed to accelerate computations on deep learning neural networks are becoming more powerful and cheaper. I expect these methods to become more widespread over the next ten years. Theoretically, they will be able to replace current algorithms with universal ones, fit even for structured data, which will make solving ML problems much easier. I could write an entire book on neural networks.

TYPES OF ML PROBLEMS

Classical machine learning can be divided into three types:

- supervised learning
- unsupervised learning
- reinforcement learning.

Supervised learning means that each set of inputs (independent variables or features) has a value (dependent variable) that the model must predict. Examples of such tasks are presented in the table below (Table 8.1) [50].

There are two main classes of problems here: a regression problem, where you need to predict an indicator with a continuous scale (for example, money, probability, etc.); and a classification problem (task), where you need to understand the class that an object belongs to (whether or not there are people in a photograph, whether or not a person is sick, who is in the photo, etc.). There are also a number of tasks related to language translation, speech recognition, and geo-positioning, which have become widespread thanks to deep neural networks.

[25]   [50]   [51]

Table 8.1. Types of ML Problems

Input (independent variables)	What needs to be predicted (dependent variables)	Application	Task class
Picture	Are there human faces? (0 or 1)	Photo tagging	Classification
Loan application	Will they repay the loan? (0 or 1)	Loan approvals	Classification
Audio clip	Transcript of audio clip	Speech recognition	
English sentence	Russian sentence	Language translation	
Sensors on industrial equipment	Is it about to fail? (probability)	Preventive maintenance	Regression
Car camera and other sensors	Position in relation to other cars	Self-driving cars	

The concept of "regression" was first put forward by Sir Francis Galton after he read Darwin's *On the Origin of Species*. He decided to research the relationship between child height and parent height. According to his findings, children of very tall parents tend to be less tall when they reach adulthood, and children of extremely short parents tend to be less short when they reach adulthood. Galton called this reverse growth "regression" (i.e. to move in the opposite direction) [51]. In 1885, he published his "Regression towards Mediocrity in Hereditary Stature," and his concept would soon be applied to all problems with one-sided stochastic dependence.

Unsupervised learning implies that there is a pattern in the data, but you don't know what it is (there is no dependent variable). It could involve dividing a dataset into clusters (cluster analysis), searching for anomalies, autoencoders (for example, to reduce the dimension of the feature space), principal component analysis, or collaborative filtering (recommendation systems).

Reinforcement learning is a model of learning through interaction with the environment. This is a special case of a learning model that involves a "teacher." Here, the teacher is not a dataset, but rather a reaction of the environment to an action we have performed. This kind of learning is often used in the development of bots for games (not just shooter games, but chess games too), to control robots, etc. Unlike classic machine learning, there is no dataset here. The agent (for example, a robot) performs an action in the environment and receives feedback in the form of a reward. It thus learns to perform actions that maximize the reward. This method can be used to teach a robot how to walk or play chess, for example.

Each type of problem in classic ML has its own algorithm. Depending on the task and the data, a variant of the model that is most likely to produce results is proposed by the hugely popular scikit-learn library. I used this library when I started studying ML models in Python for Kaggle competitions.

ML TASK METRICS

If there is a non-random pattern in the data, a corresponding model is selected for the task. And if there is sufficient data, then it is not a particularly challenging task to train the ML model. The first step is to work out how to measure the effectiveness of the model. This is crucial: if we create a model that helps in real life, it must have a clearly defined goal. And the goal is expressed in the metric. For example, if you want the model to predict demand for goods, then the goal will be to reduce the discrepancy with reality (forecast error). If you need to determine whether a given photograph contains an image of a dog, your goal will be to increase the percentage of photographs with the correct answer. All Kaggle tasks have a metric that is used to select the winner.

Ignoring this step is a rookie mistake that even fully fledged analysts still sometimes make. I can tell you from my experience at Retail Rocket that choosing the wrong metric can be very costly. This is the foundation of machine learning. And it's not as easy to choose the right metric as it may seem at first. For example, there are a number of COVID-19 throat swab tests. One of them gives more false-positives (where the patient is not actually sick), while another gives more false-negatives (which miss patients who are actually infectious). Which testing system do you choose? If you choose the first one, then you'll be forcing many people to self-isolate, which will in turn affect the economy. If you choose the second one, then infected people will be allowed to go about their daily lives and spread the virus. You've got to weigh up the advantages and disadvantages. You'll run into similar problems when developing recommendation systems: one algorithm gives more logical recommendations for the user, while the other gives recommendations that would bring in greater profit for the store. (This means that the machine learned through weak but important signals that seem illogical to us, and that its recommendations lead to increased sales, although this cannot be explained by logic due to the limitations of the human mind.) Which algorithm do you choose? If you run a business, you should choose the second. The thing is, though, when you're trying to sell this recommendation system, managers who make purchasing decisions often like the first one better. And that's easy to understand – a website is like a storefront and it needs to look appealing. You end up having to change the first algorithm, which works fine as it is, to ensure greater profitability and make the recommendations look more logical. Focusing on a limited number of metrics makes it hard to develop new algorithms.

A metric can be considered the difference between what a model predicts from the input data (independent variables, or features) and what it actually is (the dependent variable, or outcome). There are many nuances when it comes to calculating metrics, but this difference is always key. Typical metrics for ML tasks depend on what class they are.

For regression, we need to use mean squared error (MSE). This is the sum of the squares of the differences between the predicted and actual values from the dataset divided by the number of examples in the dataset:

$$MSE = \frac{1}{n}\sum(y - \hat{y})^2.$$

There are a host of other popular metrics, including RMSE, MAE and R^2.

For classification tasks, the most popular metrics can be easily obtained from a misclassification, or confusion, matrix. When I interview a candidate for a data scientist position, I often ask them to plot such a matrix (see Table 8.2) and derive metrics from it.

Table 8.2. Misclassification matrix

	Actual: 1 (True)	**Actual: 0 (False)**
Predicted: 1 (True)	100 (TP)	10 (FP)
Predicted: 0 (False)	15 (FN)	90 (TN)

Let's say you need to solve a classification task – to determine whether or not a person has a cold. You've got a dataset with the following features: fever, sore throat, runny nose, sneezing, and sensitivity to light. Each example has an identifier: 1, or True (the person has a cold); and 0, or False (the person does not have a cold). You build a model that gives you a result for each example: 1 (meaning the person is sick) and 0 (meaning the person is healthy). To see the errors in your model, you need to compare its output with the actual values. Doing this allows us to draw up a misclassification matrix. The predicted values are placed in the rows, and the actual values are placed in the columns. The cells contain the number of cases for each class: 1 for when the prediction was correct, and 0 for when it was not. In the table, I have included 100 examples of when our predictions were correct.

The brackets contain information that will prove useful for representing metrics: TP = True Positive (1); TN = True Negative (0), FN = False Negative (the model counted 0, but was in actual fact 1), FP = False Positive (the model counted 1, but was in actual fact 0). Let's display the metrics:

```
Accuracy = number of correct predictions / number of examples =
= (TP + TN) / (TP + TN + FP + FN).

Precision = TP / (TP + FP).

Recall = TP / (TP + FN).

F measure = 1 / (1/Precision + 1/Recall).
```

The most commonly used metrics for classification are precision and recall. Unlike accuracy, they don't depend on the imbalance of classes. This happens when the ratio of zeros and ones in the dataset is nowhere near 50:50.

Another interesting classification metric is AUC-ROC (Area Under Curve of Receiver Operating Characteristic), which is used when the classification algorithm gives a probability that could belong to any class – 0 or 1. In order to calculate the Recall and Precision metrics, we would have to make different threshold values for the probabilities (to distinguish between classes) and calculate them. This is where AUC-ROC, which shows the effectiveness of the classifier regardless of the threshold value, comes in. To build it, you need to take a set of threshold values from the segment [8–0;1] and calculate two numbers for each threshold value:

TPR (True Positive Rate) = TP/(TP + FN) and

FPR (False Positive Rate) = FP/(FP + TN).

Mark these numbers as points in the plane of coordinates TPR and FPR and you'll get the following curve (Fig. 8.3).

The area under the curve is the AUC. If the AUC is close to 0.5, then your classifier is not really any different from a random coin toss. The closer it is to 1, the better. This metric is often used in research papers and Kaggle competitions.

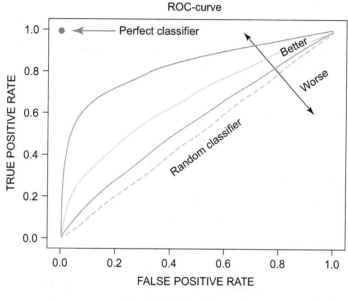

Fig. 8.3. ROC curve

Other tasks, such as ranking search results or for recommendations, have their own performance indicators. You can learn about them in specialist literature.

So, we've got a metric. We can now use it to compare different models to gauge which is better. Let the learning begin!

ML FROM THE INSIDE

Almost all machine learning models that are used for supervised learning come down to two things: defining the loss function (in the case of one example) or cost function (in the case of multiple examples); and the procedure for minimizing it.

For example, with linear regression, this will be the root-mean-square error in the form in which we defined it earlier. There are a number of optimization procedures we can use to find the minimum loss function. One of the most widespread is gradient descent.

Optimization typically looks like this:

1. The coefficients of the model (which need to be collected) are initialized to zero or given random values.

2. The value of the loss function (for example, standard deviation) and its gradient (a derivative of the loss function) are calculated. We need the gradient to understand what needs to be done to minimize errors.

3. If the loss function has changed significantly and we haven't reached the maximum number of repetitions of the calculation, then we recalculate the coefficients based on the gradient and repeat step 2.

4. Optimization is considered complete when we return a model containing the coefficients we have calculated.

Visually, gradient descent looks like this (Fig. 8.4):

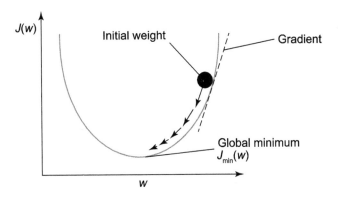

Fig. 8.4. Gradient descent

We have a loss function, and from an arbitrary point, we move towards its minimum sequentially, step by step.

There are two more versions of this algorithm: stochastic gradient descent (SGD) and mini-batch gradient descent. The first is used for working with big data, when just one example from the entire dataset is used for a single training iteration. A batch version of this algorithm can also be applied as alternative, whereby a subset of the dataset is used instead of a single example.

LINEAR REGRESSION

This is the simplest and most popular regression model. We actually use it at school when we learn the formula for linear dependence. This is the formula I was taught in school: $y = a \times x + b$. This is so-called linear regression. It has just one independent variable.

Data scientists typically work with multivariate linear regression, which uses the following formula:

$$y_i = \beta_0 + \beta_1 x_{i1} + \beta_2 x_{i2} + ... + \beta_p x_{ip}, \ i = 1, \ ..., \ n.$$

It consists of the sum of the products of each coefficient, the value of the corresponding feature and an additional intercept. The result is a straight line when we are dealing with a single independent variable, and a hyperplane when we are dealing with N features. When training linear regression, the hyperplane is constructed in such a way as to minimize its distance from the points (the dataset). This is the standard deviation. The first thing I ask a person applying for a data scientist position is: "Here are the results of an experiment. The points are marked on the plane with two axes. A line has been plotted to approximate these points. How do you know whether the straight line has been plotted optimally?" This is a good question for understanding the essence of linear regression.

If the data at the input is normalized during linear regression, its influence on the dependent variable (and thus the result) increases proportionally to the feature's coefficient. A positive coefficient is when an increase in the value of a feature increases the value of the dependent variable (positive correlation). A negative coefficient is when there is a negative correlation or negative linear independence.

LOGISTIC REGRESSION

This is the most widely used model for solving binary classification tasks (tasks with two classes).

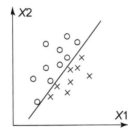

Fig. 8.5. Dividing line in a classification task

Let's say we have to separate two classes: noughts and crosses. I mark them on a coordinate grid, with the values of the X1 and X2 features being plotted along the axes (Fig. 8.5). Clearly, you can draw a straight line between the noughts and crosses to separate them: the noughts are above the line, and the crosses are below it. This is how logistic regression works – it looks for a line or hyperplane that separates classes with minimal error. In terms of results, it gives the probability that a point belongs to a certain class. The closer a point is to the dividing surface, the less "confident" the model is in its choice (probability approaches 0.5). Accordingly, the further the point is from the surface, the closer the probability is to 0 or 1, depending on the class. There are two classes in our present task. Thus, if the probability of belonging to one class in 0.3, then the probability of it belonging to the second is 1–0.3 = 0.7. Probability in logistic regression is calculated using a sigmoid function (Fig. 8.6).

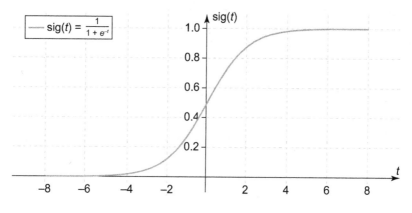

Fig. 8.6. Sigmoid function

In this graph t is substituted with a value from a normal linear formula with coefficients, similar to linear regression. The formula itself is the equation of the dividing surface I described above.

This is the most popular model both among researchers, who love it for its simplicity and interpretability (the coefficients are the same as for linear regression), and among data engineers. Unlike other classifiers, this simple formula is easily scalable at high loads. And when banner ads catch up on the internet, it will likely be thanks to logistic regression, which has been used at Criteo, one of the largest retargeting companies in the world [54].

[54]

DECISION TREES

Decision trees are right behind linear methods in terms of popularity. They are a descriptive tool (Fig. 8.8) that can be used to classification and regression tasks. The best classification algorithms (Catboost, XGboost and Random Forest) are based on decision trees. The method itself is non-linear and represents the rules of conditional sentences: "if... then..." A decision tree consists of internal nodes and leaf nodes. Internal nodes are conditions on independent variables (rules). Leaf nodes are answers that contain the probability of belonging to a given class. Answers are obtained by moving out from the root of the tree. The goal is to get to a leaf and determine the necessary class.

Decision trees are built on completely different principles than those we have considered in linear models. My kids like to play "question and answer." One player thinks of a word and the others have to guess what that word is by asking "yes–no" questions. The player who guesses the word correctly with the fewest number of questions wins. It's the same with decision trees: the rules are constructed in such a way as to move from root to leaf in as few steps as possible.

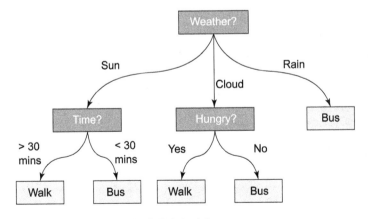

Fig. 8.7. A decision tree

This requires choosing a feature at the outset. Dividing a dataset by its value (thresholds are selected for continuous datasets) yields the biggest drop in Shannon's entropy (or the largest information gain). This involves enumerating all features and their values at each step. The process is repeated several times until there is nothing left to divide and only observations of a single class remain in the data sample – this is the leaf. There is always the risk of overfitting here, when the resulting tree is too familiar with the sample, having memorized all the data in the leaves. In practice, when constructing decision trees, data scientists limit the depth and maximum number of elements in the leaves. And if all else fails, they can "prune" or "post-prune" the tree, from leaf to root. The resulting decision is then based on the question: Will the tree really be negatively affected if the two leaves are combined? A separate dataset that was not part of the training model is used for this [55].

LEARNING ERRORS

A correctly chosen model tries to find patterns and generalize them. Performance metrics allow you to compare different models and training approaches by way of simple comparison. You have to agree that if you have two models with forecast errors of 15% and 10%, respectively, then it is obvious that you should go for the second model. And what happens if data that was not in the dataset gets into the model during testing? If training the model has provided us with high-quality generalization, then everything should be in order and the error negligible. If not, the error can be extremely large.

[55]

Training the model can lead to two types of error:

- The model did not notice any patterns (high bias, underfitting).
- The model performed an overly complex interpretation – for example, it identified a quadratic relationship where it is actually a linear one (high variance, overfitting).

Fig. 8.8. Left to right: correct training, underfitting, overfitting

Let me try and demonstrate. Figure 8.8 shows the results of experiments in the form of dots (remember your physics classes at school). We need to find patterns, which involves plotting lines describing them. Everything in the first picture in the figure is good: the straight line adequately describes the data, and the distances from the dots to the line are small. The model has identified the pattern correctly. The second clearly shows nonlinear dependence (for example, quadratic), meaning that the line drawn through the points is incorrect. What we have here is underfitting – we have made a mistake in the order of the function. The opposite is true for the third picture. The model is too complex for the linear dependence that we can see from the dots. Data outliers have distorted the results. This is a classic example of overfitting, a simpler model (a linear one, for example) should have been used.

This is, of course, an artificial scenario, with one independent variable on the horizontal axis and one dependent variable on the vertical axis. In such simple conditions, the problem is immediately evident from the graph. But what if we have several independent variables, say, ten? This is where validation comes to the rescue.

Validation is used to identify such errors when working with models, just like with a black box. The simplest approach is to randomly divide the dataset into two parts: a large part that is used to train the model, and a small part that is used to test it. The split is usually 80:20. The trick here is that when the model is put into action, the real error will be similar to the one we obtained from the test dataset. Another kind of validation involves dividing the data into three parts rather than two: one in which the model is trained; a second in which the model's hyperparameters (settings) are selected; and a third in which the test score is obtained. In his *Machine Learning Yearning* [60], Andrew Ng sees this as the primary validation model. Now let's discuss the diagnostic algorithm itself. Say we have two figures – the mean squared errors for the training dataset and the test dataset. Now, let's compare them:

- The test and training errors are almost identical. The error is minimal and thus satisfactory. Congratulations! The model has been trained correctly and can be put into operation.

- The test error is significantly larger than the training error. You are, nevertheless, satisfied with the training error. Overfitting is evident here – the model is too complex for the data.

- The training error is high. This is an example of underfitting. Either the model is too simple for the data or there is insufficient data (in terms of sheer size, or certain features are missing).

K-fold cross validation is more complex. It is widely used in high-level work, scientific research and competitions and involves randomly dividing the dataset into k (for example, eight) equal parts. We then extract the first part from the dataset, train the model on the remaining parts, and count the errors in the training and extracted data (test error). This sequence is repeated for all the parts. We are left with k errors that can then be averaged and make similar comparisons to those described above.

[60]

WHAT TO DO ABOUT OVERFITTING

There are a few simple things we can do to deal with overfitting. First, we can try to find more data (hello, Captain Obvious!). This is extremely naïve advice, as we typically work with the most complete dataset possible.

The second thing we can do is to remove outliers from the data. This can be done through distribution analysis: descriptive statistics, histograms, box and whiskers plots, and scatter plots are all useful.

Third, we can remove features (independent variables). This is particularly effective when using linear methods, which are particularly sensitive to feature multicollinearity. In other words, certain features are dependent on one another. The nature of this dependence can be natural or artificial. An example of natural dependence would be the number of purchases made and the amount of money spent. Artificial dependence is when the analyst adds new features to the dataset as a function of existing features. For example, I squared the value of one feature, while the old feature remained in the dataset. We encounter this all the time in data analytics.

In linear methods, this leads to an abrupt change in coefficients when a new feature is added that is dependent on features that are already a part of the model. For example, analysts use linear regression to gauge whether or not a customer will make another purchase. The model already contains the feature "number of purchases made" – say it has a coefficient of 0.6. The next step is to add the amount spent on purchases to the model. The coefficient of this feature will be 0.5, while the coefficient of purchases is now negative: –0.1. This is an odd situation, as it is obvious that the more purchases a customer has made, the more likely he or she is to make purchases in the future. Yet here we see that the number of purchases has a negative effect. This is because the correlation (dependence) between the number of purchases made and the amount spent in extremely high – the latter has created this effect. The coefficients themselves can be important if you want to understand why a certain situation has arisen. Multicollinearity can lead to wrong conclusions. Interestingly, statistical analysis and machine learning have different goals. In statistical analysis, the coefficients of the model are important, as they explain the nature of the phenomenon. This is not as important for machine learning, where the priority is to achieve good metrics – how this is done is of little consequence.

There are a number of ways to deal with multicollinearity: removing dependent features, compressing space using principal component analysis, and ridge regression. The first method involves the step-by-step inclusion or exclusion of features. With step-by-step inclusion, the first step is to select the feature with the smallest area if you are building a regression model based on that feature alone. This requires going through all the features and selecting just one. The next step is to select the next feature, and so on. You'll know when to stop when the model error in the test dataset does not decrease by an acceptable amount. Step-by-step exclusion works in the same way.

Principal component analysis (PCA) is a linear space compression method – an unsupervised learning method that only works for linear dependencies. The method itself sounds complicated: reducing the number of features while losing as little information as possible through projection into an orthogonal space of a lower dimension. Geometric interpretation will help us understand. Let's look at how the number of orders depends on the amount of money spent on a scatterplot. The figure shows an elongated cloud (Fig. 8.9). Now let's superimpose a new coordinate system on top of it with axes X1 and X2:

X1 is drawn longitudinally, and X2 perpendicularly, to the cloud. Now we can take the value of each point in this new coordinate system. More than this, we can leave the value along the X1 axis and get just one X1 feature instead of two that are correlated with each other. We can discard X2, as the spread (variability) of values along this axis is far lower. We have thus found a completely new feature, X1, which carries information about the user's past purchases while at the same time replacing two old features. This is essentially how PCA works. The method allows us to obtain the required number of features (spatial dimensions), performs all the necessary operations and tells us how much information has been lost

due to thus transformation (the proportion of the explained variance).
This indicator allows us to choose the number of dimensions in output.

Fig. 8.9. Principal component analysis (PCA)

The fourth way to deal with overfitting is to stop the training process
early (Fig. 8.10).

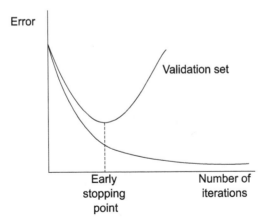

Fig. 8.10. Terminating training early

This requires counting the number of errors in the training and dataset at each iteration step. The training needs to be halted when test errors start to increase.

The fifth method is regularization. Regularization is the sum of the coefficients of the model multiplied by the regularization coefficient. It is added to the error function that the ML model optimizes. There are several types of regularization: L1 – the sum of the coefficient modules; L2 – the sum of the squares of the coefficients; and elastic net – the sum of the L1 and L2 regularizations with separate coefficients. The goal of regularization is the pessimization of coefficients with large values. This ensures that one feature is not weighted disproportionately. Regularization coefficients are known as hyperparameters. They also need to be selected so that a smaller error is obtained. L2 regularization is the more popular of the two methods.

And last but not least, we have ensemble methods.

ENSEMBLE METHODS

The "no free lunch" theorem states that no single algorithm will be optimal for all tasks. Analysts can spend their time collecting model after model to help best solve a given problem. But what if we were to combine different models into one large model? We would have a new algorithm – an ensemble of algorithms. These can be extremely accurate, even if you use "weak" algorithms that are only negligibly more reliable than a toss of a coin. The development of computing power (more memory, increasingly powerful processors, etc.) has made combining algorithms easy to do.

While there are many ways to combine simple algorithms into ensembles, we will deal the two most popular only – bagging and boosting. Bagging (or bootstrap aggregating) was first put forward by Leo Breiman in 1994. The idea is to create several datasets, all of which differ slightly from the original. There are two ways to do this: randomly selecting samples from the original dataset (sampling); and randomly selecting a subset of features from the original dataset. These methods are typically combined. The sampling of data is done with replacement, meaning that the relevant lines are not deleted from the original dataset. As a result, certain data will be present in the new dataset several times over, while other data will not be there at all.

Base algorithms for bagging should be prone to overfitting. One example here would be deep decision trees with many branches. A basic algorithm is then trained on each training dataset. The result of the ensemble is obtained by averaging the training results on all datasets. The most well-known algorithm is Random Forest, which is easy enough to write yourself, although there are a number of ready-made implementations that can be used [56].

Boosting is built on entirely different principles. It involves using simple algorithms that are only slightly more reliable than a coin toss, for example shallow decision trees. This is how it works: the first tree is trained, then the second tree is trained based on the errors made in the first tree, then the third tree, and so on until we reach the required level of accuracy. All the trained trees are assigned a weight that is proportional to their accuracy. These weights are used when you need a response from the voting model: the higher the weight, the greater the impact on the result (for example, AdaBoost).

The most widely used algorithms based on gradient boosting (Gradient Boosting Decision Tree) are XGBoost [57], LightGBM [58] from Microsoft и CatBoost [59] from Yandex. These are the algorithms that win Kaggle competitions most frequently.

The difference between boosting and bagging is that the former is a serial process, while the latter is a parallel process. Bagging is thus considered

[56]   [57]

the faster option. It can be parallelized across cluster nodes or processor cores. This is important, for example, when you need results quickly. Random forest is best for this. If you need accuracy, boosting is the way to go, but you'll need to spend a long time (days or even weeks) studying it and selecting the numerous model parameters (hyperparameters). Random forest is easier to get to grips with out of the box. One of the secondary functions of these ensembles is that a list of features sorted in order of their impact (feature importance) is created. This can be useful if you want to use another model and there are too many features in the dataset.

[58]   [59]

Chapter 9

THE PRACTICE OF MACHINE LEARNING

HOW TO LEARN MACHINE LEARNING

I went to a very run-of-the-mill school in my hometown of Tver in Russia. In my final year, I would spend four hours every evening surrounded by textbooks preparing for the Moscow Institute of Physics and Technology (MIPT) admission exams, doing practice academic Olympics tests. Two hours on maths, two hours on physics. I got used to the routine. The books were really good – my best friends, really!

It is my firm belief that the only way to get fundamental knowledge about any subject is from a book. But life moves at a far quicker pace than it did 20 years ago, and it's often not enough these days to simply read a textbook from cover to cover. You've got to get take what you can from wherever you can – and this is where good online courses are useful. I personally use Coursera – they were the first to come up with a quality commercial product backed by Stanford professors. I've completed around a dozen courses on various subjects there. And it has the best machine learning course I've ever come across – "Machine Learning" [61] by Andrew Ng, the founder of Coursera. I think the course did a lot for the popularity of this platform. More than three million people have taken the Machine Learning course so far. Andrew has also released a free book on machine learning [60].

The difference between Andrew's course and all the others is that it strikes a good balance between theory and practice. I've got a degree in physics and mathematics from MIPT and even I don't like it when a practical course is full of formulas and calculations. A good course should have minimal theoretical information to allow students to take the first practical steps as quickly as possible. At the end, the student should not only understand *how* to do something, but they should also know *why*. Books are where you go for a deep theoretical knowledge, not courses.

[60]   [61]

Another plus of Andrew Ng's course is that you get to program the algorithms yourself, which helps you understand how they work from the inside. This in turn removes the fear of machine learning – to the point where you no longer see it as a kind of magic, but rather as a craft. I think that someone who is comfortable with school-level mathematics and technical English should be able to complete the course without much effort [61]. There's nothing on decision trees and ensembles, but, otherwise, it's a thoroughly comprehensive course. By the way, Xavier Amatriain also recommends Andrew Ng's Machine Learning course on his Quora.com page.

How else can you get a good grasp of machine learning? By writing algorithms yourself. Xavier recommends the following actions [62]: find a good book on machine learning, read the introductory chapters, choose an algorithm from the book that you find interesting and write it in a programming language that you know. If you don't get something, you can have a peak at a finished implementation of the algorithm in the code of any library (although you shouldn't do this too often). I noticed a long time ago that hard-to-grasp information is the kind of information that tends to stick once you understand it. Don't be afraid to reinvent the wheel, as this knowledge will come in handy in the future. I took Xavier's advice myself a few years ago and wrote my own small learning library in Scala [63]. I was reading a book on program design in Scala at the time and decided to combine what I was learning from the book with a course on Coursera. I used vectorized calculations for the library in much the same way that Andrew Ng had.

If you think this approach is too complicated because of the complexity of the programming required, then Andrew has some advice for you. We programmers have a dirty little secret – most of the time, we'll search for a solution to problems on stackoverflow.com. Stack Overflow is essentially a question-and-answer site for programmers. When we find what we're

[62]    [63]

looking for, we often simply copy the code from the forum into our own program. Andrew suggests that we shouldn't copy the code. Rather, we should retype the code manually or, better still, try to figure out why it is correct. This, he believes, will help the developer or analyst grow faster as a professional. Not that there's anything wrong with copying, he says, as many great artists started out this way.

ML COMPETITIONS

On October 2, 2006, Netflix announced its first ever "Netflix Prize," with $1 million in prize money up for grabs for whoever could improve the company's recommendation system by 10% according to the RMSE method. The prize was eventually collected by BellKor's Pragmatic Chaos team in September 2009. The contest had lasted almost three years due to the difficulty of the task.

Similar contests have been held by the ACM Special Interest Group on Knowledge Discovery and Data Mining (ACM SIGKDD) as part of the KDD Cup programme. A new contest is held every year with its own organizers, data and rules.

These developments led to the creation of a platform for commercial machine learning competitions – Kaggle.com. Kaggle was founded by a team of three in 2010 and sold to Google in 2017. These days, it provides an abundance of services, but first and foremost is the machine learning competition, which offers some serious prize money. The competition format is almost identical to Netflix's: a company publishes its data and the rules of participation. On the closing day of the competition, the points of all entrants are tallied to determine the winner. The winners get prize money, while the company gets a solution. A description of the solution is often published on the forum.

Machine learning competitions are a way to improve practical ML skills and master the creation of features based on datasets. The events are open for everyone, and the experience generally proves to be valuable.

Sounds great, right? Well, there is a flipside to this. The solutions can't be used wholesale, only certain ideas can be taken from them. For example, Netflix stated [65] that the winning entry consisted of 107 sub-algorithms, of which only two gave a significant result: matrix factorization (SVD) and restricted Boltzmann machine (RBM). The company had some difficulty implementing these two algorithms into its system. The Pareto principle proved true once again: 80% of the result was produced by 20% of the effort (the two algorithms). I'll say it again – the Netflix developers did not introduce the entire monster as a whole, but took just a few of its elements. The winning algorithm simply cannot be introduced in its complete form. It's too resource-heavy and complex, and it would cost ridiculous amounts of money to maintain and support it.

This is the main drawback of solutions obtained in competitions like these – there are no restrictions on the calculations and the simplicity of the result. Solutions will often simply not be feasible. But I would still urge you to take part in such competitions, as they can be extremely beneficial. Look for solutions on forums and repeat them. Learn how to make features. It's not easy, but they are the heart of ML. Don't worry about where you place – if your solutions produce results which are around 5% worse than the winner, you've done a great job. Even if you're only just above the median, this is still good. You'll take a lot away from the experience.

If I had to choose between two candidates – one who has won multiple prizes on Kaggle and has dozens of models under their belt, and another who has only entered two competitions but came up with a problem and was able to solve and implement it and then use metrics to prove how it could make money for the company – I would choose the second.

Even if they won't have to repeat all of these steps at the new job, I can still see that they are able to take a step back and see the whole picture.

[65]

And this means we will be on the same page with the people who will introduce the final product. The candidate will have no difficulty understanding the limitations and requirements of collaborating departments.

ARTIFICIAL INTELLIGENCE

Artificial intelligence (AI) is one of those terms that is in vogue at the moment. This is the first time that I have mentioned AI in this book, although I use it all the time. I first came across the phrase "data mining" in the early 2000s when I was still working at StatSoft. It's really just marketing jargon that means run-of-the-mill data analysis made up of several components. It was a running joke in the office that real experts do all the data mining by cobbling together a couple of algorithms. It wasn't long before a new buzz phrase appeared, *machine learning*, which specialists liked better because it actually described a new field. Yet another oft-used term is *big data*, although the hype around this appears to have subsided somewhat – it turns out that the technology itself couldn't live up to the high hopes that had been placed on it. I've been to plenty of ACM RecSys conferences and I don't remember ever hearing the expression *big data* there, and some of the corporations that take part have massive amounts of data (Amazon, Google and Netflix, to name but a few). Companies only use these words for branding purposes and selling their services to show that they are "with it." If they don't, their competitors will pass them by.

AI has become a hot topic with the advent of deep learning. The principle of a neuron working as a building block of a neural network has been borrowed from biology. But you've got to admit that this is no reason to see the neural network as something even close to insects in terms of intelligence. Right now, the operations carried out by neural networks can in no way compare with what even the most primitive beings are capable of (such as synthesizing new life or independent decision-making). If we are to come close to creating an intelligence that is somewhat similar to that of an animal, we need to work on synthesizing and training biological neural networks, rather than electronic ones.

Artificial intelligence is a rather abstract term, in my opinion, so I prefer to use more specific language like "computer vision." It is in this area that the most significant breakthroughs have occurred, thanks to neural networks. Computer vision is used everywhere today – from tagging people on mobile phones and social networks to self-driving cars. Governments use it to perform police functions, and commercial organizations use it to solve their problems. I personally love it when the marriage between hardware and software brings practical results. Take the Stingray robot, for example, which kills sea lice on farmed salmon using computer vision and a laser [73]. Salmon lice are responsible for the mass death of fish during artificial breeding. For example, it caused global salmon supplies to dip by 9 percent in 2016 [74]. The underwater robot solves the problem: once it spots a parasite on the body of a fish, it destroys it with a laser.

Robotics is another area where huge breakthroughs have been made. The advancements here have not been limited to the use of computer vision only. When I visited the MIT Museum in Boston, I noticed that the Boston Dynamics project can trace its roots back to an MIT lab in the 1980s. Even then, the researchers at the best university in the world were working on computer and robotic control. They had a robot jumping on a stick without falling. Boston Dynamics broke away from MIT in 1992. Now the company is famous for its robots, which have become YouTube stars in their own right, garnering record numbers of views. The South Korean company Hyundai recently purchased Boston Dynamics for $1 billion. To be honest, it's at times like this that I just can't work out what' going through the heads of Russia's super-rich – surely it's far more worthwhile to invest in projects that could make you the next Elon Musk than it is to pump money into football clubs. Projects like Boston Dynamics may still be poorly commercialized today, but their time will come. Humanity is moving in the right direction.

[73]   [74]

Will AI replace people? I believe it will. And it will be businesses that make this happen. Business follows the self-serving principle of "if there's a way to save money, then let's go for it!" Once, in order to save money, many Western companies started opening manufacturing facilities in Southeast Asia, where the cost of labour was much cheaper. Robotization means that fewer workers are needed per product unit, and then it makes better financial sense to produce the goods in the country where the products are sold. One example of this is the creation of the Speed-factory robotic factories by Adidas, which were opened in Germany and the United States in 2016 and 2017 [75]. The goal was to bring production closer to the customer. In 2019, however, the company decided to close these factories. Despite this setback, the trend is clear for all to see – the robotization of production will replace more and more people.

REQUIRED DATA TRANSFORMATIONS

Before feeding data into ML models, we need to carry out a number of important transformations on them:

- standardize the data (reduction to a single scale)
- remove outliers
- prepare categorial variables
- work with missing data
- sample unbalanced classes.

With linear models, you can normalize the data, since data is often presented on different scales. Say you've got two features in a dataset – the price of an apartment ($30,000 to $1,500,000) and its size (20–500 square

[75]

metres). These are completely different ranges, which means that the model's coefficients lose their physical meaning. It will be impossible to compare the effect of a given variable on the model. Regularization also presents a problem, namely, the unnecessary pessimization of the coefficients. There are different options for standardization. One is to subtract the mean and divide the result by the standard deviation of the variable. The output will be a variable with a mean equal to 0 and a standard deviation equal to 1. Standardization does not affect the error of the linear model (if it is performed without regularization). However, certain methods are sensitive to the scales of variables, for example principal component analysis (PCA, which we covered in the previous chapter).

Outliers can also introduce a significant error into the model. The regression line will look different if you remove the outliers, which is particularly important when you don't have much data. Removing outliers is no easy task. The simplest way is to delete data that lies outside a certain percentile (for example, the 99th percentile). Figure 9 shows an example of how an outlier can change a straight line; the dotted line is the linear regression line for data with outliers, while the solid line shows the data with the outliers removed. As you can see, the straight line "turns" at the point where the outliers are removed.

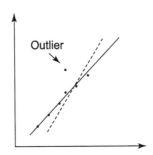

Fig. 9.1. Removing outliers changes behaviour

We have already covered categorical variables in the chapter on data. There are certain nuances when it comes to their use. Binary variables (yes/no, 0/1) typically do not present any problems. If you're working with linear models, all you have to do is reduce them to 0 and 1 (the dummy variable). This is called label encoding. As for decision trees, you need to look at the documentation of the method you want to use – how you want the categorical variables to be represented. In most cases, when you are working with a categorical variable that has three or more values, you will need to split it into several binary variables. For example, if you have a variable with three values (Yes/No/Don't know), you will need to split it into three variables (i.e. the same as the number of values). You can give these variables the same names as the values: Yes/No/Don't know. Each variable is assigned a value of 0 or 1. For example, if the answer is "Yes," the variables will be: Yes = 1, No = 0, Don't know = 0. This encoding procedure is called "one-hot encoding." It is necessary because, unlike other continuous numeric variables, the relationship between variable values is not entirely clear, which means that it is impossible to compare values. Some methods support categorical variables with multiple values – Yandex's CatBoost, for example. Another option for encoding dynamic categorical values (such as words of a text) is the so-called "hashing trick," which is used as a way to reduce the number of variables when there are a great many values.

It often happens when working with data that some variable values are empty (missing data). Depending on the system you are using, the data itself may contain empty spaces or the value None or Null. This is a fairly straightforward problem to solve if you are working with categorical variables – all you have to do is enter a new value and name it "unknown." It becomes a little trickier when you are using continuous numeric variables, as you have to work out whether there is a pattern behind the empty values. If there is no pattern, you can either delete the data or replace it with an average value. If you want to learn more about working with lost data, you can't go wrong with Andrew Gelman's book [66].

Whenever we train a model to distinguish between two classes, we are always up against the problem of these classes being imbalanced. This happens in medicine when testing the population and diagnosing rare diseases: if the dataset contains data from 10,000 people and only ten of them are sick, then then algorithm is extremely difficult to train. Another example would be ad banners on the internet, when there are many impressions, but few clicks. The problem is that it is easier for the models to ignore the data of minority classes and simply predict values for the larger class. However, this will lead to an accuracy error of close to 100%. So, what should we do? Google's machine learning course [67] recommends using downsampling to reduce the largest class and assigning a proportional weight to these lines. This will help the model converge faster, since the minority class will have a greater influence on learning, and the relative weights will allow us to immediately use the probability we get at the output for classification.

THE ACCURACY AND COST OF ML SOLUTIONS

Production costs are related to the manufacturing quality (accuracy) of the parts. The same can be said of machine learning. The first version of a solution has a certain degree of accuracy (Fig. 9.2). A great deal of time and effort is then spent on improving the initial result. The sad truth of the matter is that the improvements are not proportional to the effort expended (the Pareto principle at work once again!). In my experience creating recommendation systems, I have noticed that the cost of each improvement increases exponentially. The same can be seen in Kaggle competitions.

This can be factored in when the first version of a product is created. You don't need to shoot for super-precision right off the bat. It's better to go for an acceptable level of accuracy at the initial stages. The second method is to create a solution, implement it in the working system and only then decide whether the business needs to improve the metrics or not. It might be worth spending your time on a different product instead

[66]   [67]

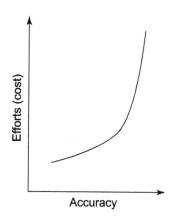

Fig. 9.2. How the cost of a solution depends on its accuracy

of endlessly polishing one – the customers won't notice anyway, or appreciate your efforts.

THE SIMPLICITY OF THE SOLUTION

William of Ockham once wrote: "It is futile to do with more things that which can be done with fewer." This principle of parsimony known as *Occam's razor* allows us, for example, to build a chain of hypotheses in order of increasing complexity – and it is this order that in most cases will prove successful. It can also be used when choosing an ML model. It's always better to go from simple to complex, from linear to nonlinear models such as neural networks.

Why the simpler, the better? When we have an ML model, we always have to think about the cost of running and maintaining it. The model consists of computational resources – and complex models require more resources. Highly skilled specialists are needed to service complex models, and they command higher salaries. And, most importantly, it is extremely difficult to make changes to a complex system, and the whole process takes time and money. At Retail Rocket, we had a simple rule when testing hypotheses: if there are two models that are almost exactly the same in terms of efficiency, then we will always choose the easier one.

Some ML algorithms have a "feature importance" option. This principle can be used when cutting features. I've already talked about interpreting the coefficients of linear models – if they are standardized, then the modulus of the coefficient (its numerical value regardless of the sign) indicates how strongly the variable has contributed to the model. For non-linear estimation, you can use the Random Forests algorithm to determine the significance of the features. This data can also be used for cutting features. The fewer features used in the model, the easier it will be to maintain. Using more features will only make the model more complex. And if you can cut the least significant features without losing much in the way of accuracy, then it will be easier to use the model in the working system. The thing is that each feature requires special attention and separate lines of code. This has to be monitored, and if you can manage to cut the number of features from 20 to 10, then maintenance costs will also go down... and there will be fewer potential sources of error.

Another thing that distinguishes the working versions of ML models from Kaggle contest entries is their simplicity. That said, achieving this simplicity may take more effort than developing a super-complex model on Kaggle. Beginners often overcomplicate things, trying to build a spaceship when a scooter will do.

THE AMOUNT OF WORK INVOLVED IN CHECKING THE RESULT

Lesson 8 of the Quora recommendation system [68] talks about the importance of being able to answer the question of why the system produced the recommendations it did. We run into similar issues at Retail Rocket too. There was once instance where sandpaper was recommended as an alternative to toilet paper. I should say here that the algorithm suggested it on the basis of the actual behaviour of the customers. But, of course, the suggestion looked like a prank, only we weren't laughing because we had to deal with each case manually. We eventually wrote scripts and instructions for our tech support team so that such incidents could be dealt with quickly or explained to the customer without the need to involve the data scientists.

Why do things like this happen? Well, when you are dealing with data-driven products that are intended for the outside world, you may run into situations that the user could never expect. If the system's simple and includes tools for locating and debugging faults, then they can be resolved quickly.

MECHANICAL TURK / YANDEX TOLOKA

All resources are good when it comes to projects that use ML models. You may have read about a company called ScaleFactor recently that allegedly used artificial intelligence to provide accounting services [69]. The company managed to raise $100 million in investments, but it turned out that the work was being done the tried-and-tested way by ordinary accountants.

I first heard about "manual labour" in ML in a video from the STRATA conference, where LinkedIn employees were talking about the Skills project. To create a dataset, they used the Amazon Mechanical Turk to get thousands of people to enter the data for the project. The model itself was simple – logistic regression. But a high-quality dataset was needed. Of course, they could have gone for the text analysis method, but you can get the same result for cheaper through these kinds of services.

I've already mentioned that one of the advantages of ML is its phenomenal speed compared to humans. Services like Amazon Mechanical Turk allow you to use the work of thousands of people to solve a problem. This could

[68]   [69]

involve training examples, such as in the case of LinkedIn, or checking millions of store recommendations, which is what we did. By the way, everyone loved our assignments on recommendations, as they found them interesting. Search engines use these resources to check their search results. Yandex launched its "Toloka" system and made it publicly available.

This is how these services work. The customer uploads the task together with a dataset for it, writes instructions and sets a price. Control questions can be added to the dataset in order to weed out freeloaders who could have completed tasks faster by randomly clicking on answers. This is why I recommend using control questions. Once the formalities have been completed, the participants can carry out the tasks and get paid for their work. In my opinion, it's difficult to make money there, but it's worth doing as a side gig (and there you have it – in the 21st century, people are slaves to AI). The number of participants depends on the price offered for the task.

Each task requires its own specific tool. If you spend a long time doing it by yourself, you still won't have enough data. This is where services such as Toloka can be a good solution. They allow you to scale the task effectively and get results of an acceptable quality. Sure, you've got to pay for it, but the time you'll save will more than make up for it.

ML AND BIG DATA

At the 2016 ACM RecSys conference, I noticed that neither Netflix not Quora recommended using distributed machine learning systems [68]. The reason for this is simple – distributed machine learning systems run far slower than concurrent computing on the same machine. We found this out for ourselves when calculating the GBRT (Gradient Boosting Regression Tree) model using our compute cluster and the MLLib library in Spark. We were trying to do this on a single machine, but there was just too much data for the memory to handle, so we used a distributed algorithm. That's all well and good, but it took two hours to calculate the model. This is far too long, especially given the fact that the model was not complicated at all. Then we optimized the data and tried calculating it on the local Smile library in Java. It took just five minutes.

Problems with distributed algorithms occur due to slow network speeds. The various nodes of the cluster have to constantly coordinate with each other and transfer data and parameters over a regular local network. Memory speed is approximately 50 times faster than a gigabit network, meaning that local computing on one machine is much faster. Plus, one machine is much cheaper than an expensive cluster.

RECENCY, FREQUENCY AND MONETARY

I didn't know much about customer behaviour patterns until I read Jim Novo's book on the subject [71]. In the book, Jim described so-called RFM segmentation – **R**ecency, **F**requency and **M**onetary – a concept was completely new to me.

Recency means the time that has elapsed since a customer last engaged in a specific behaviour. Recency is important for segmentation – the more recently a customer has done something, the more likely they are to do it again. For example, let's say Recency is the amount of time since a customer placed an order. You want to compare two customers: one whose most recent order was 30 days ago, and one whose was 70 days ago. Who do you think is more likely to place another order? That's right, the first one (30 days).

Frequency is the total number of actions performed by the client. It is important because the more actions the customer performs, the more likely they are to repeat them in the future. The authors of this method state in their books and on their websites that there is no cutoff time when it comes to measuring Frequency intervals. From my own experience, I can tell you that it is best to limit these intervals. For example,

[71]

count Frequency for the 360 days prior to the date of analysis. Let's say then, that Frequency is the number of orders placed within the last 360 days: the first customer placed ten orders, while the second placed five. The first customer is, of course, more likely to place an order in the future.

Monetary is the amount of money a client has spent across all transactions. Like with Frequency, we need to try and limit the time during which the value is measured. And the more money spent, the greater the likelihood that the client will place another order in the future. Monetary is rarely used in practice, however, as it is highly correlated with Frequency. This is why RFM segmentation is usually referred to simply as RF segmentation.

So, we're left with two parameters for segmentation – Recency (R) and Frequency (F). Both of these can predict client behaviour with a certain degree of accuracy. And if we combine them into a single parameter (RF), then the prediction will be even more accurate.

Here's the sequence of steps you need to take (according to Jim Novo's model):

- R is broken down into five tiers. This gives us five values (1 to 5), with 5 meaning the order was placed recently.

- F is broken down into five tiers. This gives us five values (1 to 5), with 5 meaning the client has placed a large number of orders within a specified period of time (the period has to be calculated too).

- An RF grid is built. The grid contains a two-digit combination of R and F, with 55 representing the best customers, and 11 the worst customers.

- The probability of a repeat action is calculated for each segment.

- This gives us 25 RF segments into which customers will be segmented according to the results of the previous steps.

In terms of RFM, the best customer is the one who regularly places orders for large amounts of money and who has made a purchase very recently (Fig. 9.3). This fundamental principle has helped create features that predict the likelihood of future actions. And it can be extended to other actions (i.e. not just purchases): the likelihood of getting sick; the likelihood of a user returning to a website; the likelihood of going to jail; the likelihood of a person clicking on a banner, etc. I performed reasonably well in a Kaggle competition using only these variables and a simple linear model. To obtain better results, I used binary encoding instead of real numbers. Segmentation can be used as a basis here (I talked about this earlier). You can take either R or F separately, or RF as a whole.

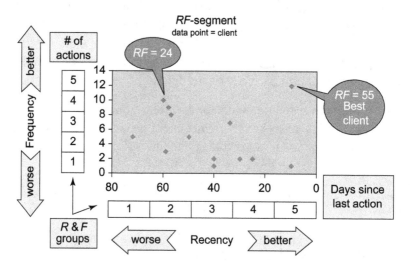

Fig. 9.3. RF segmentation

CONCLUSION

There are two free resources that I would recommend to supplement any theoretical books you may have on this topic: Andrew Ng's [60] book on the practice of machine learning and Google's *Rules of Machine Learning* [72]. They will take your understanding to new levels.

[60]   [72]

Chapter 10

IMPLEMENTING ML IN REAL LIFE: HYPOTHESES AND EXPERIMENTS

> "Every experiment may be said to exist only in order to give the facts a chance of disproving the null hypothesis."

> *Sir Ronald Fisher,*
> *The Design of Experiments (1935)*

ML models are brought into the world, exist for a while and then die. Life changes, that's just a law of nature. If a living thing does not change, it will eventually die. By improving and optimizing the model, we give it new life and new hope. Hypotheses (or ideas) and experiments that confirm or reject hypotheses can help us do this. I talked about how to kill hypotheses as early as possible during my speech at MIT in 2016. The presentation was a huge success, so I thought I'd include my ideas and conclusions on the subject in this chapter.

HYPOTHESES

A hypothesis is an idea for how to improve a product. It doesn't really matter what that product is – a website, product or store. Many companies now employ product managers, whose job includes creating and maintaining a list of such hypotheses and prioritizing their implementation. A list of hypotheses is called a "backlog," which is an important strategic element of the company's development. Just how to come up with hypotheses and prioritize them is a topic for another book. In a nutshell, this is how it should ideally look: product managers interact with the market, work with existing and potential customers, analyse the solutions of their competitors, and carry out focus groups in order to understand how profitable a given change (hypothesis) may be for the company. A list of hypotheses is created on the basis of the results of this research, and the hypotheses prioritized. Businesses need financial metrics in order to prioritize hypotheses – the more accurate, the better. But this is not as easy as it sounds, and it is often a matter of taking a "shot in the dark." The biggest commercial successes in history have been revolutionary, not evolutionary. Just look at the first iPhone.

Prioritizing hypotheses serves the main goal of achieving success as quickly as possible. Following this logic, ideas that are more likely to produce this result should be first on this list, right? Well, there are different levels of complexity when it comes to implementing hypotheses, which means that you have to take labour intensity and the cost of setting up the necessary infrastructure (servers, hiring additional personnel, etc.) into account when prioritizing hypotheses. Let's say the first hypothesis promises to bring in around $150,000 per year, and you'll have to hire two developers and a data scientist for one month to implement it. Meanwhile, the second hypothesis promises $25,000 at a cost of five day's work for two additional staff. Which hypothesis would you pick first? I always leave these decisions to management. I can't give a clear-cut answer here.

What if we give the task of coming up with hypotheses and prioritizing them to individual departments? On the one hand, this seems like the perfect solution. After all, not having to go through the IT department will ensure that things get done quicker, right? But let's imagine that a company is a living organism and its strongest department (say, IT) is its arms. The department has a good list of hypotheses, and the priorities are more on the mark than those produced by other departments – it has strong arms! Now let's imagine a triathlon competition. In the Olympics, you have to swim 1500m, then get on a bike and ride 40km and finish of with a 10-km run. Strong arms are needed for the first stage, but then you'll need strong legs for the next two. If you've been skimping on leg day, you'll lose to the more well-rounded competitors. Or you might not finish the race at all! It's the same in business – you can't rely on one department. You need to take a balanced approach. I fell into this trap myself at Retail Rocket, stewing in my own juices trying to prioritize my hypotheses by myself. Sure, one of our departments was incredibly strong, but the other teams just couldn't keep up with us. If I could go back, I'd insist on collaboration on everything, including the product and the market.

You can't test all the hypotheses on your list. Most of them will remain just that – hypotheses. Don't fret about it, it's actually a good thing, as it means the most profitable ideas will be brought into fruition first. Every hypothesis eats up resources. We're not fortunate to have infinite resources, so we can't test all ideas. I'll say more – nine out of ten hypotheses don't pan out. But you have no idea that a hypothesis will not produce the desired result until you are well into the testing process. I believe that it is best to kill a hypothesis as early as possible – as soon as the first sign that the idea won't take off presents itself. Not only will this save you resources (a lot of resources!), but it will also allow you to move on to the next hypothesis quicker.

I've compared various types of hypothesis and their effects. Evolutionary hypotheses, where one parameter is slightly optimized, have a less profound effect than revolutionary hypotheses, where the approach is fundamentally different. That said, evolutionary hypotheses are more likely to bear fruit.

HYPOTHESIS TESTING: PLANNING

Suppose we have a ready-made hypothesis that management has given the green light to as the most promising. We've got all the resources we need and are eager to get going. What other information do we need? First, we need to know what the goal of the hypothesis is – what quantitative metric will it optimize? We get that quantitative metrics are not ideal, but we need them in order to track changes. We can give ourselves a huge pat on the back if we can significantly improve the metric.

Second, we need to understand how and in what conditions we plan on testing the hypothesis. There are two types of testing in machine learning: offline testing and online testing. Offline testing provides metrics on data that already exists (I talked about this in the chapter "Machine Learning Algorithms"). Online testing involves collecting metrics that are of interest to you and comparing them using statistical tests.

In his 1925 monograph *Statistical Methods for Research Workers*, Ronald Fisher (the founder of hypothesis testing) outlined concepts such as the statistical significance criterion, the rules for testing statistical hypotheses, analysis of variance, and experiment planning. This work defined our current approach to experiment planning. You've probably heard about how the COVID-19 vaccine was tested – in a double-blind, randomized, placebo-controlled trial. This is the most reliable clinical trial used in evidence-based medicine. Randomized means that the test subjects were split into experimental and control groups at random. In order for the experiment to retain its integrity, it is extremely important that researchers do not have the ability to place patients with mild symptoms in the experimental group and those with more severe symptoms in the control group. Special randomization (mixing) methods are used to make any differences between the groups statistically insignificant, which, in turn, makes the study results more accurate. It was Ronald Fisher who came up with a way to plan and conduct such experiments. He worked for a time at the Rothamsted Experimental Station. When planning an experiment with fertilizers [76], Fisher was not aware of the numerous factors that could affect the research results. He found that, when faced with the question "Which fertilizer is better?" it made no sense to compare the growth of plants in different greenhouses that used their own fertilizer. You need to compare the growth of the same plant in the same greenhouse using different fertilizers. Moreover, even in the same greenhouse, sunlight will fall at different angles on different areas, and the humidity can also be uneven. So, you have to toss a coin to decide which seedbeds will be used for fertilizers A and B. Fisher called this approach to experiment design the principle of randomization. This is the only way to determine whether the difference between the fertilizers is significant. And the only way that we can say the two fertilizers were tested in as close to equal conditions as possible is through the

[76]

principle of randomization, as it eliminated all variables that were out of our control from the equation.

Before Fisher, test subjects were divided into groups systematically, which could distort the results. Interestingly, many in the scientific community did not accept Fisher's method. They were convinced that the systematic approach they had always used was the correct one. In addition to the usual A/B tests, Fisher also proposed methods for carrying out more complex multivariate tests. The fact is that problems often arise even with ordinary tests involving two groups, so hardly anyone goes as far as conducting multivariate tests, where several changes are tracked at once. That's why I going to focus on simple, two-group tests in this book.

To carry out a test, we thus need a metric and we need randomization. Tests are carried out with a control group. In medical trials, the volunteers are typically split into two groups: the first group receives the study drug, while the second is given a dummy drug called a placebo. Marketing trials work in much the same way. In the days of mail-order catalogues, promotional discounts were sent to one group of customers, while dummy letters (containing no discounts whatsoever) were sent to the second. When online stores fire out emails to customers, they typically don't send anything to the control group. Amazon is a pioneer of digital marketing. It used an A/B test (split test) to determine whether its new website positively affected consumer behaviour, whereby half of the visitors to the site would see the old version and the other half would see the new version. Before a test goes live, you need to check every facet of its operation. This is done using simulation tests and real tests. Another option is A/A, which I'll talk about later.

WHAT IS A HYPOTHESIS IN STATISTICS?

Statistical hypothesis testing involves two important concepts: general population and sample. General population refers to the subjects of the study – the thing that the study aims to make conclusions about. Sample refers to the part of the general population that we were able to observe.

Suppose we have a huge bowl with balls of different sizes in it. There are hundreds of thousands of balls in the bowl. We want to find the average diameter of the balls. We can't count every single ball in the bowl, that would take too much effort. To save time and money, we'll take a random sample with replacement (meaning that we will return each ball after we have calculated its diameter) of a certain number of balls. In this example, the bowl full of balls represents the general population; the average diameter is the unknown parameter that we want to determine; and we do this by taking a random sample from the general population. The parameter in the general population is true, and the sample parameter is an estimate of the true parameter.

When I hear the word "distribution," I imagine a histogram showing the frequency of occurrences of a given event. In our example, a histogram indicating the diameters of the balls. We're working with continuous numerical values, and the histogram itself is divided into ranges that are usually of equal length (0–10, 10.01–20, and so on). It's difficult to make decisions based on histograms alone. Hypotheses typically estimate a given distribution parameter such as the mean or median. This is then used to build a histogram (Fig. 10.1).

It's extremely difficult to compare these types of histograms (distribution histograms) with one another, so statistics of distributions are used.

Both the general population and the sample have their own distribution of balls. The closer the sample distribution is to the population distribution, the better. It is extremely important here that the balls are pulled out at random here. We have no idea whether all the balls with one diameter were poured into the bowl first, followed by balls with another diameter. This would leave us with the largest balls on the surface. And if we mostly take balls from the surface, our sample distribution will be skewed towards the larger end, thus giving us incorrect conclusions. The balls need to be returned to ensure that we are working with the original population distribution, as each selection will be independent of the previous ones. Logic tells us that the more balls we pull out, the more the sample distribution will be representative the general population distribution, and the more accurate the parameter estimate will be. How many balls are needed for an acceptable level of accuracy? The answer lies in statistics (more on that later), but, for now, let's make the task even more complicated.

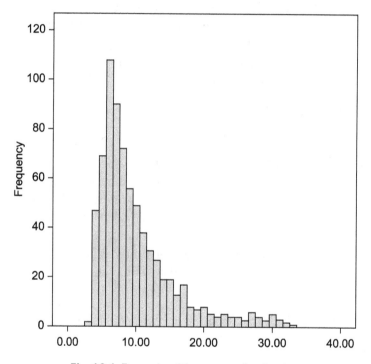

Fig. 10.1. Example of frequency distribution

Now we've got two bowls, and we need to compare the average diameters of the balls in each of them. It's time to start formulating hypotheses. This involves formulating a main hypothesis (H_0) and an alternative hypothesis (H_1) in terms of statistics and experiments:

- The null hypothesis H_0 states that there has been no change in the metric as a result of the experiment, and all observed changes are random.

- The alternative hypothesis H_1 states that there has been a change in the metric as a result of the experiment and the observed changes are not random.

Testing a hypothesis is like a court case. We are supposed to believe that the defendant is innocent until strong evidence is produced that proves them to be guilty. It's the same with hypotheses [77]. We start out thinking that hypothesis H_0 is true until we find evidence to refute it in favour of hypothesis H_1.

We can now reform these general statements for our two-bowl problem as a two-sided hypothesis:

Hypothesis H_0 states that the average diameter of the balls in the two bowls is equal, $\mu_1 = \mu_2$.

Hypothesis H_1 states that the average diameter of the balls in the two bowls is different, $\mu_1 \neq \mu_2$.

We can also formulate them as a one-sided hypothesis:

Hypothesis H_0 states that the average diameter of the balls in the first bowl is less than or equal to the average diameter of the balls in the second bowl, $\mu_1 \leq \mu_2$.

Hypothesis H_1 states that the average diameter of the balls in the first bowl is greater than the average diameter of the balls in the second bowl, $\mu_1 \geq \mu_2$.

I believe it is better to use one-sided hypotheses. After testing an idea, we try to improve the metric. Here, we are interested in whether it has improved or not (Hypothesis H_1). Now, let's look at how statistics can be used to do the comparison.

[77]

THE STATISTICAL SIGNIFICANCE OF HYPOTHESES

Like the court system, statistical hypotheses are not infallible. We can use a table to explain the errors that statistical hypotheses make. There are two types of error (Table 10.1): Type 1 errors, where we reject a true null hypothesis H_0 (an innocent person has been found guilty); and Type 2 errors, where we incorrectly accept this hypothesis (a guilty person has been found innocent).

Table 10.1. Statistical Hypothesis Errors

	Don't reject H_0	**Reject H_0**
H_0 true	H_0 correctly accepted	H_0 incorrectly rejected (Type I error)
H_1 true	H_0 incorrectly accepted (Type 2 error)	H_0 correctly rejected

In the language of statistics, errors are described using probabilities:

Probability of a Type 1 error: α. Researchers typically use $\alpha = 0.05$ (5%).

Probability of a Type 2 error: β. The rate of error $(1 - \beta)$ is called the power, which is the probability of finding an improvement, if any.

To simplify the process of hypothesis testing, Fisher [76] introduced the p-value, which is a measure of proof against the null hypothesis H_0. The smaller the p-value, the stronger the evidence against the null hypothesis. It is important to note that the p-value is not the probability that hypothesis H_0 is correct. Rather, it only works towards rejecting the null hypothesis.

In traditional, or, as I call it, Fisher statistics, the p-value is a universal number that it understandable to statisticians and allows them to reject the null hypothesis. The *p*-value was not a thing before Fisher arrived on the scene. Larry Wasserman's *All of Statistics: A Concise Course in Statistical Inference* [77], tells us that researchers typically use the following interpretation of the *p*-value (for α = 0.05) (Table 10.2).

Table 10.2. Interpreting p-values

p-value	Evidence
< 0.01	Very strong against H_0
0.01–0.05	Strong against H_0
0.05–0.10	Weak against H_0
> 0.1	Little or no evidence against H_0

Now let's look at a graphical interpretation of the two-sided hypothesis. Figure 10.2 shows a comparison of the distribution of the null and alternative hypotheses for our two-container example. Each distribution represents a probability density. In effect, this is two histograms with the area under each curve being equal to 1. On the null hypothesis chart, we mark two vertical lines so that the area of each tail is equal to α/2. If we have a one-sided hypothesis, only one line with area α is constructed. This line divides the distribution of alternative hypotheses into two parts – β and (1 – β). The areas under them are exactly equal to a Type 2 error and the power of the criterion, respectively.

The graph clearly shows that the further the peaks (averages) of these distributions are, the higher the power and the lower probability of a Type 2 error (that the null hypothesis will be accepted incorrectly). This

[76]   [77]

is most logical, as the further the averages of the distributions are from each other, the more obvious the difference between the hypotheses becomes, thus making it easier to reject the null hypothesis. On the other hand, a "narrow" distribution means an increase in power, which again makes it easier for us to reject the null hypothesis. Increasing the data size only serves to "compress" these distributions.

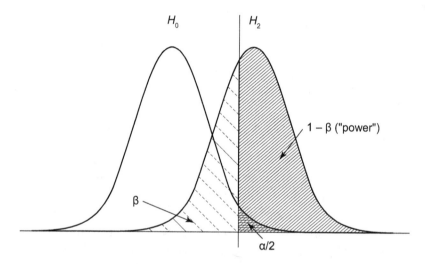

Fig. 10.2. Power

This is precisely how sample size calculators work. The calculator enters the minimum detectable difference in parameter values and the value of α and β errors. The result will be the amount of data that needs to be collected. The pattern here is simple – the smaller the difference you want to detect, the more data you will need.

An alternative to the p-value is the confidence interval – the interval within which the parameter we are measuring is located with a certain degree of accuracy. A probability of 95% ($\alpha = 0.05$) is typically used. If we have two confidence intervals for the test and control groups, the point at which they intersect will tell us whether there is a difference between them. P-value and confidence interval are two sides of the same coin. The interval is useful for presenting data on graphs. It is often used in alternative methods for evaluating A/B tests: Bayesian statistics and bootstrapping.

STATISTICAL CRITERIA FOR P-VALUES

As we have already learned, the *p*-value is a universal metric for hypothesis testing. To calculate the *p*-value, you need a null hypothesis, statistical criteria, a one- or two-sided test and data.

To determine the *p*-value, you need to know the distribution of the selected statistic (statistical test), assuming that the null hypothesis is correct. The cumulative distribution function (CDF) of this statistic is then used to calculate the *p*-value, as the figure demonstrates (Fig. 10.3):

- Left-tailed test: *p*-value = cdf(x).
- Right-tailed test: *p*-value = 1 − cdf(x).
- Two-tailed test: *p-value* = 2 × min(cdf(x), 1 − cdf(x)).

There's no need to try and reinvent the wheel when we have ready-made calculators at our disposal in statistical packages and software libraries. The important thing is to choose the right statistical criterion.

The choice of criteria depends on the task at hand:

- Z-test – for checking the mean of a normally distributed quantity.
- Student's t-test – the same as a z-test, but for small samples (t < 100).
- Pearson's chi-squared test – for categorical variables and all kinds of binomial tests. This is useful for calculating conversions (for example visitors to buyers) when you need a binomial test, such as whether a visitor to an online store made a purchase or not.

An independent two-sample Student's t-test is well-suited for our two-container example or for comparing the average purchase amount.

One problem with all of these tests is that they are distribution-specific. For example, the Student's t-test and the z-test require normally distributed data. This kind of data forms a bell shape on a histogram. But the distribution of the average basket size in an online store does not. Sure, you can transform this data by taking the logarithm and assembling it into a bell shape, but this is usually not convenient. The go-to alternative for non-normal data is nonparametric tests.

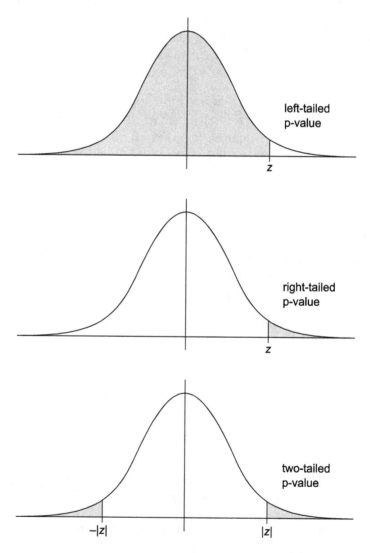

Fig. 10. 3. Left-tailed, right-tailed and two-tailed tests

However, according to STATISTICA (a dictionary of statistical terms) [78], nonparametric methods are better suited to small samples. There's no point using nonparametric statistics if you've got a lot of data (for example $n > 100$). With large samples, the sample averages obey normal probability law, even if the original variable is not normal or there was an error in the measurement. Nonparametric tests have lower statistical power (they are less sensitive) than parametric tests, and if you want to detect small changes, you need to be careful when choosing the criteria.

In our problem with containers, we can apply the independent two-sample Student's t-test. The second alternative is bootstrapping, which is an extremely versatile tool.

BOOTSTRAPPING

Bootstrapping is one of the most interesting ways to evaluate metrics in A/B tests. It is one of our favoured methods at Retail Rocket for continuous parameters such as average purchase value, average cost of goods and revenue per visitor (RPV).

Bootstrapping [79] works by using multiple samples from the data that are then used to calculate statistics. The algorithm looks like this [80]:

1. Set the number of samples k that we intend to take from the source dataset. The number must be at least 100 – the more the better.

2. Each time the sample (k in total) is repeated, elements with replacement are randomly selected from the original dataset – the same number as in the original dataset (to preserve the variation of the parameter [81]). During this procedure, some elements of the original

[78]   [79]   [80]

dataset will be selected several times over, while others will not be selected at all.

3. The parameter we need is calculated for each sample.

4. We now have k values that can be used to calculate the confidence interval or statistical test.

In A/B tests, we work with two groups – a test group and a control group. Both need their own bootstrap. The required metric in each sample and group is calculated, as is the difference in metrics between groups. This gives us k values of the distribution of the difference in the two groups. The significance of the A/B test is calculated by formulating the null hypothesis H_0: the two samples are the same, so the difference between them is zero. If the Type 1 error rate is $\alpha = 0.05$, the test is two-tailed and we need only to calculate the percentiles (quantiles) for the segment $[\alpha/2, 100\% - \alpha/2]$, that is $[2.5\%, 97.5\%]$. This is easy to do if we sort our series of k values of the difference of metrics and determine the value of the percentiles at the ends. If 0 is located between these values, then the null hypothesis cannot be rejected; if it is located outside these values, then it must be rejected.

Let's go back to our example with two containers. We have a sample of 1000 balls from each container. If you remember, we need to determine whether or not there is a difference in the average diameter of the balls between the containers. For the bootstrap procedure, we take k = 300 samples for both groups. Then we immediately calculate the average in each sample and the difference between them. This gives us 300 numbers. We sort these numbers in descending order and then select two – one at the 2.5th percentile (2.5% × 300 = 7.5, or the seventh highest number) and one at the 97.5th percentile (97.5% × 300 = 292.5, or the 293rd highest number). If both numbers are positive, or if both are negative, then the difference is statistically significant.

[81]   [82]

The word "bootstrap" comes from the expression "to pull oneself up by the bootstraps" and is often traced back to *The Surprising Adventures of Baron Munchausen*, in which the hero pulls himself out of a swamp by his hair. These days, bootstrapping refers to this sort of "self-pulling," where we get something useful for free.

The advantages of bootstrapping are that it is independent from the sample distribution, the only parameters you are working with are the number of samples, and you can easily calculate any metric. The disadvantages include high computational requirements. Working with thousands of samples is resource-intensive. The third alternative for A/B tests is Bayesian statistics.

BAYESIAN STATISTICS

I first learned about the Bayesian approach to A/B tests when I read an article by Sergei Feldman on the website of one of our competitors, RichRelevance [82]. I was particularly impressed by the comparison of the two approaches to formulating the results of A/B tests:

- We rejected the null hypothesis that A = B with a p-value of 0.043.

- There is an 85% chance that A has a 5% lift over B.

The first belongs to traditional Fisher statistics, while the second belongs to Bayesian statistics. In the article [82], Feldman notes the following drawbacks of p-values for working with hypotheses:

- P-values are a difficult concept to grasp and explain. I learned all about them back in 2002, but I still have to crack open a book every time to remind myself of what exactly they are.

- P-values use a binary approach – you can either reject the null hypothesis or fail to reject the null hypothesis by comparing the p-value with the value $\alpha = 0.05$

Classical mathematical statistics (the frequentist approach) treats parameters as fixed unknown constants, while Bayesian statistics treats them as probabilistic quantities [83]. This is somewhat similar to the difference in the approaches of classical and quantum physics. I personally prefer the probabilistic approach of Bayesian statistics, as it is clearer and more natural than the p-value. I was so intrigued by it that I spent ages looking for a good book on the subject. William Bolstad's *Introduction to Bayesian Statistics* [83] turned out to be just that book. I appreciate a good book, and in this case, I can call the author a Teacher with a capital *T*. Bolstad's built an extremely robust system for deriving formulas and proofs. I read his book from cover to cover, did almost all the exercises inside and then wrote the first version of the software library for A/B testing at Retail Rocket. I came upon an interesting fact about Bayesian statistics when I was reading Antonio Rojo's book on Ronald Fisher [76] – it turns out that Bayesian statistics was widely used to evaluate statistical significance even before Fisher came onto the scene. Proponents of the two approaches (Fisher's traditional statistics and Bayesian modelling) continue to argue about which method is better.

Bayes' theorem looks like this:

$$P(A \mid B) = \frac{P(B \mid A) \times P(A)}{P(B)},$$

where:

- P(A) is *a priori* information that we have about A before the experiment. These are our beliefs (perhaps even intuitive beliefs) before we carry out a given experiment.

- P(A|B) is posterior probability, the probability of proposition A after taking the evidence B into account, which leads to new (posterior) conclusions.

- P(B|A) is the likelihood of event B given that hypothesis A is true.

- P(B) is the total probability of event B.

[76]   [83]

Bayes' theorem allows you to "reverse cause and effect": a known fact of an event can be used to calculate the probability that it was the result of a given cause.

To estimate the parameters, the formula can be written differently:

$$P(\theta \,|\, data) = \frac{P(data \,|\, \theta) \times P(\theta)}{P(data)}.$$

We want to find out the distribution of parameter θ (for example, the average diameter of a ball) after we have obtained the data from our experiment. Before the experiment, we assume that the parameter obeys distribution $P(\theta)$. All the calculations for binomial tests – for example, comparing conversion rates – are listed in [83]. It's the same for continuous normally distributed quantities, where we can calculate the average diameter of the balls in the containers or the average basket in online stores. Both of these are relatively easy to calculate, as they both use conjugate distributions. To calculate the A/B test, posterior formulas and sampling are required – similar to the process used in bootstrapping.

An important problem in Bayesian statistics is the choice of *a priori* judgment. And this is where classical statistics comes in. *A priori* information has its own "weight" (n equal sample size), which is expressed in the number of data points. Bolstad's book also contains formulas for estimating the "weight" of prior distributions expressed in the number of data points. Looking at the literature on the subject, I was able to come up with the following rules. If you don't have any information, use uniform distribution. If you do, then it is better to use normal distribution, where the prior average is your premise, and the standard deviation of the prior denotes how confident you are in that premise. The "weight" of your confidence is best evaluated using the formulas in Bolstad's *Introduction to Bayesian Statistics* [83]. This will give you an idea of how much data you need to change your point of view. I prefer to have "confidence" play a smaller role so that the experiment can yield a result faster. Think of *a priori* assumptions as a magnifying glass that is focused on the confidence point. If the data does not confirm your assumptions, then the focus will shift closer towards the correct solution. If it does confirm your assumptions, then the test will give a positive result faster, as the focus was on the right place – you were not mistaken. For example, when testing different versions of recommendation algorithms to see if the conversion rate has improved, it is safe to use the current conversion rate (before the experiment) as the prior average. The standard deviation of the prior should not be too narrow.

Another problem with Bayesian statistics is that it is bound to the distribution of the original quantity, which you have to know. In this regard, bootstrapping is better, but typically takes longer than the Bayesian method.

A/B TESTS IN THE REAL WORLD

I've already described the main advantages and disadvantages of testing algorithms. If you want more detailed advice, I would recommend the article *Seven Rules of Thumb for Web Site Experimenters* [84] by Ron Kohavi, Alex Deng, Roger Longbotham, and Ya Xu. A word of warning: unfortunately, there is no shortage of "experts" (and entire schools) giving theoretical advice on the internet, and this muddies the waters incredibly. But even scientific papers can be full of errors, especially if they have not been published in journals or presented at reputable conferences. And what about respected bloggers? I'm a fan of simplicity and believe that you can figure out testing and analysis methods on your own. Just start with the simplest thing, which would be Fisher's statistics with p-values. I'll let you in on a secret here – if your test truly is significant, and there is enough data in the samples, then all three methods will show statistical significance. Here are the errors that I typically ran into:

- the test has been configured incorrectly
- the random number generator works poorly
- the statistical criterion is invalid
- the peeking problem
- post-analysis was not performed
- a decision has been made when the null hypothesis cannot be rejected.

The most common issue is that the test has been configured incorrectly. Say you've come up with a hypothesis, have a metric and have written a technical description of the test. If it's an ML model, then you will have conducted offline tests beforehand and everything was fine. Once you have implemented the test and laid out its working system, it must be checked. With a website, this means clicking on the necessary links and checking that the two groups are shown the correct versions of the pages. Now let's imagine that the test is running and there is an error in it. A month goes by and it is time to calculate the results. Human nature dictates that we will look for mistakes if the results are not what we expected or wanted, and be satisfied if they are. However, if there is a mistake in the test, then a great deal of time has been wasted and the test has to run again. To deal with this, we developed an entire business process at Retail Rocket for running tests with verification instructions. Such mistakes are extremely costly.

A bad random number generator for dividing users into test and control groups can also be an issue. A/A tests are a reliable means of detecting such a problem. Another option is simulation. With simulation, you need to replicate the developer's code (which assigns the segments) and check it against old user logs. In other words, you need to simulate an A/B test. Random number generators are notoriously unreliable, so we had a team of engineers write their own version. The source code was later posted online [85].

An invalid criterion can also produce an error. In this case, I would recommend carrying out simulation tests on the chosen statistical criterion for verification purposes. You can do this using distribution generators or existing logs of user actions (if there are any). For example, if you have two random generators with the same master data, you need to make sure that the chosen criterion does not show significance. Then

[84]   [85]

introduce a small difference between the generators and make sure that statistical significance appears. I would also recommend carrying out a power analysis to find out how much data is needed for the minimum required statistical significance to appear. For example, you may decide to implement an improvement only if it improves the metric by 1%. In this case, you would take two generators with this difference and simulate the criterion to figure out how many data points are needed for the difference to be noticed. This is your minimum sample size.

Peeking at test results is an issue I have faced many times over the years. This happens when you haven't collected enough data, but you still want to see the results. The statistical significance of the test is random, and it "jumps" at the beginning. We see this with simulations and in real-life situations. I first came across this at Ostrovok.ru, where A/B tests were displayed on the dashboards of office monitors. I got a call from the CEO asking why the significance levels of a test we had recently launched were jumping back and forth. You can't assume that the test has been successful at this point. If you make a decision here, it is bound to be a mistake – if you wait for the test to "settle down," it will show a lack of statistical significance. As far as I see it, the only way to solve the peeking problem is to define the minimum detectable difference in metrics that suit you. A sample size calculator or simulations can then be used to calculate the sample size. Once you have obtained the required amount of data, you can look at the result and make the appropriate decisions. Here you will face a dilemma: if the difference is too small, you will need a colossal amount of data. And this is bad for business, because collecting large amounts of data takes time, something businesses do not have. I would suggest that you decide beforehand how long you are willing to wait and factor this into the minimum detectable difference. The minimum test duration is also limited by the consumer decision-making cycle. For instance, if we know the average time to make a purchase decision is three days, then the test should last at least two business cycles, or six days. You can keep an eye on the test in the meantime, but only in order to detect any technical errors that may have been missed.

A good post-analysis of the hypothesis test can give you an insight into what else can be done to improve the metric. As I noted above, it is quite natural to want to look for an error when a new version of a product had failed, and it is also natural to not look for errors when a test has been successful. At Retail Rocket, we discovered errors of both a technological and ideational nature. This is typically accomplished using pivot tables and searching for problems in a multitude of slices. It is extremely satisfying when you find a mistake or come up with a modification of a hypothesis that works in the next test. This same process can be used for tests that have yielded the desired results, to look for new ideas for how to improve a product.

A/A TESTS

I first heard about A/A tests from DJ Patil. I had never used them before. A/A tests check the last mile of everything you have done for the test: the random number generator, the data collection scheme, and the statistical criterion you have chosen for the metric. The test really does divide the audience into two parts, but the control and test groups use the same version of the product. In the end, you should have a valid test without rejecting the null hypothesis, since the version of the product is the same.

The first thing we need to check is how well the random number generator that will be used to divide the participants into groups in the test works. Assignment to groups can be done in two ways: by assigning a random number, or by hashing information about the subject. When a user visits a site, their ID number is usually recorded in the cookies. This number is used to recognize the user when they come back to the site. In A/B tests, ID numbers are hashed, meaning that they are turned from text into a number, with the last two or three digits being used to divide users into groups: for example, users whose IDs end in 00–49 are placed in the control group, and those with 50–99 are placed in the test group. We use a similar principle in our Retail Rocket Segmentator project [85]. In A/A tests, you get the same distribution as in the test! If it is set at 50/50, then this is what you should get at the output. Even small discrepancies of 3% in the data can jeopardize the entire test. Say you've got 100,000 for your test and you want to split them in half but get 48,000 in one group and 52,000 in the other. This indicates that there's a problem with the "randomness" of your generator. You can also test these distributions in simulations when you know the exact algorithm. However, in my experience, small design nuances that we don't know about can lead to "shifts" in distributions. This is why I prefer A/A tests.

You also need to be careful to make sure that users are included in groups evenly – we don't want any displacement along different sections of users. For example, say you've got two groups of users in your test: companies (10% of the sample) and individuals (90%). After dividing them into groups, you notice that the ratio has changed – to 7% and 93%, respectively, in the control group, and to 12% and 88% in the test group. There are two possible explanations for this. First, there is pattern in the assignment of customer identifiers, and this data is used when assigning groups. Second, the number of companies in the sample is too low. The second issue is easier to deal with – you need to try and collect more data. If the observed difference disappears, then everything's good. If it doesn't, then you need to do something about the procedure for assigning users into groups. Note that such tests are more likely to yield valid results when you're using a 50/50 split, rather than something odd like 90/10, where only 10% of users are in the smaller group.

The third thing you need to keep in mind is that no matter what metric you are looking at your statistical criterion should show a lack of statistical significance, as we are showing users the exact same thing. In my experience, binary (binomial) tests yield faster and more accurate results than tests that use a continuous scale. Website conversion (the percentage of visitors who make a purchase) will work better than average purchase price (average basket size). As I see it, there are two reasons for this: 1) conversion has a lower variability (there are only two values here – whether the user made a purchase or not); and 2) there may be outliers in metrics that use a continuous scale. "Outliers" are rare events, such as when a customer places an unusually large order. And they will skew the metrics towards whichever group it is in. Not exactly the result we're looking for, is it? This is why we usually cut a small percentage of data "from the top" (ignore the most expensive orders) until the A/A test is completed. We do it at Retail Rocket. In theory, you can use the median instead of the mean, as it is more resistant to outliers.

A FEW MORE WORDS ABOUT A/B TESTS

I'd like to talk a little here about interleaving tests, multiple tests and multi-armed bandits. Interleaving tests involve mixing the outputs of two groups into one, with the person who set up the test knowing when and which elements from the groups (test or control) were shown and to whom. This is what search engines do to test and refine algorithms. The user is shown the results of their search queries, with the control algorithm being used for some results (say even-numbered ones), and the tested algorithm being used for the rest. That is, it is the research results, rather than users, that are divided into groups. This is often done randomly, with data being stored for each query. We carried out such tests for product recommendations. In fact, our internal A/A tests helped us see that there was an issue with our random number generator, which we were using differently to the one at Retail Rocket Segmentator [85].

We also use multiple tests, although I do agree with the authors of the book *Seven Rules of Thumb for Web Site Experimenters* [84] when they say that it is better to make tests simpler and the segments "fatter" because this will lead to faster and more reliable decisions. Take a two-group (50/50) and a four-group (25/25/25/25, or split proportions) test, for example. The first test will yield a result at least twice as fast, as there is twice as much data in each segment.

Multi-armed bandits are extremely popular right now. The procedure was taken from reinforcement learning [86]. Imagine a slot machine hall

[84]   [85]   [86]

in a casino – the kind of slots where you pull a lever to potentially win a prize. Some machines pay out more frequently than others. The testing algorithm assumes that you are using the explore–exploit strategy. The "explore" part refers to a user consistently pulling the lever of all the machines, while "exploit" means pulling the levers of those machines that give the bigger payouts more often. By combining these two strategies, we can find the best combination of machines by how many times their levers need to be pulled – people are far more likely to play slots that pay out money more often. For example, one machine pays out 10 times more frequently than another. This is used as an alternative to A/B tests, which give us one winning option only. The advantage of this method is that when a new algorithm is introduced, we just add it to the list of machines. The "explore" category is necessary because the environment changes and slots that pay out often may start to run dry, and vice versa. In the long term, multi-armed bandits perform better than A/B tests, although I believe that they are generally less reliable. This is why I recommend that you turn to them only after you've mastered A/B tests, as they can be used to calibrate multi-armed bandits.

SETTING UP AN A/B TEST

An interesting thing happened to me once. We were looking for people to invest in Retail Rocket and Yandex.Market invited us for a meeting. One of the blokes at Yandex asked if we were using offline tests as is usual in machine learning. I said we were not. My partners buried their faces in their hands. We never did get to work with Yandex. I'm not sure why they passed on us, but I imagine they thought I didn't know what I was talking about. In desk research, offline tests are the only way to test the effectiveness of recommendation systems. But I did read up on the subject after that meeting with Yandex. We derived all the formulas for metrics that researchers in the scientific community typically use and found that offline tests were weakly correlated with the usual A/B tests that I ran. It turned out that my original strategy for developing algorithms based exclusively on A/B tests was right. So why do we need offline tests at all?

Let me remind you what an offline test is – it is a simulation of an A/B test using old data. If I have a dataset (log) of the actions of old users, then I can train the algorithm on one part of it and check its effectiveness on the other. Ideally, it should produce similar results to a real A/B test. But why does it diverge in our case of product recommendations? The way I see it, there are two reasons for this. First, product recommendations change the way users behave, which means that calculating recommendation metrics based on old data has poor predictive power. Second, our primary metric is guessing which products customers will buy. The decision cycle can take days. If all we had to do was predict clicks on a given product, then everything would be much easier.

There are two situations where I use offline tests for recommendation systems. First, the metrics must change in accordance with the ideas that are embedded in the new algorithm. For example, if an algorithm improves the "variety" of the products in the recommendations, then the corresponding metric should go up. If the algorithm "pushes" new items up, then the average "age" of products in the recommendations should go down. Second, if the change in metrics does not happen as expected, this indicates that there is an error either in the idea or in its implementation. These things need to be thought out in advance so that you're prepared for all eventualities before you take a look at the metrics. This way, you are less likely to "overlook" an error. For example, the new algorithm will increase the variety of products in recommendations (more different types of products will be shown), but at the expense of predictability. If the metrics show that the opposite happened, you have a problem and need to find it.

And, finally, I strongly recommend that you look at the results with your own eyes. For example, you can prepare a visual report. This involves selecting several dozen of the most popular products, as well as a number of random products, building old and new recommendations for them, and putting them in a consolidated report with pictures and product names.

Look at it honestly, and let others criticize it. What bits do we like, and what bits not so much? Are there any products that the new algorithm should have worked better with? Have the recommendations improved? I use these reports to look for errors that the metrics sometimes miss. I guess you could say that they are the ultimate truth.

EXPERIMENT PIPELINE

We know that companies need to have a list of development hypotheses ranked in order of importance and managed by business development managers or product specialists. The first hypothesis on the list is taken and, if needed, modelled and verified using offline tests. The final step is A/B testing, followed by post-analysis of the results. The decision is then made on whether or not to implement the hypothesis.

If you can streamline this process, you've got a true experiment pipeline. Conceptually, it's similar to an industrial conveyor – a hypothesis goes through a number of statuses: accepted, modelling, offline testing, online testing, analysis, rejected, implemented. This is more of a mechanical than a creative process. I had it packed into Trello columns where the card moved went from left to right. This approach allows for scaling experiments, and it has its own metrics such as "time between statuses," "work started," "rejected/implemented," etc.

You've probably realized by now that it takes a long time for a hypothesis to move through the experiment pipeline. A/B testing is especially time-consuming. I'd wager that you're thinking it would be nice to "kill" unsuccessful hypotheses before they have even made it halfway through the pipeline. It's always good to reject hypotheses as early as possible so you don't end up wasting time on a dead-end project. This is how we managed to reduce the average time for hypotheses to pass through our experiment pipeline at Retail Rocket from 90 to 45 days.

Chapter 11

DATA ETHICS

Data is used everywhere these days. But is this a good thing in terms of our security? There's a concept in programming called a "greedy algorithm." A greedy algorithm is one that is focused on obtaining immediate short-term benefits. Commercial companies are typically driven by "greedy" algorithms and want to extract a profit from everything they possibly can, including the data that we leave behind, knowingly or otherwise. I'd like to talk about data ethics in this section. We've all experienced it – you're talking to someone about a top-loading washing machine, say, and a few minutes later an ad for these washing machines appears in your social media feed. Someone's been eavesdropping on you and used your data, right? Not exactly! It's a myth, but the very fact that our movements are being tracked gives food for thought. Is it legal? And, if it is, is it really ethical?

HOW WE ARE BEING WATCHED

Our digital footprints can be divided into two types: explicit and implicit. Explicit data is data that we provide voluntarily: whenever we fill out an online questionnaire or sign an online agreement or application, we check a box agreeing to the processing of our data. Implicit data is the information we leave about ourselves – our so-called "digital footprint" – through our online activities: our geolocation through mobile communications; the face recognition systems on CCTV and traffic cameras; the location of our cars through license plate recognition; the names of the people in our phone's contacts; the pages we have visited on the internet, etc. There is far more implicit data than there is explicit data, and consumers and providers are rather careless with it. Even more worrying is the fact that, unlike explicit data, which is protected in the Russian Federation under the Law on Personal Data, implicit data does not enjoy any kind of legal protection. This is not the case in the European Union following the recent adoption of the General Data Protection Regulation (GDPR) [107].

Implicit data has been used to identify and subsequently arrest people who have taken part in violent protests using videos taken at the events, or to identify and fine those who were in breach the self-isolation regime during the COVID-19 pandemic using CCTV footage. Just fifteen years ago, you'd have been forgiven for thinking that this kind of technology had come straight out of a sci-fi book. Andrew Ng, the main person behind image recognition algorithms (and whose name has cropped up on several occasions in this book) has said that this kind of technology is like a double-edged sword: on the one hand, it serves good; on the other, it is easy to abuse.

Face recognition technology is rather sophisticated today – all you need is a good dataset and access to a camera. In their article "We Built an 'Unbelievable' (but Legal) Facial Recognition Machine" [91], a group of journalists from *The New York Times* described how they collected a small dataset of publicly available photographs of people who work near Bryant Park in Manhattan. They then ran the photos through Amazon's commercial facial recognition service and got 2750 face matches over a nine-hour period from their dataset. The total cost of the experiment was $60! In theory, it's not difficult to build such a dataset using social networks: you've got names that correspond to pictures. There used to be a shareware service called findface.ru (now findface.pro) in Russia, where you could upload a photo of a person and get their name. The social network VK (like Facebook) was used as the dataset.

Another source of implicit data is when our smartphones pinpoint our exact geolocation. In late 2019, *The New York Times* published a series of articles on various issues of data collection and use as part of "The Privacy Project" [87]. One of these articles, entitled "One Nation Tracked" [88], describes how the journalists were able to get hold of a massive dataset containing the locations of 50 million mobile phones and 12 million Americans living in several major U.S. cities, including Washington, DC, New York, San Francisco and Los Angeles. Each line of

[87]    [91]    [107]

the dataset includes the exact location of a single smartphone over the course of several months in 2016/17. The journalists carried out a study of the dataset and produced a superb animation to represent the data. One would be forgiven for thinking that the data has been completely anonymized and is thus safe. Alas, this is not the case. Paul Ohm, a law professor and privacy researcher at the Georgetown University Law Center, said in the article that describing location data as anonymous is a completely false claim that has been debunked in multiple studies. "Really precise, longitudinal geolocation information is absolutely impossible to anonymize," he notes, adding that, "DNA is probably the only thing that's harder to anonymize than precise geolocation information." In most cases, a person can be identified by repeated journeys between two points – home and work. Would any other phone be making that very same journey to and from work on an almost daily basis? The article confirmed my belief that the use of implicit data is poorly protected.

But we were being tracked even before everyone and their mother had smartphones, through our web activity. Cookies are small pieces of data stored on the user's computer by the web browser while browsing a website. The term "cookie" was coined in June 1994 by Netscape Communication's engineer Lou Montulli. Back then, cookies provided a solution to the problem of reliably implementing a virtual shopping cart. Within two years, cookies had gained immense popularity and become the industry standard. Several types of cookies currently exist, and any web analytics course will provide you with a detailed description of each and every one of them. But I am only interested in two types of cookies in this book:

- Persistent first-party cookies – cookies that are stored by the website (or domain) you visit. Imagine you have visited Amazon.com, for example. Your browser will save cookies of this type to the Amazon.com "folder."

[88]   [89]

■ Persistent third-party cookies – cookies that are stored on domains that are not the domain (or website) you are visiting. They are typically saved through third-party content on the page, such as images from other domains. For example, the DoubleClick ad system save its cookies to the DoubleClick folder, even though you are on Amazon. com.

First-party cookies are used to store your data and login information, as well as for website analytics. For example, first-party cookies allow you to log in quickly on websites, remembering your passwords. Third party cookies are a little sketchier. They can be used to track your movement between sites, for online advertising, and to transfer your data to third-party resources. Let's take the RTB (Real-Time Bidding) protocol [89] as an example. RTB is used to instantly display personalized ads via banners and videos. Large companies such as Google and Criteo have already bought up much of the available advertising space on content sites (which make up 2.5 million of the 4 million sites on the Russian internet) in order to resell it via auctions. The idea is simple – the advertiser that has made the highest bid on a given ad impression will have their banner displayed on the publisher's site. This is how the bidding process works:

1. The user visits a website that contains ad slots.

2. Before the page has finished loading, the ad platform sends the following information to advertisers [89]: your IP address, your cookie ID, your interests (Google does this), the address of the webpage you are on and what it is about, the type of device you are using and even your location. The list goes on.

3. Bids from advertisers are calculated (the information described in step 2 is sent within a few hundred milliseconds). The advertisers' servers use their own mathematical models to do this. These models process both the information received from the advertising platform, but also information that they already have. This information can be collected by analysing user actions on the site, which is what Criteo does [90], selling services to ensure that potential buyers (users who visited the site but didn't buy anything) come back.

4. The advertising platform holds an auction for all bids and selects a winner.

5. The winner's banner is displayed on the site.

There is also programmatic advertising, which is when an advertiser buys a segment of an audience from a service, for example Yandex or Google, based on internal ("buying up" users who have bought nappies from my store) or external ("buying up" users who have bought nappies on the internet) data. Ads are displayed through the same RTB mechanisms. These ads are not as personalized, but they reach the segments the marketing managers need to reach. For example, a large online store may "sell" part of its audience with small children to a nappy manufacturer. This audience would then see a nappy advertisement.

Third-party advertiser cookies are needed in order to take full advantage of all the information available in the RTB machine, and they must be matched with the cookies of the advertising platform (this is called "cookie matching"). This requires third-party cookies from two sources – the advertiser and the advertising platform (say, Google) – on the page the user is viewing (not necessarily the advertising platform). The cookies themselves are obtained by requesting a transparent (and thus invisible to the user) single-pixel image. This is usually done using a small JavaScript code that is called up when the user views the page. It is during cookie matching that the client ID is matched between the advertiser and the advertising platform. This gives the advertiser much more information about the user. For example, an online store can transfer a customer ID to Google so that it can be seen in Google's RTB auctions. This ID is then used to pull the necessary information from the store's internal database, such as how many purchases the customer has made, when the customer last placed an order, what product categories they are interested in, etc. The store then uses this information to make

[90]   [93]

a bid – how much it is willing to pay for the customer to see its ad – and selects a suitable advertising banner. RTB advertising would be significantly less useful for the store if it didn't have this inside information about past purchases.

The same cookie matching mechanism is used to collect and sell customer data behind the customer's back. The next time you're surfing the internet, open the list of network requests in your browsers developer tools tab and see how many different systems collect information about you. There'll be social networks with their buttons, comment sections under the articles you're reading, etc. All this is used to collect information about you. This is why third-party cookies have come under attack from browsers and lawmakers. According to the study *The GDPR is a Cookie Monster* [93], before the introduction of the GDPR in the European Union, a single webpage would leave approximately 80 third-party cookies – that is, around 80 analytics services and advertising trackers would simultaneously receive information about your browsing history.

Your user identification in the cookies of any online service is sacred. The service can use this ID to uncover your entire internet history. Cookies themselves are unreliable, which is why they sometimes "go bad." They can be displaced as a result of browser restrictions or deliberately erased by the user. This is why services are breaking their backs to increase their survivability, duplicating storage in all kinds of browser archives. If the JavaScript code can't find the main cookie but can find it in these archives, then it will restore it using the information in the archive. The next step is to link all your devices into a single device, thus obtaining an even more extensive browsing history and giving the service more complete data about your internet activity. The easiest way to do this is through user logins: the user logs into the main site from a computer and a mobile phone, since it is the same account, which links the cookies in the main computer and the mobile device to the site account.

What if the user deliberately removes the cookies? This is what online scammers do when they want to get a loan, for example. Special services have been set up to bring these people to justice. These services use digital footprints that don't need cookies to track user activity, relying instead on information that can be obtained from the browser in real time. If the digital footprint has been well-designed, then it will be able to distinguish one user from another with a high degree of accuracy, and hence track down potential scammers. This is exactly what juicyscore. com does, for example, by collecting hundreds of user characteristics, from technical to behavioural traits – even down to typing speed.

We've already talked about tracking and selling mobile phone location data. Smartphones have their own unique ID for online advertising in mobile apps, an alternative to internet cookies called Mobile Advertising ID. This ID is called AdID in Google's Android, and IDFA in Apple devices. It is essentially the same as a cookie, and the user can reset the ID to clear their history at any time. These IDs are only available in mobile apps, not browsers [94].

Internet service providers are another source of data. Before the wide-spread introduction of the secure https protocol, internet service providers could see the entire browsing history of their users – all the information in the address bar of the browser. Now they can only see the domains of the sites you visit thanks to DNS queries [92], which are used to ask for the IP addresses associated with the domain names. I don't think internet service providers have a significant impact on the data market – unless we are talking about browsing sites with specific content.

For retailers, it would be a dream come true to be able to see all the data of a potential customer and at the optimum time send a trigger message to influence their behaviour. We've already discussed how this is done online. It's decidedly more difficult to do it offline, so you have to use loyalty cards. Retailers reward customers for this with discounts (you can often see two prices on price tags – the regular price and the discounted price for loyalty card holders), and customers share information, which

[92]    [94]

allows you to link individual purchases together. Incidentally, when you log in to the websites of major retailers, your online cookies are linked to your loyalty card, which in theory makes it possible to send you personalized ads even after all you've done is popped to the shop for a loaf of bread.

GOOD AND BAD DATA USAGE

Let's think about it, is data usage a problem? In the cartoon *The Little Goat Who Counted to Ten*, the animals were upset at the goat for wanting to count them. But his counting ability came in handy when everyone needed to know how many passengers were on the ship. I've always said that 95% of the people suffer because of what 5% of the "bad" guys do – a small group of good-for-nothings undermines trust in everyone else.

Take mobile phone geolocation. If you have such a dataset, you can plot transport routes more effectively, find the best places to open stores, track the workload of facilities on Google maps by the hour, etc. All good uses of data, right? But when it comes to tracking the movement of individuals without the involvement of the regulatory authorities, such use of data is potentially dangerous. Even if the data is impersonal, it is theoretically possible to figure out which person is being tracked.

Now let's talk about internet browser cookies. Their main purpose is to make web browsing hassle-free by performing such functions as remembering your passwords, for example. The next step is web analytics – each user is assigned a unique ID which is recorded in the cookies. We can calculate the effectiveness of ads by tracking user activity: if a user clicks on an ad, leaves the site and then comes back to make a purchase. Third-party cookies can then be used to personalize the site and provide targeted advertising. These are all relatively harmless uses of your data, right? Well, cookies and your personal data provide powerful tools for price discrimination. For example, some sites offer Mac and iPhone users goods at higher prices. Others (Amazon, for example) offer bigger discounts for first-time visitors. The article "How Online

Shopping Makes Suckers of Us All" [95] even cites the example of users in the greater Boston area being shown lower prices than those in the more remote parts of Massachusetts on identical goods. This is for the simple reason that Boston residents have more options than people living in the suburbs. Another thing that your cookies could be used for is to transfer or sell your data to third-party services.

I once proposed an idea at a hackathon hosted by Ostrovok.ru – to collect additional data by saving personalized advertising impressions from Yandex.Direct that were displayed to users. This required placing Yandex.Direct ads in the website footer. We then wrote a parser that saved the text of the ads along with the user's cookies. We were thus able to glean information about the user's broader interests. And it worked! The overwhelming majority of ads were for other hotels and booking systems, which was of no interest to us. However, some of the impressions contained ads for services that were not competitors of Ostrovok.ru. Having proven the viability of the test, we ended the experiment and deleted all the data. What I took away from this little exercise was that it is possible to intercept data on the user's private interests, and it is not as difficult as it may seem at first. This is another example of the bad faith use of personal data.

The story of what happened to the Russian internet statistics counter LiveInternet.ru (li.ru) is quite revealing here. As the article "Why are Russia's Most Popular Websites are Getting Rid of LiveInternet?" [96] explains:

> "German Klimenko talks about his project with one of the banks. From what we can gather, this is more or less how his Fastscoring+ system works: if you've visited a health website with a li.ru counter and searched for medicine to treat a serious illness, then the bank that Klimenko works with won't give you a loan – no one is interested in lending money to someone who is seriously ill."

This really struck a nerve with me. Outraged, I decided to write a post on my website. If you think about it, German Klimenko gave out this controversial information in order to promote his project. Yet this is not the only service that has exactly the same kind of data – the difference is they keep silent about it. Where's the guarantee that it won't be used when deciding on someone's creditworthiness?

I think the main reason why user data is abused is because many services on the internet are free. Almost every single content project and social network is financed through ads. Nothing is ever totally free – websites and online services need to pay for servers, cover their employees' wages, etc. Of course, websites can run subscription plans whereby users can avoid seeing ads (YouTube does this). Services that follow an ad monetization model are tempted to make at least some revenue on user data (because advertising only brings in so much money).

In addition, data leakage is always a possibility when "free" services that provide analytical services (such as Google Analytics) are installed on a website. And I am convinced that they don't always use customer data for its intended purpose – I mean, they've got to make money on something, right? Any free service is a Trojan horse, just keep that in mind at all times. Sooner or later, "private" analytics services will be all the rage, but they won't come cheap, meaning that many websites won't be able to afford them.

THE PROBLEM OF DATA LEAKAGE

I've already mentioned that Netflix is rather generous when it comes to access to data other than the customer's payment information. But what exactly do we mean when we say "personal data"? The customer's

[95]    [96]

name, address and telephone number? Yes, this is all explicit personal data and can be used to match a real person with their virtual ID. On the other hand, if you want to find a real person, all you need is that person's geolocation. Geolocation can thus be considered personal data as well. Here's another example: data from the Netflix Prize was removed from the public domain after the article "How to Break the Anonymity of the Netflix Prize Dataset" [97] proved that comparing information from this dataset with public movie ratings databases could reveal the identities of people and the ratings they had given. The U.S. Federal Trade Commission subsequently filed a lawsuit against Netflix. The dataset was eventually removed from the public domain and the second Netflix Prize was cancelled. We certainly kept this episode in mind at Retail Rocket when we were publishing our dataset [33] on Kaggle. com, encrypting all text descriptions completely. The trade-off was that the data was difficult to work with for researchers, but it did solve the problem of confidentiality.

By data leakage, I mean the unauthorized transmission of any personal information outside the company's security perimeter. Leaks can occur within a company when an employee gains access to data they do not have the authorization to see. Let's take a look at how this can happen. When designing a data warehouse, contact details (phone number, email address, etc.) and customer name are often stored in plain text. To minimize the risks, this data must be encrypted – for example, using a hash function. This deals with the problem of data leaking from the warehouse. If tech support needs to identify the cause of a problem for a client whose address is contained in the data warehouse, all they have to do is hash it so that they can then work directly with the warehouse using this hash. This is, of course, extremely cumbersome, as you'll have

[33]   [97]

to create a separate email recovery operation when compiling a customer mailing list. But that's the price of data security.

Data security is extremely important in this age of complete digitalization. Burglars these days don't break down doors and blow up safes; they break into databases and surreptitiously copy the data they need. And we're not just talking addresses, names and passwords. They could be after simple text files as well – a message or letter containing information about a person, or even an audio recording from a voice assistant. The article "The Dark Side of Our Voice Assistants" [98], for example, raises the issue of parts of our audio messages that are not automatically recognized being sent to people (a service like Amazon Mechanical Turk) for decryption. While the recordings are evidently sent in an anonymized form, information can be found about the users that they would definitely not want to disclose. Voice assistants are usually only activated after certain words (wake words) are uttered, and only then do they start to transmit your voice over the internet for recognition. A team of researchers developed an architecture to test this, publishing their findings in an article entitled "LeakyPick: IoT Audio Spy Detector" [99]. It turned out that the LeakyPick project was even able to detect encrypted audio messages sent from voice assistants. The researchers also identified 89 words that could unknowingly trigger an Amazon Echo Dot to transmit audio to the cloud.

Perhaps the biggest personal data leak in history is that linked to the investigation into the poisoning of Alexei Navalny in Russia, which was based entirely on confidential data on the movements of certain people and their phone call records. This demonstrates gross negligence in information security, despite the adoption of the law on personal data.

[98]   [99]

DATA ETHICS

The issue of data ethics can be divided into two parts: ethical standards and data loss prevention. Both require attention and carry certain risks (not always legal risks, but certainly reputational risks).

Former Amazon data scientist Andreas Weigend wrote an entire book about data entitled *Data for the People*. He has this to say about data confidentiality:

> "... the ultimate goal is to educate people. I want them to understand that there are trade-offs [...] I want people to be aware of the spectrum of options available to them, and the consequences of choosing specific ones. I want to empower people to manage their data responsibly, including decisions on their privacy. A company must honor these decisions and treat its customers with integrity and respect. I hate it when a company tries to manipulate its customers, pulling the wool over their eyes."

This is an excerpt from an interview Andreas gave in 2005 [100] – 15 years have passed and we're still in the same position.

The fact of the matter is that there is a tacit data use agreement between companies and their customers, the finer details of which unfold as the market matures and customers become savvier. I agree with Andreas that need to educate themselves. I think that it is high time we started teaching the basics of data security in schools. Information privacy laws force companies to publish their privacy policies on their websites. As part of its "Privacy Project," journalists for *The New York Times* carried out a study of such policies called "We Read 150 Privacy Policies. They Were an Incomprehensible Disaster" [101]. The study involved analyz-

[100]   [101]   [102]

ing the length and readability of privacy policies from 150 websites and apps. The title of the article gives us a good idea of how it went! It turns out that the BBC had the most readable agreement – a high-school education and 15 minutes of your time are all you need to get through it. Airbnb's, on the other hand, requires a legal education and 35 minutes of your time. While the agreements have become more readable since the introduction of the GDPR in the European Union, they are still "created by lawyers, for lawyers" [101]. They often contain technical information about how data is collected, yet say nothing about transferring this data to third parties – something that directly affects the user. I recommend checking the article out, it's got some great infographics and animations.

Data scientists and ML experts have got their own unwritten code of ethics too. Top of the list is never use data for personal gain or to satisfy your curiosity. The only time you can actually work with people is when you're providing technical support. We (data scientists) have access to pretty much everything when it comes to confidential customer data, and it's not difficult for us to pull up a person's entire history if we want. There's even a word for this – LOVEINT (love intelligence) – which was coined back in 2013 following a scandal at the US National Security Agency [102] where agents had been using spy technology to track their lovers or former lovers. Obviously, you should never do this under any circumstances whatsoever. Access restrictions and lockouts are easy to bypass, so it's good when there are internal ethical prohibitions in place.

Carelessness with personal data is also unacceptable. This includes transferring personal data internally outside the security perimeter – through public email services, for example. Data leakages are far less likely to happen if you follow this rule.

And it goes without saying that you should be wary of using controversial features in your model such as gender, race, signs of serious illness, age, etc. This is a hot topic in the United States right now, and artificial intelligence experts have to keep these things in mind at all times, especially following the Black Lives Matter and Time's Up movements. For instance, Andrew Ng hosted a group discussion event where participants tried to come up with a list of ethical guidelines for AI development

[103]. Biases in datasets are often the result of societal prejudices. The *Harvard Business Review* published an interesting article on this called "What Do We Do About the Biases in AI?" [104], which described a case of discrimination in a British medical school identified back in 1988. The UK Commission for Racial Equality determined that the computer program the school was using to decide which applicants would be invited for interviews was biased against women and those with non-European names. And it had been trained to match human admission decisions, doing so with 90–95% accuracy. The program itself was not the program, rather it was the dataset, which was created by people who had made the admission decisions in previous years; the program simply identified the pattern and repeated it. There's no easy way to deal with this kind of bias, but it can be done. For example, by diversifying your team. In Russia, the least we can do is to create conditions in the hiring process that will not discriminate against women.

HOW USER DATA IS PROTECTED

Things are getting better on the privacy front. Here are some of the most significant events that have affected the privacy market, including harmful cookies.

First, we have the appearance of ad blockers in desktop and mobile browsers, which not only keep you from seeing various ads, but also block certain third-party cookies that are used when transferring data to third parties. In the US, 27.0% of internet users will block ads in 2021 on at least one of their internet-connected devices [105]. In Russia, 44% of internet users in Russia block use ad blockers. It's more difficult to block ads in mobile browsers for the simple reason that there are fewer

[103]   [104]

ad blockers out there. Let's not forget that most content resources make their money on advertising, which means that ad blockers cut into their profits. Now, most sites didn't use aggressive pop-up ads anyway, but the ones that did had an impact on the entire industry because they effectively ushered in the era of ad blockers. The knock-on effect of this was that search engines started to lose money. To counter this, they would skew search results so that the sites that used aggressive pop-up ads would be further down the list. Users would not be bothered by all these pop-up ads and would thus not install software to block them.

The next step was to introduce default third-party cookie blocking for browsers. "Prevent cross-site tracking" is automatically enabled in Apple's web browser. The Interactive Advertising Bureau, an international organization that develops industry standards and provides legal support for the online advertising industry, carried a study entitled the "IAB Europe Guide to the Post Third-Party Cookie Era" [106] which found that 30% of all ad impressions are rendered on Safari and Firefox – browsers that block third-party cookies by default. Another 65% of ad impressions are set to be blocked by Chrome, whenever Google gets around to doing it. While Google did announce in January 2020 that it would stop supporting third-party cookies within the next two years, it continues to drag its feet because, unlike Apple (Safari) and Mozilla (Firefox), it makes money from ads, including through RTB, which needs third-party cookies to enhance information.

This doesn't apply to in-app advertising – Mobile Advertising ID will continue to work as before. But you can reset these mobile cookies in the system settings. I've also noticed that with each update of Apple's iOS, apps are given fewer and fewer rights to access client data by default. For example, you can now change access to location services (Never, Ask Next Time, While Using the App) or individual photos.

[105]  [106]

I'd also like to draw your attention to one technical nuance: in today's systems, it is extremely difficult to delete data completely. The thing is, in addition to the main working databases, where your data can be deleted through your ID, there are numerous lower-level systems where the information is kept – for example, the storage and backup systems. These systems are optimized for storing, rather than editing, data. Deleting a given user's data is thus so difficult that no one will ever actually take the time to do it. And even if you manage to get all your data deleted, the company can still restore it whenever it wants.

However, the most interesting developments took place at the legislative level. Russian websites are obliged to publish information in accordance with Federal Law No. 152-FZ "On Personal Data" dated July 27, 2006. EU websites must comply with the General Data Protection Regulation (GDPR), which entered into force on May 25, 2018. The GDPR aims to regulate the processing of personal data and ensure its transparency for the client. It contains a clause stating that the data protection documents on company websites must be concise, easily accessible and easy to understand. The GDPR was used as template for similar legal instruments in other countries, such as the California Consumer Privacy Act (CCPA), which protects the rights of California residents. An article appeared a few years ago comparing the GDPR and the Russian Federal Law No. 152-FZ [107]. I was shocked to discover that cookies and IP addresses are considered personal data under the GDPR. Russian law does not agree. In my opinion, this is the key difference in how personal data is treated. And following all these stories of data trading, I would say that the GDPR's approach is the correct one.

Let's compare the effectiveness of the laws on the protection of personal data from the point of view of the user. Open the UK and Russian websites of Decathlon, the sporting goods retailer (decathlon.co.uk and

[101]   [107]   [108]

decathlon.ru). The Russian site has a link called "Data Protection" at the bottom of the page. Click on it and you'll be taken to a page with a bunch of legalese on how your data is used. There are no unnecessary details here. At the bottom, you'll find a regular mailing address where you can send a letter asking for your personal data to be deleted. The UK version, which is still subject to the GDPR (until it leaves the EU), is far more impressive. First, when you open the site for the first time, you'll be greeted by a window giving you the opportunity to either agree with the data processing rules or follow a link where you can check boxes for individual services to process your data. It looks similar to the security settings you see in smartphone apps, and everything is written in clear and understandable languages (unlike Federal Law No. 152-FZ). By the way, the Dutch version of the website allows the user to disable the Retail Rocket service – Decathlon is a client of ours, but the GDPR gives it every right to do this.

The data disclaimers on the Amazon and Target websites are just as bad as the ones I saw on Russian websites – a point also noted by researchers at the Privacy Project [101]. On Target.com, I clicked on the link to prohibit the sale of my data under the California CCPA. I was then asked to fill out a lengthy form telling me that this option was only available to California residents. The authors of "This Article is Spying on You" [108] ran an experiment using an article from *The Times* on how abortion can impact fertility. They found that if you visited the website from an IP address in the United States, then your data would be sent to 50 services, compared to just 16 if you accessed the site from an EU IP address. The number of third-party cookies for US users was 100, and just 28 for users in the EU. The impact of the GDPR is clear – your data is far less likely to end up in the hands of bad faith actors. Research into the impact of the GDPR [93] has shown that the number of third-party cookies found on news websites in Europe has declined by an average of 22% since the introduction of the law.

The advantages of the GDPR compared to other laws on data protection are clear, and I hope that Russian laws catch up in the near future.

Chapter 12

CHALLENGES
AND STARTUPS

In this chapter, I want to talk about the problems facing modern ecommerce companies and how to fix them. And I think you might be able to take something from my experience as a co-founder of Retail Rocket.

WEB ANALYTICS IN ADVERTISING

Web analytics aims to understand user behaviour on the internet. I would divide it into two parts: analysing the effectiveness of advertising; and analysing user interaction with websites.

Let's start with analysing the effectiveness of advertising. Anyone who is familiar with the legendary business mogul John Wanamaker (1838–1922), a visionary in retail (he opened the first ever supermarket and is credited with the creation of the price tag) and the father of modern advertising, will likely have heard his famous saying: "Half the money I spend on advertising is wasted; the trouble is I don't know which half."

I used to believe wholeheartedly that internet advertising would put an end to this practice of wasting money and would be far more effective than TV commercials and ads in newspapers and magazines. I mean, you've put a commercial on TV. Great, but how do you go about measuring its effectiveness? Well, there's a few ways – from changing the sales schedules as of the moment the commercial appeared on TV, to carrying out consumer surveys in order to gauge whether or not awareness of the product has increased. With print advertising, you can also use promo codes for discounts or gifts, which generally provide a more accurate measurement of an ad's success because you can literally count the number of promo codes that have been used.

Online advertising has made things so much easier. Links are always marked with special tags, for example UTM codes. Pay attention to them when you click on ads. When you click on an ad and are taken to a website, the cookies from that site are stored on your computer. This allows the site to recognize you when you return to there. The mechanism can be used to track your purchases days or even weeks after clicking on the ad. This is far more accurate than with traditional TV and print advertising, right? Well, that's exactly what I thought back in 2005 when I had just started looking into the effectiveness of online advertising. There weren't as many ads and cross-clicks back then, so it was easier to track their impact.

There are so many ads these days – so many! And users often click on a number of ad sources before actually making a purchase. You could start with an internet search, then browse an online store that was recommended from search advertising for a bit and then leave the site. You might come back to the site a few days later thanks to so-called re-targeting advertising (Criteo, which have mentioned already, does this), register, drop the item you were looking at in your cart and then leave the site. A few hours (or even minutes) later, you'll probably get an email saying something like "You left items in your cart." So, you click on the link and complete your purchase. So, what do you think: which type of advertising was responsible for you making the purchase? Obviously, if you hadn't searched for the item in the first place, you'd never have placed the order, right? But what about the other types of advertising – retargeting and the "complete your purchase" email reminder? Did they have an effect too?

Standard web analytics tools tend to give the nod to last click attribution. In our example, this would be the email reminding you that you have left items in your cart. But you would never have even received that email if you hadn't gone through the first two steps. This is called the problem of reattribution, where different advertising sources "fight" among themselves for an order. How can we calculate the effectiveness of an ad if several clicks from different advertising sources were made before the target action (i.e. the placement of an order) was made? Carry out an A/B test: show half of the users a retargeting ad, and the other half nothing. Send half of them an abandoned cart email, and the other half nothing. But what if retargeting and abandoned cart emails are mutually dependent? In theory, we could set up a complex multivariate test. But this is not feasible in practice. It's difficult to carry out these kinds of

A/B test for online advertising, not to mention expensive, as you have to turn off part of the ads, which causes a drop-off in revenue.

Many great minds are struggling to create alternative ways of calculating the effectiveness of advertising. Perhaps they'll be able to come up with a system based on a probabilistic approach, for example, one that gives more weight to the initial clicks. In order to build such a model, you'll need to do a number of A/B tests, which is not cheap. And then you'll only have a model that is specific to your product, not a general model that can be extended to the entire industry.

There are two more terms you are likely to come across in web analytics: end-to-end analytics and cohort analysis. End-to-end analytics is usually understood as working with a client on an individual level: from placing the advertisement in the first place, to shipping the order, to tracking the customer's subsequent actions. This is done with the help of unique customer IDs that "walk" the customer through the various systems, from advertising to logistics. This allows companies to calculate the costs of advertising and order processing down to each individual client, albeit with some approximation.

A marketing cohort is a group of consumers that have performed a specific action within a given period of time. Cohort analysis refers to tracking these groups of clients. Its main purpose is to calculate Lifetime Value (LTV), the amount of money that a client brings in over a certain period of time. Let's say you've set this period at three months and decided to calculate LTV on the first day of each month (Fig. 12.1). Each settlement month, the analyst "looks" at customers who registered with the site

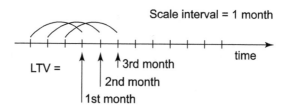

Fig. 12.1. Calculating LTV

or placed an order three months ago, counts the number of purchases they made over that period, and then divides this by the total number of customers in the cohort. To do this, customers who placed their first order two or four months ago cannot be included.

INTERNAL WEB ANALYTICS

Internal web analytics do not typically receive as much attention as advertising. Significantly more money is spent on ads than on the website itself, so management wants to know how effectively this money is being spent. But the actions of visitors to the site (the focus of internal analytics) are extremely important. Internal web analytics includes developing a purchase funnel, analysing completed forms and questionnaires, merchandising, site functionalism, click maps, recording user actions (for example, Yandex.Webvisor), etc. These tools help give you a much better picture of your target audience.

A purchase funnel looks just like a regular funnel: visitors "fall through" it until they perform the target action, usually placing an order. In the average online store, the order conversion rate is typically around 1%. That is, only 1 in every 100 visitors reaches the bottom of the purchase funnel and places an order. A great deal of time is spent trying to up this number, because if the order conversion rate improves, then you earn more without increasing advertising costs.

But there's advertising, and then there's advertising. What's better, a small stream of visitors who are just about ready to make a purchase? Or a large number of visitors, the overwhelming majority of whom will leave the site immediately? The order conversion rate may be higher in the first instance, but it will also be more expensive. This is why I'm not a fan of "measuring" conversion rates. The way I see it, cost per order is far more important, as it allows you to objectively compare the financials of two online stores in a first approximation. A purchase funnel can also be thought of as a sequence of micro-steps from targeted actions:

1. Visiting at least one webpage after arriving on the lading page (non-bounced visitor).
2. Adding an item to the basket.
3. Clicking on the "checkout" button.
4. Checking out.

By optimizing each step, you can increase the number of visitors who make it to the end of the purchase funnel.

One of the best things I learnt about internal web analytics when I was studying the Omniture SiteCatalyst (now Adobe Analytics) system was merchandising analytics. Merchandising analytics is a way of measuring the effectiveness of an online store's virtual shelves. Online stores are made up of several types of webpages: home page, search page, product category page, product information page, shopping basket, order steps, user personal account, etc. Every page type contains product blocks (Fig. 12.2) – for example, five products displayed horizontally on rotation or a large product list on category pages. Products in product blocks contain the following attributes: a picture, a snippet of information about

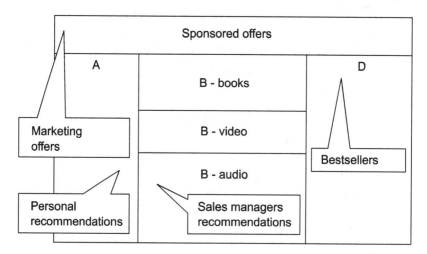

Fig. 12.2. Example of merchandising in an online store

the product, its price, the name of the product, and an "add to cart" or "quick buy" button. What can you do with the design of the product block? You can make the picture bigger, remove certain elements, etc. But if you want to see what has changed in the metrics, then merchandising analytics is the way to go. Here, blocks of goods in online stores are the equivalent of regular shelves in brick-and-mortar stores.

This is how merchandising analytics works: all links to products (pictures, names, the "add to cart" button) are marked with special invisible tags that can contain the page type (home page, search page, etc.), block name (horizontal, listing), and link type (picture, name, "add to cart" button). Every time a user clicks on a block, the system remembers the product, block, and user. It then monitors the user's activity for a set amount of time (for example, 24 hours) to see what they do with the product after clicking. If they added it to their cart or placed an order, then this metric is assigned to the invisible tag that belongs to that link. You end up with a table that looks something like this (Table 12.1).

Table 12.1. Calculating the effectiveness of merchandising

Name of tag	Clicks	Added to cart	Orders
Homepage / first-line recommen-dations / picture of item	1000	350	20
Search / Listing / Name of item	15,000	3000	500
Product page / "Similar products" / picture of item	50,000	15,000	2000

I normally enter this information into Excel and split the tag into three fields (page type, block type and link type), which allows me to address the following range of problems:

- How does each page type contribute to sales? For example, 15 years ago, I was able to determine that the Ozon.ru search page was responsible for half of all cart additions on the site.

- How does each recommendation block contribute to sales? At the time of my departure form left Ozon.ru, the recommendation system accounted for approximately 38% of all cart additions on the site.

- Where do users make the most purchases – after clicking on the product picture or the product name? According to my research, users click on pictures more often, but it is product names that generate the most sales.

Once the data scientist has these numbers, the company can carry out all manner of "what if" experiments: What if we made the product pictures bigger? What if we removed pictures from searches altogether? What if we swapped product blocks? What if we changed the recommendation algorithm in the product block? Merchandising metrics give you far more room for maneuver when it comes to modifying your site.

Now, let's look at some of the finer details of merchandising analytics. First, we have the same problem of tag reattribution that exists in advertising: a user searches the site, clicks on a product, comes back later to click on a link to the same product in the recommendation block and then purchases it. Should the purchase be attributed to the search page or the recommendation block? You can choose either in this case. And there is no clear answer as to which attribution method is best. I tend to attribute such sales to the search page. Second, the computing power required for merchandising analytics are far more expensive than for advertising analytics. This is why Omniture SiteCatalyst refused to increase the tracking time for user actions from 24 hours to seven days, so I had to use the "add to cart" metric instead of the order metric, as users typically do not place an order within 24 hours of visiting a site for the first time, but they do add the product to their carts. Pay attention to how various web analytics vendors work with merchandising: Yandex.Metrica does not carry out merchandising analytics at all and has no plans to do so; Google Analytics has Enhanced Ecommerce; and Adobe Analytics has merchandising tracking [114]. I've looked at the documentation for how Google and Adobe implement their merchandising analytics systems and I can say that Adobe does it far better. I borrowed this idea myself and wrote my own algorithm to calculate the effectiveness of recommendations given by online stores. Retail Rocket continues to use the algorithm to this day.

The page click map is an interesting tool, but it needs to be set up correctly if you're working with dynamic blocks where products are rotated. I would typically try to use merchandising analytics instead and draw the map in the editor. This allowed me to make an aggregate click map for a product page. But the store carried around 500,000 products in total. No click map can cope with this, but merchandising analytics can.

Another useful tool is to "video record" user activity. Yandex.Metrica does this using its "webvisor" service, which records all the actions of a small sample of users, even down to mouse movements. You can then watch the recordings back in the program interface. This reminded me of the book *Why We Buy: The Science of Shopping* by Paco Underhill, in which the author explains how he sets up a huge number of cameras in his client's stores, watches videos for days on end, and provides recommendations on how to rearrange the store space in order to ensure that more visitors make a purchase. Webvisor can be used in exactly the same way. Unfortunately, the tool itself is underrated, either because not many people know about it or because it is a bit fiddly to use. This is a good alternative to expensive usability systems such as eye trackers.

If there's one piece of advice I can give you on web analytics, it's this: don't read the user manuals, read the implementation manuals instead. This is where you find out what's "under the hood" – you'll get all kinds of ideas on how to work with some of the trickier features of the web analytics system you're using. I would also advise you to try and use a consistent methodology where possible. I really like the "functionalist" approach to web analytics [109]. An approach like this can help you make more systemic decisions, even with regard to the simplest of tools.

[109]   [114]

DATABASE MARKETING

Email has been around for years, and we still use it. Before the internet, we had mail order, which originated in the United States in the 19th century. Then there was direct marketing, which involves selling products through direct communication channels (mail, email, telephone). This is markedly different from regular advertising, which aims to appeal to the general consumer rather than a specific target audience. Direct marketing involves working with clients on an individual level. There are generally two types of activity in direct marketing: selling to an existing customer base and building new customer bases. The first is database marketing.

Imagine you've got an existing customer database with contact details, correspondence records, order numbers, etc. You send these people catalogues in the mail on a regular basis. You've been instructed to organize another mail-out to try and solicit additional orders from customers. The simplest approach is to send the same thing to everyone – a discount offer, for example. This is quite expensive to do, as each letter costs money to mail out and the discount you're offering will affect the company's margins. You've also got to keep in mind that some customers will place an order anyway, with or without a discount. This is where it makes sense to split customers into groups. There is no point sending customers who are likely to order an item even if it isn't on discount a promotional offer (if absolutely necessary, you can offer them a small discount on something). This is not true of customers who don't typically order products that aren't on offer, so it is definitely worthwhile sending them a discount. Customers who have not ordered anything for a while shouldn't receive any kind of promotional offer.

A customer scoring mechanism would be useful here. For our sales promotion, we need to calculate the probability that each customer in our database will make a purchase. Using this scale, we can then divide customers into groups, each of which will be offered a unique discount. For example:

- The group of most active customers (probability of making a purchase > 70%) receives a discount of 3%.

- The group of reasonably active customers (probability of making a purchase 40–70%) receives a discount of 10%.
- The group of customers who order items intermittently (probability of making a purchase 20–40%) receives a coupon worth $10.
- The group of customers who haven't ordered anything for a long time (probability of making a purchase < 20%) doesn't receive anything.

You can compile a model like this using logistic regression with RFM features, which we covered in the chapter on machine learning. At this stage, we divide clients into groups and start developing a test plan. Our model could be wrong despite good metrics obtained from the existing data. To check this, you need to do an A/B test with a control group. This involves randomly selecting 20% of the customers in each group and splitting the resulting group in half. One half of the group will receive a promo offer – this will be the test group. The second half will receive a letter only (depending on the sales promotion) – this will be the control group. This needs to be done with every group, with the possible exception of the group of customers who haven't ordered anything for a long time. Once your plan is ready and you've printed all the letters, send them out to your customers. Have your analysts wait for a while (a month or two) before they start tallying the results: sales against expenses. You'll be left with a table that looks something like this one (Table 12.2) for each group.

Table 12.2. Calculating profits from test mail-outs

Group	Mail-outs		Customers		Gross profit	
	Test group	Control group	Test group	Control group	Test group	Control group
Most active	1000	1000	120	100	110,000	100,000
Reasonably active	3000	3000	170	150	140,000	130,000
Rest	5000	5000	180	150	110,000	120,000

It is thus worth offering discounts to your most active and reasonably active customers, but not anyone else. This is what happened: the coupon for $10 proved popular among the third group of customers, but their average purchase value was less than that of the control group. This was not enough to recoup the money spent on the sales promotion. The result (profit) of the control group turned out to be better. In my experience, customers respond better to a fixed-amount coupon than they do to a discount, but the average purchase value is always lower than that of customers using discounts. This topic is covered in great detail in *Drilling Down: Turning Customer Data into Profits with a Spreadsheet* [71], my favourite book by Jim Novo, and is also covered in *Strategic Database Marketing* [110] by Arthur Hughes. Real-life scenarios can be more complicated: perhaps you are testing several types of discounts, coupons and gifts on groups at the same time. I ran similar promotions for Ozon.ru customers who hadn't bought anything for a long time and managed to get over $100,000 in additional sales.

Over the years, direct marketing has become synonymous with junk mail, but this is not an area that aims to appeal to the general consumer. Traditional direct marketing is not as popular these days, of course, thanks to the widespread use of email. It's far more expensive to send out a physical letter than it is to drop someone an email, no matter how many cost-cutting measures you employ. And our inboxes have been overflowing ever since! But let's stop and think about it for a second: is bombarding us with emails likely to increase sales? In the short term, yes. But, in the long term, you end up "eroding" your customer base. You lose the goodwill of your customers – people get annoyed when they are spammed with emails all the time. Some will unsubscribe from your mailing list, while others (the majority) will send your message to their "spam" folder out of exasperation. This affects the company's reputation, and any subsequent emails you may send will be automatically

[71]   [110]

directed to the spam folder. But, more often than not, people just stop responding to your emails.

At Ozon.ru, I devised a test to find out how frequently we should send emails to customers, and what the best day for sending these emails was. This involved sending daily emails to some clients, and weekly emails to others. It turned out that the optimum scheme was to send out emails once a week, every Tuesday. It was also at Ozon.ru that we sent out a newsletter every morning listing the latest book releases. This was until we realized that daily mail-outs was a bit much, so we switched to weekly newsletters containing a selection of books once a week. Our support team started to get letters from disgruntled customers asking why the book recommendations were coming in less often now. One customer even wrote that it had become a tradition in their office for everyone to read the Ozon.ru newsletter together. After that, we added an option to the subscription – customers could now choose how often they wanted to receive the emails, daily or weekly. Some people want regular newsletters, others not so much, and it's good to take this information into account. For example, it would be wise to reduce the information pressure on those customers who have not placed any orders as a result of past mail-outs. Every email, even if it remains unopened, tries the customer's patience. And that patience is likely to overflow sooner or later.

The next step in the evolution of email marketing was trigger emails and the customer interaction chains they create. A trigger email is a response to any action or inaction of the customer. Here are some examples:

- Sending an email to a customer who has registered on the website but has not placed an order within the past three days. Statistics show that the likelihood of a customer placing an order drops by 10% every day.

- Sending an email to a customer who has added an item to their cart but not taken any further action for one hour after that.

- Sending an email with links to drill bits to a client who bought a drill last month. Statistics show that 50% of customers who have bought a drill will buy drill bits at some point within the next 30 days. Drill bits are consumable items.

The list could go on. So, what we do is we test all options and collect them into a single chain of interaction with customers. I was first introduced to such schemes when I was working at Ozon.ru by some French consultants who worked for PPE Group. Retail Rocket has implemented a similar system using data on customer interaction with the site.

STARTUPS

Startups were all the rage a few years ago. I've spent pretty much my entire career working with startups, rather than global corporations. And I even got in on the ground floor in one of them as a co-founder, so I think I've got the right to speak on this topic. What drives people who want to start a new business? When it comes to startups, professional experience in the field you want to get into is crucial, as you generally don't need to attract massive investments. This is certainly not the case for people who don't have the necessary experience. Experience or not, if you're launching a startup while trying to hold onto your nine-to-five, you can forget about weekends and free time. The usual path is to bring the product to the MVP (Minimum Viable Product) stage and then start actively seeking investments and pitching the project to potential investors at conferences.

Venture investors look for projects whose value will grow exponentially. They invest in many startups, where maybe one will flourish and recoup the costs. Looking for an investor is an adventure in itself: there are sure to be some characters who want to make money off you. It happened to me once where a relatively well-known figure in ecommerce asked for 5% of the company for setting us up with an investor. Finding a good investor is quite the achievement. By "good investor," I mean someone who not only gives you money on favourable terms, but who also remains hands-off when it comes to the day-to-day management of your business, and who helps you out with their connections by finding potential clients, etc. A good investor can also introduce the founders and managers of a startup to the management of other portfolio companies. For example, Index Venture (an investor in Ozon.ru) took us to London and introduced us to such projects as Betfair, Last.fm and Lovefilm. Investors and founders at Wikimart.ru arranged trips to California so that we could meet the folks from Color, Netflix and eBay. You might say this is all hipster posturing and money down the drain, but, personally, they inspired me to do great things. It's one thing to watch a recording of a video conference, and it's another thing entirely to talk face-to-face with people from legendary companies and see that they're dealing with the same problems that you deal with, just on a bigger scale.

When negotiating a deal, venture capitalists want to give less and get more, while the founders want to sell less for as much as possible. The terms of the deal are what the negotiating is all about, and they form the basis of the future relationship between the founders and the venture capital fund. Unfortunately, sometimes they end badly [111]. But this is not always the case. For example, Retail Rocket has a great relationship with Impulse VC, which has been with us since the very beginning.

Are there any arguments for going ahead with a project no matter what happens? There certainly are, and some very compelling ones at that. The experience of creating a startup gives you an understanding of what is important and what is not, and far quicker than if you were in a regular corporate environment. The flip side of this that people don't talk about is you can't just up and leave your own company like you can a normal job – you're tied to it by a golden chain, as it were. It's a matter of what your price is: those who leave first get less. I know people who have left startups before they were sold to strategic investors, losing out on a big payday in the process. There are many reasons why someone may choose to leave a startup: fatigue, the desire to move onto other projects, disagreements with partners, etc. The more people are involved in the management of the company (investors and co-founders), the more likely

[111]

you are to run into a "too many cooks in the kitchen" scenario, where arguments take up more time than actions.

It's never a good thing when business turns into politics. But a startup is different from a family business, for example, because the founder will inevitably lose his or her clout, especially when the company goes public or is sold to a strategic investor. If you are so attached to your project that you just can't share it, then seeking investment is probably not the way to go.

At the time of writing the previous chapter, one of the companies I had worked for (Ozon.ru) had gone public, while another (Wikimart.ru) had folded back in 2016. Ozon.ru was founded in 1998, and I started working there in 2004. The company was growing by approximately 40% per year at the time. No one talked about startup culture or anything like that, we just got on with our jobs. Wikimart.ru was founded by two Stanford graduates who had come up with the idea while they were still studying and scored their first investment before they had received their diplomas. The culture in the company was entirely different. They hired some really smart people, although none of them had experience in ecommerce. That, in my opinion, was a mistake. You can't run a warehouse if you don't have any experience running one. This is why Wikimart.ru's financials were worse than those of Ozon.ru. The second difference between the two companies was that Wikimart.ru was financed by the American Tiger Global Management investment firm, while Ozon.ru was bankrolled by Baring Vostok Capital Partners, a Russian private equity firm whose international footprint is much smaller. The economic sanctions against Russia cut off the flow of Western capital for Wikimart.ru, with Tiger Global Management refusing to finance the project any further. Third, Wikimart.ru started off as an alternative to Yandex.Market, aggregating current offers from sellers, before switching to a delivery model. The market wasn't ready for this kind of model at the time, although this is not the case anymore, with a number of major internet retailers (including Ozon.ru) having adopted it.

Another feature of startups is the high staff turnover. Employee salaries are one of the biggest overheads of a business. When a company grows, so too does the number of staff it employs. It's like cell division, and it can get out of hand very quickly – when everyone has an assistant, and these assistants have their own assistants, and so on. This is where the company starts to lose its focus. Then an economic crisis hits and investors start to demand that you cut costs to keep profits up, so you inevitably have to let people go. My first experience with this was in 2008, when Ozon.ru took the decision to lay off 10% of its employees. There was no one really that I could let go, so I just removed my department's job ads from wherever they had been posted. I remember the Ozon.ru CEO going through lists of employees at the building's turnstiles, which recorded the times that everyone came in and left the office, and getting rid of those who were spending less time at the office. I was there at Wikimart.ru too when they were forced to make mass layoffs after the news came in from Tiger Global Management. Just like Ozon.ru, they had to trim the workforce by 10%. At Ostrovok.ru, however, I was among the managers tasked with reducing the budgets of our departments by 30%, so I let one third of my team go. Commendably, Ostrovok.ru did everything by the book, as laid out in the Labour Code of the Russian Federation, meaning that people were given severance packages. The way I see it, staff cuts are a normal part of the life of a startup – something to deal with teething troubles. Unfortunately, however, when they start to cut staff costs, people are often fired indiscriminately. Considering that some departments have far more staff than is really needed, while others are more conservative when it comes to hiring, the principle of "cut 10% everywhere" is clearly flawed.

MY PERSONAL EXPERIENCE

I first started raving about startups when I was at Ozon.ru. They were a hot topic back then. I'd had this idea for an apartment remodeling project codenamed "jobremont" (*remont* is the Russian word for "repairs" or "renovations"). This is how it would work: a user places an order for a renovation job, triggering an auction among apartment renovation companies, and then selects the offer that best fits their needs.

I wanted people to be able to log in to the service using their mobile number, rather than their email address. Mobile phone authentication only became a thing about five years later. I posted on habr.ru and got some pretty positive feedback. I even met with potential investors twice. At the second meeting, it was suggested that I develop something else, as they had already invested in a similar project called remontnik.ru. I turned the offer down, although I did go through remontnik.ru when I wanted to remodel my flat. Six years later, I started working on my new project – a recommendation system for online stores.

We first decided to develop a recommendation system when I was working at Ozon.ru. I'd accumulated a sizeable database on the site's customer traffic, and like any curious analytics engineer from MIPT or the Faculty of Mechanics and Mathematics at Moscow State University, I started to think about how I could use this data. It's the age-old question: What came first – the chicken or the egg? The data or the idea to develop a recommendation system? We, that is the data scientists and engineers at Ozon.ru, were fascinated by the question. What can I say? We were young and full of ambition back then. What's more, we'd heard that 35% of sales on Amazon.com came from recommendations, and we would obsess over attaining similar figures ourselves. And when someone who's good with tech gets an idea into their head, then there's no stopping them, especially if they're surrounded by likeminded people.

Amazon talked about recommendation services back in its 1999 Annual Report: the word appears ten times in the document. Online stores weren't really a thing in Russia back then. Amazon is such an influential company that the article "Two Decades of Recommender Systems at Amazon.com" [112] by Greg Linden – the man who created its recommendation system – is one of the most cited articles according to Google Scholar.

[100]   [112]   [113]

The meeting we had at Ozon.ru with Andreas Weigend, a leading data scientist at Amazon who now teaches at Berkeley and Stanford and provides consulting services for a number of ecommerce giants, left a lasting impression on me. He told me that, "the last click the user makes will give you more information about them than you had before." I couldn't get these words out of my head, even though I already knew that sociodemographic data was far less useful than behavioural data. In his article "I Search, therefore I am" [100], Weigend said that the search terms that people use can offer "a revealing view into the mind and the soul of a person" ("We are what we search for," "A powerful compression of people's lives is encoded in the list of their search queries"). This information would come in handy later at Retail Rocket when writing "short-term" personal recommendations.

Anyway, the Ozon.ru website did have a recommendation system at the time. It had been created by the website's developers, and we decided to expand its functionality. Of course, Amazon.com served as a great example of how recommendation systems were implemented. A lot of ideas were thrown around: for example, including the recommendation's weighting in the widget so that potential buyers can see what percentage of people bought the recommended product. This functionality is not available on Ozon.ru and Amazon.com, but I recently found an example of such a system on the website of the German retailer of musical instruments and pro audio equipment thomann.de when I was looking for an electronic drumkit.

The following types of recommendations were available:

- people often buy x with this product
- people who visited this page purchased
- search recommendations
- personal recommendations.

There was an interesting story with the "people often buy x with this product" algorithm. Statistically, it didn't work particularly well. Then one of our analysts came across Greg Linden's article "Amazon.com Recommendations: Item-to-Item Collaborative Filtering" [113] and wrote his own cosine method in C# with the help of multi-threaded programming – because implementing a cosine of the vectors of customer interests on an SQL server is not much fun. After this, I came to believe in the Great Cosine in the *n*-dimensional space of vectors of client sessions, which would serve me well in the future.

One of the tasks that caused us difficulties was measuring the effectiveness of recommendation blocks. But we'd already bought the Omniture SiteCatalyst (now Adobe Analytics) web analytics tool and, with the help of merchandising analytics that I talked about earlier, we were able to overcome these issues. By the way, 38% of all cart additions were attributable to recommendation blocks.

I stopped working on recommendation systems for a while. That was until I found myself at Wikimart.ru, when a trip to the Netflix offices and a conversation with Eric Colson about the technologies they use inspired me to go back a change the technologies we were using completely. Not that the Wikimart.ru system needed any changes; all my old developments were working fine on their databases. But, as far as I was concerned, Hadoop was redefining the possible back then – scaling computations up to a thousand computers at the same time. What this meant was that I didn't need to rewrite or optimize any algorithms – all I had to do was add more computers to the cluster. Around two years later, in October 2012, I wrote the following:

ONLINE STORE RECOMMENDATIONS SERVICE

Aim

To create a simple and fast cloud-based product recommendation engine that can be embedded on a store's website without interfering with the internal architecture of that site.

Monetization

Stores can pay using the following scheme, in order of priority:

- Pay per order. Merchandising analytics can be used to accurately determine the likelihood that a site visitor will purchase a recommended product.

- Pay per click.

- Payment for additional services, such as personal recommendations in mailing lists or offline data on recommendations.

Types of Recommendations

The service can provide the following types of recommendations:

- Search recommendations (external and internal searches).

- Most popular products.

- Product recommendations ("People usually buy x after purchasing y," "people often buy x with this product").

- Personal recommendations on the website and mail-outs.

Technical Details

The service should be divided into four completely independent blocks:

- The service will collect data on the store's website using JavaScript trackers. The data is logged on separate servers.

- Product availability data will be downloaded separately (where possible) as ordinary yml files.

- Data is processed on a daily basis (or more frequently) using MapReduce. Recommendations are calculated and placed in the database or in separate files.

- A separate web service issues recommendations on the website. It is important that the recommendations include products that are in stock only.

Implementation

Typical implementation should include the installation of JavaScript code on the site:

- JavaScript trackers for collecting data. If Google Analytics is installed, then it can track important events on the site (purchases, cart additions, etc.).

- Snippets that can pull data from web services.

This was a fully formed idea of a recommendation service that can be used in any number of stores. I was approached by a fellow called Nikolay Khlebinsky at a conference in November 2012, who asked me to create such a system. The thing is, he hadn't even read my "Online Store Recommendations Service" text. He was impressed by the presentation I had given a few months earlier and had sent me some emails asking about my work. I never replied because I didn't want to give my ideas away. It was inevitable that we would eventually meet face to face, however – Nikolay is extremely persistent. The next step was to set up a partnership, registered our shares and signed a simple agreement. Nikolay would be the CEO, Andrey Chizh would be the Technical Director, and I would be the Director of Analytics. I had the first algorithms ready to go by the end of December. I'd written the first lines of the code in the food court of the Gagarisnky Shopping Centre in Moscow. My daughter was eight months old at the time and I'd taken her for a walk in her stroller. I sat outside in the cold on a folding chair I had brought with me, writing the code on my tablet. We launched the following March [116]. We had heard that a similar product (called crosss.ru) was also under development at the time, so we wanted to beat the other guys to the proverbial punch. And that's exactly what we did. Back then, the Retail Rocket partners complemented each other extremely well. We stayed in our lanes and performed our respective duties to a tee. It wasn't long before we managed to secure investments from Impulse VC – if you're looking for investments, I would suggest you look in their direction.

We were worried about the competition in the beginning, but it turned out that our main competitors were in-house IT teams. An employee or team at an online store would be tasked with developing such a system on their own and, a year or so later, they'd be knocking on our door asking us to do it for them. It was around 2020, maybe earlier, that the situation started to change and the competition really heated up. Online

[116]

stores started trusting third companies and outsourcing such functions as marketing automation and recommendations. I'd like to think that we played a big part in earning this trust.

For me, one of the biggest takeaways from this experience was that working for two companies at the same time is a bad idea: you're at the office during the day and then spend your evenings and weekdays slaving away on your own project. I was working 80-hour weeks during those first few months before I quit my job at Ostrovok.ru. I learned that when you spend your evenings coding into the early hours after you've already put in a full shift at work, you'll be spending the next day or two fixing your mistakes. Worse still, some of my oversights weren't corrected until a few years later! It was then that I decided that from that moment on, I would only dedicate myself to one thing at a time. That's why I took five months of unpaid leave to write this book.

Not all customers are able to accurately assess your efforts to create a quality product. And with recommendation systems, it is not immediately clear how much work has actually gone into it. For example, you've carried out an A/B test and the results show that two recommendation systems produce the same increase in sales. Which one do you choose? The first system provides a more logical picture of recommendations – a great deal of effort has been put into the visual side of things so that the customer knows exactly what they are looking at (the picture matches the description). There's one serious flaw in recommendation systems: as soon as you start to improve the "picture," the results of A/B tests deteriorate. I've spent countless hours trying to make everything look perfect so that the metrics don't suffer. Can our competitors say the same? I very much doubt it. But customers tend to focus on price first, that is, they will invariably go for the cheaper option. And when there's a choice between Russian-made and American-made, they'll always go for the latter. What can you do when we trust imported goods more? Russian shoe manufacturers who pretend that they are Italian or German are well aware of this. Life's not fair, and sometimes there's no reasoning with people who are convinced that your product is inferior. This is what we are up against every single day.

The next conclusion that I came to was that we needed to get rid of toxic clients, as they only cause headaches. Net Promoter Score (NPS) is a market research metric that measures customer loyalty. It is usually calculated by asking the customer a simple question: "How likely are you to recommend our company to a friend or colleague?" Answers are typically given on a scale of one to ten. It wouldn't be a bad idea to introduce a similar rating system for clients: How easy are they to work with? I've come across all manner clients, from fiercely loyal to extremely toxic. Toxic clients demotivate employees who are forced to work with them. Normal business communication is an important criterion when it comes to measuring the quality of customer service. The nest time I set up a company, I'll be sure to include a clause in the customer contract giving them the right to terminate our relationship if I get bad ratings from my employees.

Chapter 13

BUILDING A CAREER

STARTING YOUR CAREER

Your career lifecycle will probably look something like this: you get an education; find a job; develop your professional skills; and then leave. I would suggest that you start trying to work something out jobwise while you are still at university. I started working during my second year, but that was back in 1999 when there was no money to be had anywhere. Salaries were paid in dollars at the time, and I remember how happy I was when I received by first paycheck – 200 dollars! I'd been working as a programmer, but I left after a year because I wanted to try something else and keep up with my student payments. I got a job at StatSoft in the summer following my third year after spotting a flyer in the reading room of the MIPT library. It said: Russian–English translator required for software localization. StatSoft had a wonderful, homy atmosphere. I worked with a team of brilliant and ambitious people, undergraduates and graduates of MIPT and Moscow State University. When I was done with translating, I'd study the statistical package that we used and the theory behind it. I would also take part in product presentations. The first one was at the Central Bank of the Russian Federation. I can still remember it now. I never knew I could produce so much sweat! And my stomach was doing somersaults! It took me a few of these presentations to realise that I probably shouldn't eat anything beforehand. It's better to go hungry than give a speech with crippling stomach cramps due to nerves. For someone who finds it difficult to communicate with people, this was the absolute best crash course in presentations I could have taken! There were business trips to Kiev, Cherepovets, Krasnoyarsk... I took part in sales pitches and ran some courses for clients. It was like an on-the-job *Business Skills 101* course!

Of course, it was pure happenstance that I managed to land that job. But success isn't built on luck alone – you need to know how to make the best of the opportunities that luck affords you. I started at StatSoft as an intern at the same time as another physics major from the Department of General and Applied Physics at MIPT. He barely lasted a month, as he didn't care much for translating. He'd probably have been giving some more interesting things to do if he'd just hung on a little longer. By the way, the StatSoft.ru website still has a page for internship applications.

I wouldn't worry too much about chasing big money when you first start out. Be ballsy instead. If you get lucky, grab on with both hands and go along for the ride! I got lucky – I immediately fell in love with my job. Many physics graduates don't think about pursuing a career in science, so I'm glad that I'm still involved in applied physics. Try and land internships, and not necessarily in big "reputable" companies. I would say that it's actually better to start with smaller firms: you'll develop a broad outlook on your chosen field and you won't be just a small cog in a massive corporate machine, where you couldn't be further from the final product. You'll also have a much bigger hand in what the company actually does, in its sales and profits. And, to me, this is far more rewarding.

What should you pay attention to when looking for your first (as well as your second, third and every other) job? First, what will you learn there? I would recommend asking this question at the interview. If the interviewer thinks you're being a bit too forward, then the company is probably not for you. Second, your potential manager's character will have a huge impact on your development as a specialist. If he or she is a strong leader and reliable colleague, then you've hit the jackpot, my friend! Third, learn about the company's corporate culture during your probationary period – how kind or toxic it is to newcomers. I'm not saying that new recruits need to be mollycoddled, but there should at least be some kind of induction programme. The reality for me was usually something resembling indifference – I wasn't led by the hand too much, and was left to do my job. And that suited me fine. There were times when certain tasks were sent my way and others would be resentful. But it's the job of the head of department to deal with issues like this. One more thing: listen to your gut, both at the interview stage and during your probationary period. If something seems a little off, it probably is.

HOW TO FIND A JOB

There are three ways to find a job: by contacting a company directly; through professional recruiters; or by using personal connections. The latter method is usually the most successful. One person at Netflix told be that it's impossible to get a foot in the door if you don't know anyone who works there. It's easier to get access to recruiters through acquaintances at top-tier firms like the so-called FAANG (Facebook, Apple, Amazon, Netflix, Google (Alphabet)) companies. The best job offers I have ever received have invariably come from people I had worked with in the past. That's how I landed the jobs at Ozon.ru and Ostrovok. ru – through my old boss in the first case and a former employee in the second. Keep in touch with your colleagues, they could end up helping you out in the future.

It's far more difficult to get hired if you apply via the company's website or hh.ru. This is because no one has any information about you (no one has personally recommended you). And, let's face it, the most interesting positions are never published on company websites. As for going through professional recruiters, I've never found a job this way, and I've never used a headhunter when recruiting. I can only see one advantage to using these services: sometimes recruiters are hired to help fill senior management vacancies that are not disclosed to the general public.

So, how do you get an interview? And how do you prepare for it? First of all, you need to read the entire text of the job listing carefully. Better yet, read it through several times over, as every word in it has been meticulously chosen. Next, you need to rewrite your CV so that it immediately jumps out at the recruiter. And don't neglect the cover letter – they really do work! I always thought they were a bit pointless, until I started hiring myself, that is. It's your chance to tell the recruiters why you are interested in this vacancy and why you are the ideal candidate for the job. As a recruiter, I can tell you that a cover letter really demonstrates that the person wants the job. I'll often give the nod to people who have submitted a cover letter, even if there are objectively stronger candidates out there who didn't bother to write one.

You've been called in for an interview. This is usually a short phone conversation to see how suitable you are for the job. A good recruiter can get a good idea of this from just one phone call, and the opinion they form of you could work to your favour throughout the recruitment process. They will also ask you what your salary expectations are, and here's a pro tip for you: saying a number puts you in a position of weakness. This is true of the recruiter as well, so it's best to put this issue off until the final stage of negotiations. When it comes to the interview, preparation is key. I've been through the interview process with both Facebook and Quora. With Quora, I had a couple of introductory videocalls before flying to their offices in Palo Alto for two days of interviews – 13 on the first day, and another five on the second. Facebook even sent out special reminders before each interview on how to prepare. Before important interviews, I would always look for a list of questions I might be asked (or compile a list myself) and write down my answers in a notebook. Making notes beforehand will help you feel more confident in the interview. You won't be able to answer all the questions at the interview, but be sure to write down the ones that caused you difficulties so that work through them for next time. Think of it as training – you very well may be asked some of those questions during an interview with another company. Interviews are typically split into three parts: background, theory and practice.

In the first part, you talk about your experience. You'll be asked a number of questions, the most important of which is why you chose to do *x* and *y*. Good interviewers will definitely ask this question, and you should think about your answer in advance or, better still, ask someone to rehearse the interview with you. That will help identify any areas of weakness. I also pay attention to how the candidate views their contribution to the companies they have worked for.

The second part of the interview is usually theoretical – the interviewer asks simple questions to test your theoretical knowledge. For example, how a given algorithm works, when and what statistical criterion needs to be applied. Strange as it may seem, many candidates can't answer the most basic questions, ones that I included in the chapter on experiments. Learning the absolute minimum will immediately put you head and shoulders above the competition. Companies used to ask all sorts of absurd brain teasers (like "why are hatches round?") – Google was notorious for this – until a study came out showing that giving the correct answer was not necessarily a good predictor of a candidate's future success. So, brain teasers became a thing of the past.

The third part of the interview is practical. This involves sitting down at a computer with the candidate to solve a simple problem using any method they choose. Candidates for data scientist positions are required to process data and draw conclusions. Speed is important here: if you've got the practical skills, then you'll have no problem completing the task quickly. I was asked to be the guitarist in a band once. At the time, I played using tablature (diagrams that show you where to put your fingers on the fretboard) – I couldn't read chords on the fly, but I knew how to in theory. So, I'd have to learn the chords beforehand. This took forever, and I was only slowing the band down. I didn't last long in the band, of course, the rest of the guys didn't have the time to wait for me. It's the same with analytics and engineering – you've got to be able to do the simple things quickly. If you do them slowly, then you'll be holding up the whole team. This only way to get faster is through practice. And the best place to hone your skills in this area is Kaggle.

REQUIREMENTS FOR CANDIDATES

I will list the bare minimum that a data scientist needs to know (assuming that they are not involved in machine learning; that's for ML engineers).

A good data scientist such be familiar with the field they are working in – marketing, logistics, finance, web analytics, or whatever. This knowledge is important because it helps you get a grasp of issues that affect the business.

For data scientists, hardware and software are just tools. I like variety and would start, oddly enough, with Excel. It is an extremely powerful tool, and the industry standard in finance. Then there's SQL, a language for working with databases. This is most popular way to obtain and process data. My third favourite tool is basic probability theory and mathematical statistics: mean, median, variance, correlation, statistical hypothesis testing, etc. Fourth are programming tools: Python notebooks (Jupyter Notebooks) or R Notebooks.

Sometimes a position will require knowledge of certain software. Don't worry if you don't know that particular piece of software – if you've got a good base, individual skills are easily acquired.

I would divide engineers into two categories – data engineers who are responsible for keeping the system running, and ML engineers who work on ML models. This is what I believe a data engineer should know:

- How to work with Unix/Linux Shell.
- The principles of MapReduce.
- How to work with Hadoop where necessary.
- How to work with Kafka or other stream-processing software.
- How to work with DAG software (AirFlow, Oozie, etc.) – a system that works with directed graphs.

An ML engineer should know:

- Basic machine learning algorithms – the ability to write them independently. It is sometimes necessary to go beyond standard ML libraries and create your own.
- Feature engineering. This can only be learned through practice – for example, solving problems on Kaggle.
- How to use the Git version control system.
- How to work with containerized models and ML Ops tools such as ML Flow.

Additionally, both data engineers and ML engineers must have a sound command of two programming languages – Python and any of C++, C#, Java or Scala, as well as SQL.

YOU'VE ACCEPTED AN OFFER

Congratulations! Keep in mind that the probationary period (usually two or three months) cuts both ways – you are on probation with the company, but the company is also on probation with you. If you find yourself in a situation where the promises made when you were hired never materialize, then it's time to get out. This is why you shouldn't cut off ties with other potential (and former) employees as soon as you accept an offer. There's absolutely nothing wrong with interviewing for other jobs during your probationary period. Your new employer won't like it, but so what? You've got to do what's right for you. It may turn out that it's not the right job for you, or that you don't quite fit in with the company. I've had people turn an offer of employment down only to come back a few weeks later after discovering that the job they took wasn't what they had expected.

One more thing. First impressions with your employer mean a lot. It's extremely difficult to change a person's opinion of you over time. The way you present yourself during your probationary period will most likely determine how your bosses see you moving forward.

CONTINUING PROFESSIONAL DEVELOPMENT

If you land a job with a good company, you won't be left to your own devices with a job you barely understand. Ideally, you'll be given a mentor and tasked with writing a program during your probationary period. Once you've done that, you'll be invited to stay at the company. This is now the standard procedure for breaking in new recruits and interns, but when I started out only the big companies did it.

Okay, so you've completed your probationary period and become a full-fledged member of the team. What now? In a perfect world, you should have a meeting with your manager to discuss your individual workplan, a roadmap for your professional development. We do this at Retail Rocket. It is the manager's job to devise such a roadmap, and you should probably talk to them about it if nothing has been done. The roadmap should include skills and knowledge that you will need to acquire in order to obtain a salary increase or promotion. Don't be afraid of making your ambitions known. Those who do tend to achieve more. Managers are often extremely busy and your career aspirations are not at the top of their list of priorities. Our line of work demands constant development – things change very quickly, over the course of just a few years, and we have to stay on top of these changes. Having a solid development plan will ensure that you don't get left behind. Additionally, you need to maintain a balance between your work and your professional development, otherwise you are likely to get stuck in one place. My work keeps me extremely busy, but I always try and find the time to read a good book in my area of specialization or take an online course with Coursera.

We all need feedback. It helps us understand our weaknesses and what we need to do to get up to speed. At Retail Rocket, we organize weekly one-to-one meetings with management. If the company's task management is so efficient that meetings are not required, I would insist on them anyway. People tend to not speak up at team meetings. It's much easier to speak openly during one-to-one meetings and even give feedback to the manager (if, of course, you're lucky enough to have a manager who listens). I've been in both positions here – employee and manager. And I've worked in companies that use the one-to-one format, and in companies that don't. So, I would say that I'm in a fairly good position to compare the effectiveness of the two approaches. There is no doubt in my mind that these meetings are useful, and even necessary.

In some roles, people may do as they are told, but this won't cut it when you're working with your mind. Intellectual work is like art – a task can be completed in any number of ways. And when you are given a task, you need to have your own opinion about it, even if you don't voice it. This is a habit that will come in handy as you grow in stature at the company.

What separates an experienced employee from an inexperienced employee? An experienced employee needs to be told *what* to do, while an inexperienced employee needs to be told *how* to do it. As you grow as a professional, you will find that you are being told how to do something less and less often. And on those rare occasions that you are told how to do something, you can speak your mind and say, "Wouldn't it be better if I did it this way, or like this, because…" Then you won't feel like a cog in a machine, but an intellectual equal.

Our work is different from that of, say, a cashier or warehouse employee in that when they clock off, they stop thinking about work. It's different for us – we're still thinking about a task long after the working day is over, especially if we're working on something interesting. Ingenious solutions tend to take time. In my case, the saying "sleep on it" works, or I'll come up with the answer to a problem while I'm washing the dishes. That's why we don't have a dishwasher at home! If we did, I'd be scrolling through social networks instead of coming up with ideas. Richard Hamming believes that the brain needs to be occupied with a good problem the day before so that it will be easier to find a solution the next day [21]. What I'm trying to say is that it's impossible to solve problems effectively while tied to your desk for 12 hours a day. I worked two jobs at the same time when I was building up Retail Rocket. I'd work on my pet project every evening and on weekends, and it was then that I noticed how right Hamming was: if you write code late at night, you'll spend the next day cleaning it up. Our performance dips when we're tired.

These days, I can't work for more than three hours on a problem before I need to take a break and let my mind rest. When I say "let my mind rest," I mean disconnecting from work entirely. I started cycling to work a few years ago and I do it every day now, even in the Russian winter – as soon as the temperature drops below zero, I'll change to winter tires and put on my waterproof pants (which inevitably get filthy thanks to

[21]

the dirty Moscow roads). I find it takes my mind off work. If I take public transport, my head is always spinning with all kinds of ideas. But if I go by bike, I arrive home fresh and invigorated because all my attention was focused on the road.

This kind of brings me to the topic of workaholism. I first came across this phenomenon when I was in my fourth year at university after taking a class with the head of one of the departments at MIPT. She once told us that she got up at five in the morning and worked until late. A while later she just disappeared – the story was that she'd had a breakdown or something. I know people who work ridiculously hard and, under constant stress, turn to various psychotropic drugs for relief, from antidepressants to tranquilizers. No job in the world is worth risking your mental health for, and we need to do more to address this issue.

Another important aspect of our work is that it shouldn't depend too much on who we are as a person. I call this person-independence. A good manager should always have a plan of what to do if an employee leaves for whatever reason. The company needs to continue as before, so being overly reliant on a single person is always a big risk. Whenever I build a system, I always make sure that it can function perfectly without me. The same goes for my work in a company. The OLAP cubes I created at Ozon.ru continued to be used for years after I left. And the recommendation system I built at Wikimart.ru ran automatically without me. There is, of course, an inherent risk here – when everything is automated and runs smoothly, you will eventually become superfluous and can thus be let go. But let's think about it from a different angle. You've done your job, your system and system processes are working – not perfectly, but without any serious errors. Maybe there is someone who could easily replace you. You've found the perfect job! You can go about developing your career in the company, as well as at another company with no worries. And when you're ready to leave, you can do so knowing that you've built a good reputation for yourself and that your former colleagues and managers will happily write you a letter of recommendation. I've experienced all this first-hand.

HOW TO CHANGE JOBS

You'll know when it's time to change jobs when the trajectory of your professional development or ambitions no longer coincide – or are even at odds – with the trajectory of the company's development. You'll know when this happens because you'll have lost interest in what you are doing. It's happened to all of us, including me. In 2005, for example, when I'd just started working at Ozon.ru. I'd built an analytics system based on MS SQL Server and, after a while, there wasn't really anything for me to do. My manager had just left the company and the new shareholders were interfering with the day-to-day operations. What's more, they had no interest in dealing with me.

I was left to my own devices, so I eventually started working on my hobby – I'd long been working on a motion sensor alarm system for mobile phones in my free time. I was 23 years old and renting for the first time. I'd read some stories online about landlords going into apartments without permission when their tenants weren't home, so I created a kind of security system: I'd leave an old mobile phone modded with a motion sensor in the apartment that would call me if anyone went in so I could listen in to what was happening. To get it to work, I had to write a program for the controller. So, with nothing else to do, I started writing the program during my work hours. This is a bad idea, of course, and we were all in the wrong at the time. Still, I didn't get fired, and I didn't resign. Once the new management had finished its staff reshuffles, the assignments started to trickle in once again, so I put my project to one side and got down to work once again. In case you were wondering, my landlady never came round without giving me prior warning. I ended up leaving Ozon.ru five years later. I had my own office by then, right next to the CEO's. At some point, I realised that I wasn't interested in my job anymore and may as well rot away there until I retired. I thought a new role might reinvigorate me, so I headed up a project to switch the Ozon.ru loyalty programme to a points-based system, but that didn't capture my attention either. That's when I knew that it was time to leave, which is exactly what I did.

It's a well-known fact that the fastest way to move up the career ladder is to change jobs relatively frequently. Conventional wisdom used to dictate that the optimal time to spend at a single company was two years. The decision to leave is typically influenced by what drives the individual personally and professionally. There are two types of people in this respect, as far as I can tell. The first is innovators, people who are driven by the desire to create something new, but are not interested is the process of "polishing" their solution through endless optimization. The second type of person is optimizers – people who are capable of bringing new life into an existing solution, but who find it difficult to come up with ideas of their own and create something from scratch. For the innovator, as soon as he or she has set the ball in motion, their job is done – they are no longer interested and are already looking for new challenges. I belong to the first type. I'm an innovator – I come, I see, I conquer. I created an analytics system from scratch, put a team together, developed processes and then moved on. If you want to find out your type, I recommend trying both roles – innovator and optimizer – and see which you like best. This will make career decisions easier.

This is what Richard Hamming has to say about how to build your career [21]:

> "Somewhere around every seven years make a significant, if not complete, shift in your field. Thus, I shifted from numerical analysis, to hardware, to software, and so on, periodically, because you tend to use up your ideas...
>
> You have to change. You get tired after a while; you use up your originality in one field. You need to get something nearby. I'm not saying that you shift from music to theoretical physics to English literature; I mean within your field you should shift areas so that you don't go stale."

[21]

Hamming was referring to research papers, although I think his words can apply to data analysis as well. There's nothing stopping you from moving between areas, from web analytics to machine learning, from analytics to programming, and vice versa.

If you've been feeling uninspired for a while, that there's nothing for you to do at work, then talk to your superior. And if, after talking to your boss it becomes clear that nothing's going to change, then it's probably time to leave. This way, you won't be kicking yourself for staying too long and losing precious time. After all, we've only got so much of it.

DO YOU NEED TO KNOW EVERYTHING?

Our "old friend" Richard Hamming was once asked, "How much effort should go into library work?" This is what he said:

> "It depends upon the field. I will say this about it. There was a fellow at Bell Labs, a very, very, smart guy. He was always in the library; he read everything. If you wanted references, you went to him and he gave you all kinds of references. But in the middle of forming these theories, I formed a proposition: there would be no effect named after him in the long run. He is now retired from Bell Labs and is an Adjunct Professor. He was very valuable; I'm not questioning that. He wrote some very good Physical Review articles; but there's no effect named after him because he read too much."

You can't know everything, and reading takes up a lot of time. I love reading, but I never have enough time for it. Books can sit on the shelf for years before you finally pick them up and give them a read. Whenever I have a choice between passive (theoretical) and active (practical) actions, I go for the latter. Passive actions include reading, watching a video presentation, taking an online course, etc. I'm hardly a doofus – I've got dozens of certificates from Coursera. Active actions include solving a problem, completing a project (even if it's a personal project), etc. Work tasks interest me more than educational ones. Knowledge and erudition are important, but skilful application is far more important. And you don't need to know a subject inside and out in order to apply that knowledge – 20% is enough (remember Pareto!). Remember Xavier Amatriain's advice in the chapter on machine learning? Just read the introduction of a book on ML, open up whatever algorithm you want, and start coding. You'll learn what's important and what isn't through practice. You'll never be a good musician if you only know the theory.

Which employee is better: the one who took 20 different courses and did a lot of study assignments or the one who finished only a few simple projects, but saw them through to the end, from idea to implementation? In 95% of cases, I would say the second. In my experience, I have found that there are two kinds of people: theorists and practitioners. I once hired a person who knew the theory inside out, thinking that if they know the theory, they'll be able to figure out how to do it in practice. Boy, was I wrong!

So, if you don't need to read a lot, how are you supposed to learn? This is what Hamming said:

> "If you read all the time what other people have done, you will think the way they thought. If you want to think new thoughts that are different, then do what a lot of creative people do – get the problem reasonably clear and then refuse to look at any answers until you've thought the problem through carefully how you would do it, how you could slightly change the problem to be the correct one. So yes, you need to keep up. You need to keep up more to find out what the problems are than to read to find the solutions. The reading is necessary to know what is going on and what is possible. But reading to get the solutions does not seem to be the way to do great research. So I'll give you two answers. You read; but it is not the amount, it is the way you read that counts."

I remember my physics teacher getting on my back about trying to "re-invent the wheel" and using a certain formula. I always hated learning things by heart, just hated it! I found it easier to know the basic principles and learn a few formulas. Everything else is derived from them, although it takes a little longer to work things out than when you have a ready-made formula. Do know that you're allowed to bring any book you want to exams in the physics department at MIPT? You can fill your bag full of books if you want. Do you reckon it'll help? Nope! Because you've got to understand the basic principles first. You learn the principles of problem solving by... solving problems! Not reading solutions and memorizing formulas. You can't know everything. It's easier to find your own approach than to pore over volumes of books in search of "case studies." These days, case studies are looked at like a recipe – do everything it says step-by-step and everything will be hunky-dory. But that's not the way you come up with unique or nonstandard solutions.

Hamming also noticed that those employees at Bell Labs who work with their office doors open achieved more than those who worked with their doors closed. This is also an alternative to reading. Having an open mind and being receptive to new ideas and perspectives are key to success. So, what can we do to open our minds and be more receptive? For one, don't fob off your colleagues, and don't lock yourself away in your office. Sure, you'll get distracted by all their questions and requests, but you'll also be brought back to reality, a far cry from your lofty thoughts. Your colleagues are a source of information that you won't find anywhere else. They can also help you brainstorm your ideas – you can't hone them in a vacuum, after all. As co-founder and Director of Analytics at Retail Rocket, I would sometimes go into another department with my laptop and sit down. That's it, I'd just sit there, listening to what was going on there in the background while I worked. This is how I learned about problems that I never knew could even exist – and I would never have even found about them if I hadn't asked. The information I received proved invaluable when it came to making my own decisions.

EPILOGUE

The aim of this book is to give you some practical advice. And if you are able to apply at least some of my ideas in your work, then I will consider this a success.

One last piece of advice: always ask yourself the question, "Am I squeezing everything I possibly can out of the data?" At some of the places I have worked (Ozon.ru, Wikimart.ru, Retail Rocket), I was responsible for data analytics myself. At others (TechnoNICOL, Innova, KupiVIP, Fastlane Ventures), I provided consulting services, and it was here that I realized that it is not all about numbers.

To make the best use of numbers, you need, first of all, to monitor the quality of the data itself and, secondly, to effectively manage personnel within the company, prioritize hypotheses and use the necessary technology. I have tried to analyse these areas as thoroughly as possible in the relevant chapters of this book.

We learn about life through trial and error: children experiment more, adults less. Similarly, companies need to experiment in order to grow. This includes generating ideas, testing them in practice, obtaining results and repeating this cycle over and over, even if the result is not as good as you would have wanted and you are tempted to give up. Don't be afraid of failure – it is experimentation that leads to improvements.

Don't hesitate to get in touch with me through this book's website top-datalab.com/book or via email at rzykov@topdatalab.com. I'll be happy to answer any questions you may have!

BIBLIOGRAPHY

Most of the references in this book are provided via hyperlinks. Over time, some of them will stop working. I have developed a mechanism to ensure that all the references remain accessible that is available at **http://topdatalab.com/ref?link=[Reference number]**. "Reference number" corresponds to the number of the respective reference in the text (for example, for number 23: https://topdatalab.com/ref?link=23). If I learn that a link or QR code in this book has stopped working, I will restore it as soon as possible. All the reader has to do is let me know.

1. Behave The Biology of Humans at Our Best and Worst Robert Sapolsky https://www.amazon.com/Behave-Biology-Humans-Best-Worst/dp/0143110918

2. Amazon.com: Letter to shareholders 2015 https://s3-us-west-2.amazonaws.com/amazon.job-cms-website.paperclip.prod/shareholder_letters/2015.pdf

3. Amazon.com: Letter to shareholders 2015 https://blog.aboutamazon.com/company-news/2016-letter-to-shareholders

4. What is decision intelligence https://towardsdatascience.com/introduction-to-decision-intelligence-5d147ddab767

5. Focus on decisions not outcomes https://towardsdatascience.com/focus-on-decisions-not-outcomes-bf6e99cf5e4f

6. Russian Covid deaths three times the official toll https://www.bbc.com/news/world-europe-55474028

7. Understanding Decision Fatigue https://www.healthline.com/health/decision-fatigue

9. Building Data Science Teams. DJ Patil https://www.amazon.com/Building-Data-Science-Teams-Patil-ebook/dp/B005O4U3ZE

10. What's the difference between analytics and statistics? https://towardsdatascience.com/whats-the-difference-between-analytics-and-statistics-cd35d457e17

11. Debunking Narrative Fallacies with Empirically-Justified Explanations https://multithreaded.stitchfix.com/blog/2016/03/23/debunking-narrative-fallacies/

12. AB test attack: recipe 'R'+t(101)+'es46'" https://translate.google.com/translate?hl=en&sl=ru&tl=en&u=https://habr.com/ru/company/retailrocket/blog/330012/

13. Measure What Matters: How Google, Bono, and the Gates Foundation Rock the World with OKRs. Doerr John https://www.amazon.com/Measure-What-Matters-audiobook/dp/B07BMJ4L1S

14. Dogs vs. Cats: Create an algorithm to distinguish dogs from cats https://www.kaggle.com/c/dogs-vs-cats

15. ResNet-50 is a convolutional neural network https://github.com/matlab-deep-learning/resnet-50

16. Data scientists mostly just do arithmetic and that's a good thing https://m.signalvnoise.com/data-scientists-mostly-just-do-arithmetic-and-thats-a-good-thing/

17. Jung's last BBC interview on Freud and World War III https://translate.google.com/translate?hl=en&sl=ru&tl=en&u=https://www.bbc.com/russian/features-53475033

18. The Tyranny of Metrics. Jerry Muller https://www.amazon.com/Tyranny-Metrics-Jerry-Z-Muller/dp/0691191913

19. Spark/Scala Young Fighter Course https://translate.google.com/translate?hl=en&sl=ru&tl=en&u=https://habr.com/ru/company/retailrocket/blog/302828/

20. Data science management https://www.quora.com/How-do-I-move-from-data-scientist-to-data-science-management

21. You and Your Research. Richard Hamming https://www.cs.virginia.edu/~robins/YouAndYourResearch.html

22. Planning Poker https://en.wikipedia.org/wiki/Planning_poker

23. Hypothesis Testing: How to Eliminate Ideas as Soon as Possible. Roman Zykov https://recsys.acm.org/recsys16/industry-session-3/#content-tab-1-1-tab

24. Application of Kullback-Leibler divergence for short-term user interest detection https://arxiv.org/abs/1507.07382

25. Does Stylish Cross-Sell Store Need: Retail Rocket's Experience in Image Analysis for Formation of Recommendations https://translate.google.com/translate?hl=en&sl=ru&tl=en&u=https://habr.com/ru/company/retailrocket/blog/441366/

26. The most powerful idea in data science https://towardsdatascience.com/the-most-powerful-idea-in-data-science-78b9cd451e72

27. Elementary Concepts in Statistics https://docs.tibco.com/data-science/GUID-6C466605-AB68-4F81-B2BA-220BEAA05D51.html

28. Say It With Charts. Gene Zelazny https://www.amazon.com/Say-Charts-Executives-Visual-Communication/dp/007136997X

29. The Cognitive Style of Powerpoint: pitching out corrupts within. Edward R. Tafte https://www.amazon.com/Cognitive-Style-PowerPoint-Pitching-Corrupts/dp/0961392169

30. On Pair Programming. Martin Fowler https://martinfowler.com/articles/on-pair-programming.html

31. Technical Debt. Martin Fowler https://martinfowler.com/bliki/TechnicalDebt.html

32. Netflix Culture https://jobs.netflix.com/culture

33. Retailrocket recommender system dataset https://www.kaggle.com/retailrocket/ecommerce-dataset

34. Making Sense of Data Warehouse Architecture https://datawarehouseinfo.com/data-warehouse-architecture/

35. Columnar database: a smart choice for data warehouses https://www.stitchdata.com/columnardatabase/

36. System and method for efficient large-scale data processing (Google) http://patft.uspto.gov/netacgi/nph-Parser?Sect1=PTO1&Sect2=HITOFF&d=PALL&p=1&u=/netahtml/PTO/srchnum.htm&r=1&f=G&l=50&s1=7,650,331.PN.&OS=PN/7,650,331&RS=PN/7,650,331

37. MapReduce: Simplified Data Processing on Large Clusters https://www.dropbox.com/s/azf00wnjwnqd2x8/mapreduce-osdi04.pdf?dl=0

38. The Friendship That Made Google Huge https://www.newyorker.com/magazine/2018/12/10/the-friendship-that-made-google-huge

39. Apache Hadoop https://hadoop.apache.org/

40. Apache Spark http://spark.apache.org/

41. Loader of HDFS files with combining small files on Spark https://github.com/RetailRocket/SparkMultiTool

42. Python for Data Analysis. Wes McKinney https://www.amazon.com/Python-Data-Analysis-Wrangling-IPython/dp/1491957662

43. Cloudera Hadoop - Choosing and Configuring Data Compression https://docs.cloudera.com/documentation/enterprise/6/6.3/topics/admin_data_compression_performance.html

44. Google colab https://colab.research.google.com/

45. Kaggle notebooks https://www.kaggle.com/notebooks

46. Gartner Top 10 Trends in Data and Analytics for 2020 https://www.gartner.com/smarterwithgartner/gartner-top-10-trends-in-data-and-analytics-for-2020/

47. Metabase https://www.metabase.com/

48. SuperSet https://superset.apache.org/

49. Beyond Interactive: Notebook Innovation at Netflix https://netflixtechblog. com/notebook-innovation-591ee3221233

50. What Artificial Intelligence Can and Can't Do Right Now https://hbr. org/2016/11/what-artificial-intelligence-can-and-cant-do-right-now

51. Regression Towards Mediocrity in Hereditary Stature. Francis Galton http:// www.stat.ucla.edu/~nchristo/statistics100C/history_regression.pdf

52. Are We Really Making Much Progress? A Worrying Analysis of Recent Neural Recommendation Approaches https://arxiv.org/abs/1907.06902

53. Kaggle's State of Data Science and Machine Learning 2019 https://www. kaggle.com/kaggle-survey-2019

54. Unity is strength — A story of model composition https://medium.com/criteo-labs/unity-is-strength-a-story-of-model-composition-49748b1f1347

55. Introduction to Machine Learning. Second Edition. Ethem Alpaydin. https:// www.amazon.com/Introduction-Machine-Learning-Adaptive-Computation/ dp/0262043793

56. Scikit learn Ensemble methods https://scikit-learn.org/stable/modules/ ensemble.html

57. XGBoost: Introduction to Boosted Trees https://xgboost.readthedocs.io/en/ latest/tutorials/model.html

58. LightGBM https://lightgbm.readthedocs.io/

59. Catboost https://catboost.ai/

60. Andrew Ng. Machine learning Yearning https://www.deeplearning.ai/ machine-learning-yearning/

61. Coursera Machine Learning https://www.coursera.org/learn/machine-learning

62. How do I learn machine learning? https://qr.ae/pN9vA4

63. Fastml4j on Scala https://github.com/rzykov/fastml4j

64. Netflix prize https://www.netflixprize.com

65. Netflix Recommendations: Beyond the 5 stars (Part 1) https://netflixtech-blog.com/netflix-recommendations-beyond-the-5-stars-part-1-55838468f429

66. Andrew Gelman, Jenifer Hill "Data Analysis Using Regression and Multilevel/ Hierarchical Models" https://www.amazon.com/Analysis-Regression-Multilevel-Hierarchical-Models/dp/052168689X

67. Google Course of ML: Imbalanced Data https://developers.google.com/ machine-learning/data-prep/construct/sampling-splitting/imbalanced-data

68. 10 More lessons learned from building real-life Machine Learning systems https://xamat.medium.com/10-more-lessons-learned-from-building-real-life-ml-systems-part-i-b309cafc7b5e

69. ScaleFactor Raised $100 Million In A Year Then Blamed Covid-19 For Its Demise. Employees Say It Had Much Bigger Problems. https://www.forbes.com/sites/davidjeans/2020/07/20/scalefactor-raised-100-million-in-a-year-then-blamed-covid-19-for-its-demise-employees-say-it-had-much-bigger-problems/

71. DRILLING DOWN: Turning Customer Data into Profits with a Spreadsheet - Third Edition, Jim Novo https://www.amazon.com/DRILLING-DOWN-Turning-Customer-Spreadsheet-ebook/dp/B07RY5XV1J

72. Google Rules of Machine Learning: Best Practices for ML Engineering https://developers.google.com/machine-learning/guides/rules-of-ml

73. Louse laser pioneer in contention for invention award https://thefishsite.com/articles/louse-laser-pioneer-in-contention-for-invention-award

74. Lox prices in city eateries could jump due to salt-water parasite https://nypost.com/2017/01/15/lox-prices-in-city-eateries-could-jump-due-to-salt-water-parasite/

75. Adidas backpedals on robotic shoe production with Speedfactory closures https://techcrunch.com/2019/11/11/adidas-backpedals-on-robotic-factories/

76. Ronald Aylmer Fisher biography https://www.adelaide.edu.au/library/special/mss/fisher/fisherbiog.pdf

77. Larry Wasserman, All of Statistics: A Concise Course in Statistical Inference (Springer Texts in Statistics), Springer (December 1, 2010) https://www.amazon.com/All-Statistics-Larry-Wasserman-ebook/dp/B098LR91FC

78. Nonparametric Statistics Introductory Overview — When to Use Which Method https://docs.tibco.com/data-science/GUID-1669B816-C669-4F4F-919E-231A8F3CAFDA.html

79. B.Efron, Bootstrap Methods: Another Look at the Jackknife https://doi.org/10.1214/aos/1176344552

80. Bootstrap confidence intervals https://www.dropbox.com/s/6dbqxrcocmfxyvp/MIT18_05S14_Reading24.pdf?dl=0

81. Criteo Labs: Why your A/B-test needs confidence intervals https://medium.com/criteo-labs/why-your-ab-test-needs-confidence-intervals-bec9fe18db41

82. Bayesian A/B tests https://richrelevance.com/2013/05/21/bayesian-ab-tests/

83. William Bolstad, Introduction to Bayesian Statistics https://www.amazon.com/Introduction-Bayesian-Statistics-William-Bolstad/dp/1118091566

84. Ron Kohavi, Alex Deng, Roger Longbotham, and Ya Xu. Seven Rules of Thumb for Web Site Experimenters https://exp-platform.com/rules-of-thumb/

85. Retail Rocket Segmentator https://github.com/RetailRocket/RetailRocket.Segmentator

86. Reinforcement Learning: An Introduction https://web.stanford.edu/class/psych209/Readings/SuttonBartoIPRLBook2ndEd.pdf

87. The Privacy Project https://www.nytimes.com/interactive/2019/opinion/internet-privacy-project.html

88. One Nation tracked https://www.nytimes.com/interactive/2019/12/19/opinion/location-tracking-cell-phone.html

89. Google Authorized Buyers, Real-time Bidding https://developers.google.com/authorized-buyers/rtb/start

90. Explained: Data in the Criteo Engine https://www.criteo.com/blog/explained-data-in-the-criteo-engine/

91. We Built an 'Unbelievable' (but Legal) Facial Recognition Machine, https://www.nytimes.com/interactive/2019/04/16/opinion/facial-recognition-new-york-city.html

92. What ISPs Can See, Upturn, March 2016 https://www.upturn.org/reports/2016/what-isps-can-see/

93. The GDPR Is a Cookie Monster https://content-na1.emarketer.com/the-gdpr-is-a-cookie-monster

94. IAB. Cookies on Mobile 101 https://www.iab.com/wp-content/uploads/2015/07/CookiesOnMobile101Final.pdf

95. How Online Shopping Makes Suckers of Us All https://www.theatlantic.com/magazine/archive/2017/05/how-online-shopping-makes-suckers-of-us-all/521448/

96. Why are the largest Russian Internet sites removing the Liveinternet counter? https://translate.google.com/translate?hl=en&sl=ru&tl=en&u=https://vc.ru/flood/1822-pochemu-krupneyshie-saytyi-runeta-ubirayut-schetchik-liveinternet

97. How To Break Anonymity of the Netflix Prize Dataset, https://arxiv.org/abs/cs/0610105

98. Alexa, are you invading my privacy? – the dark side of our voice assistants https://www.theguardian.com/technology/2019/oct/09/alexa-are-you-invading-my-privacy-the-dark-side-of-our-voice-assistants

99. LeakyPick: IoT Audio Spy Detector https://arxiv.org/abs/2007.00500

100. I SEARCH, THEREFORE I AM, Andreas Weigend https://www.dropbox.com/s/xk6w60szuq6dpeh/WeigendFOCUS2004-en.pdf?dl=0

101. We Read 150 Privacy Policies. They Were an Incomprehensible Disaster, https://www.nytimes.com/interactive/2019/06/12/opinion/facebook-google-privacy-policies.html

102. 5 Americans who used NSA facilities to spy on lovers https://www.washingtonpost.com/news/the-switch/wp/2013/09/27/5-americans-who-used-nsa-facilities-to-spy-on-lovers/

103. Pie & AI Asia: On Ethical AI with Andrew Ng https://www.deeplearning.ai/blog/pie-ai-asia-on-ethical-ai-with-andrew-ng/

104. What Do We Do About the Biases in AI? https://hbr.org/2019/10/what-do-we-do-about-the-biases-in-ai

105. Ad Blocking Growth Is Slowing Down, but Not Going Away https://www.emarketer.com/content/ad-blocking-growth-is-slowing-down-but-not-going-away

106. IAB Europe Guide to the Post Third-Party Cookie Era https://iabeurope.eu/knowledge-hub/iab-europe-guide-to-the-post-third-party-cookie-era/

107. Comparing privacy laws: GDPR v. Russian Law on Personal Data https://www.dataguidance.com/sites/default/files/gdpr_v_russia_december_2019.pdf

108. This Article Is Spying on You https://www.nytimes.com/2019/09/18/opinion/data-privacy-tracking.html

109. Functionalism: A New Approach to Web Analytics https://www.dropbox.com/s/a75hmjzekf006ia/wpaper_005.pdf?dl=0

110. Strategic Database Marketing. Arthur Hughes https://www.amazon.com/Strategic-Database-Marketing-Masterplan-Customer-Based/dp/0071773487

111. A good founder's guide to bad VC behaviour https://technation.io/news/good-founders-guide-bad-vc-behaviour/

112. Two Decades of Recommender Systems at Amazon.com https://www.amazon.science/publications/two-decades-of-recommender-systems-at-amazon-com

113. Item-to-Item Collaborative Filtering, Greg Linden, Brent Smith, and Jeremy York https://www.dropbox.com/s/dctxbv8dk8wrsmw/Amazon-Recommendations.pdf?dl=0

114. How to use Merchandising eVars in Adobe Analytics, https://dmpg.co.uk/how-to-use-merchandising-evars-in-adobe-analytics-product-modules

116. Retail Rocket https://www.crunchbase.com/organization/retail-rocket